150 Best
Diabetes
Desserts

Edited By
Barbara Selley, BA, RD

Robert
ROSE

150 Best Diabetes Desserts

For complete cataloguing information, see page 244.

Disclaimer
The recipes in this book have been carefully tested by our kitchen and our tasters. To the best of our knowledge, they are safe and nutritious for ordinary use and users. For those people with food or other allergies, or who have special food requirements or health issues, please read the suggested contents of each recipe carefully and determine whether or not they may create a problem for you. All recipes are used at the risk of the consumer.

We cannot be responsible for any hazards, loss or damage that may occur as a result of any recipe use.

For those with special needs, allergies, requirements or health problems, in the event of any doubt, please contact your medical adviser prior to the use of any recipe.

Design and Production: Joseph Gisini/PageWave Graphics Inc.
Editor: Sue Sumeraj
Proofreader: Sheila Wawanash
Indexer: Gillian Watts
Photography: Colin Erricson & Mark Shapiro
Food Styling: Kathryn Robertson & Kate Bush
Prop Styling: Charlene Erricson

Cover image: Chocolate Marble Vanilla Cheesecake, page 192

We acknowledge the financial support of the Government of Canada through the Book Publishing Industry Development Program (BPIDP) for our publishing activities.

Published by Robert Rose Inc.
120 Eglinton Avenue East, Suite 800, Toronto, Ontario, Canada M4P 1E2
Tel: (416) 322-6552 Fax: (416) 322-6936

Printed and bound in Canada

1 2 3 4 5 6 7 8 9 CPL 16 15 14 13 12 11 10 09 08

Contents

Preface

This book of desserts is for people living with diabetes and for their families and friends — just about everyone! By 2010, 10% of the population of the United States and Canada will have diabetes, so it's a rare person who does not know someone with this disease.

The recipes selected for this book were not specifically developed for people with diabetes, but we have chosen ones that can be worked into most people's meal plans. Many are special-occasion treats, but some can fit in more often.

To help you include these recipes in your meals, each recipe has a breakdown of calories, carbohydrate, fiber and other nutrients, plus America's Food Exchanges and Canada's Food Choices.

In the introduction, we look at

- who has diabetes, and why we should be concerned about this disease;
- food and nutrition recommendations for people with diabetes; and
- "budgeting" for desserts: how you can plan to include these treats in your meals.

In addition, in case you don't wind up with the same number of cookies as we did when preparing a recipe, we've included a "cookie calculator" that allows you to recalculate a single serving.

Following the introduction, you will find a table of nutrient values for common dessert ingredients, as well as two worksheets, so you can figure out how to fit your own favorite desserts into your meal plan. Would you like to know the Exchanges or Choices for a serving of a favorite recipe? The worksheets on pages 18–29 will help you estimate them.

Throughout the book, you will find "Barb's nutrition notes" and other tips that will help you prepare and enjoy these recipes.

Whether you're controlling your diabetes through diet and exercise alone, or with the help of oral medication or insulin, I hope you'll enjoy the recipes in this book and find the tips helpful.

Introduction

Who has diabetes?

In North America, 6% to 7% of adults and children have diabetes — about 20.8 million people in the United States and over 2 million people in Canada. These numbers have been rising steadily in recent years and are expected to reach 10% of the population by 2010.

Diabetes is a serious disease. Untreated, it can lead to a wide variety of sometimes life-threatening complications involving the heart, eyes, kidneys, nerves and circulatory system.

Diabetes affects us all. Because about one person in fifteen lives with diabetes, almost every one of us knows someone with the disease.

WHAT IS DIABETES?

There are three main types of diabetes. In each instance, blood glucose (sugar) levels are above normal because glucose isn't being metabolized properly.

- In **type 1 diabetes**, the pancreas doesn't produce insulin, the hormone that allows the body to use glucose as fuel. About 10% of people with diabetes have type 1.
- **Type 2 diabetes** is much more prevalent, affecting about 90% of people with diabetes. It occurs when the pancreas doesn't produce enough insulin, or when the body can't use it properly, a condition known as insulin resistance. Until recently, type 2 diabetes was generally considered to be a condition of middle age, but it is now occurring in children and teenagers.
- **Gestational diabetes** occurs in about 4% of pregnant women. While it usually disappears after the baby is born, both mother and child are at higher risk for type 2 diabetes later in life.

In addition to those with known diabetes, millions of North Americans of all ages have **pre-diabetes**: their blood glucose readings are above normal, but the levels are not high enough for a diagnosis of diabetes. Although pre-diabetes can develop into type 2 diabetes, we now know it's possible to prevent this progression.

What can I do to manage diabetes?

Whether you have type 1, type 2, gestational diabetes or pre-diabetes, the cornerstones of effective management are:

- managing food intake to control blood glucose;
- increasing physical activity;
- achieving or maintaining a healthy weight;
- quitting smoking if you smoke;
- monitoring blood glucose;
- taking medication (insulin or oral medications) if required; and
- maintaining blood pressure in a healthy range.

It is important to become educated about diabetes and to work closely with your physician, dietitian, pharmacist and other members of your health care team.

For more information about diabetes, its prevention and its treatment, contact the American Diabetes Association at www.diabetes.org or the Canadian Diabetes Association at www.diabetes.ca.

What should people with diabetes eat?

Healthy eating recommendations for people with diabetes are very similar to those for the general population. It is not necessary to prepare separate meals or buy special foods.

The following information is general. Your dietitian's recommendations for you may differ in some ways.

Carbohydrate

Carbohydrate, found mainly in grain products, vegetables, legumes (dried peas and beans), fruits and milk products, should make up about 50% of your calories. You may be surprised to learn that it's okay for people with diabetes to eat sugar (see opposite).

Fiber

To achieve the recommended fiber intake of at least 25 grams per day, carbohydrate food choices should consist mainly of whole-grain products, legumes and vegetables.

WHAT'S THE STORY ON SUGAR?

There are many types of sugar. Milk, vegetables and fruit all contain naturally occurring sugars (such as lactose, glucose or fructose). Added sugars (such as granulated sugar, honey or corn syrup) are those added either when food products are manufactured or when we ourselves prepare our meals and beverages.

People with diabetes used to be advised to avoid added sugars altogether, but we now know this ban was unnecessary. Added sugars, however, do not provide vitamins and minerals, so they should replace only small amounts of carbohydrate from other sources. The key word is "replace." Any food eaten in excess of what you need will lead to weight gain and/or elevated blood glucose levels.

Current guidelines allow for people with diabetes to consume up to 10% of total daily energy (calories) as added sugars from all sources, including processed foods. If you eat 2,000 calories per day, this translates to 50 grams of carbohydrate — a little over 3 Other Carbohydrate Exchanges or Carbohydrate Choices (equivalent to 10 teaspoons/50 mL) of sugar).

Remember that this 50 grams includes both sugar you can see (added to your coffee, for example) and hidden sugar in sweet foods.

What's the story on low-calorie sweeteners?
There's a wide range of sugar substitutes and artificial sweeteners in the marketplace. On page 149 you can read about the various types and how they are used.

Fat

Fat should make up no more than 30% of your calories. At 2,000 calories per day, this is equivalent to 66 grams. Remember, this includes fat from all sources: meat, fish, poultry, eggs, oils and spreads, nuts and seeds, and combination foods such as cookies and muffins.

- **Saturated and trans** fats together should make up no more than one-third of your total fat intake, or 22 grams if you consume 2,000 calories per day.
- **Polyunsaturated** fat should also not exceed one-third of total fat intake, and should include omega-3 fatty acids from fatty fish and plant sources, such as canola oil, walnuts and flaxseed.
- The remaining fat you consume, at least one-third of daily fat intake and preferably more, should come from **monounsaturated** sources, such as canola oil, olive oil and soybean oil. Often called "healthy fats," monounsaturated fats can help lower your LDL ("bad") cholesterol.

Protein

Protein from all sources (meat, fish, poultry, eggs, dairy products, legumes and other plant sources) should make up about 15% to 20% of your calories. At an intake of 2,000 calories per day, this is equivalent to 75 to 100 grams of protein. Higher amounts are not recommended, as they may increase the work that the kidneys need to do.

Sodium

People with diabetes should follow the recommendation for the general population: a maximum of 2,300 mg of sodium per day, about the amount in 1 teaspoon (5 mL) of salt. This does not mean, however, that you can add a teaspoon of salt to your meals. Up to 75% of the sodium we consume comes from processed foods, not from what we use in cooking or add at the table. So, when you're grocery shopping, it's important to check sodium on the Nutrition Facts panels.

What nutrients are found in dessert ingredients?

Carbohydrate

Carbohydrate in desserts comes mainly from flour, other grain products (such as rolled oats) and sugar. Fresh and dried fruit, chocolate and cocoa supply smaller amounts. Here are some other points to keep in mind:

- Whole-grain ingredients, such as whole wheat flour, rolled oats, oat bran and wheat bran, help boost fiber intake.
- All sources of sugar — whether granulated sugar, brown sugar, fructose, honey, maple syrup, corn syrup, jam or jelly — contain about 5 grams of carbohydrate per teaspoon (5 mL).

Fats and oils

Soft non-hydrogenated margarine and canola oil are the best choices. They are low in saturated fat, contain no trans fats and supply omega-3 fatty acids. However, some recipes do not work well with these preferred fats, calling instead for butter or shortening. Although they contain the same total amount of fat as margarine or oil, butter and shortening are high in saturated fat. Shortening also contains trans fats (the levels are lower than in the past, but still significant).

If you have a choice in a recipe between margarine and butter, for example, always choose to use soft non-hydrogenated margarine. If a recipe specifies butter or shortening, it likely will not work if another fat is substituted. In that case, limit your enjoyment of the recipe to special occasions.

Sodium

Sodium is a nutrient you don't usually need to be concerned about in desserts:

- While salt, baking powder and baking soda are all high in sodium, only a very small amount is present in a single serving.
- Margarine and butter containing salt add sodium, but again the amount is small.
- Flour, sugar and fruit contain almost no sodium; milk and eggs have moderate amounts.

How can I "budget" to allow room in my meal plan for desserts?

We plan ahead when we budget money. It's just as important to plan ahead when you will be having a dessert or another food item you don't routinely eat. The key is to find a food or foods somewhere else in your meal that contains the same Food Exchanges or Food Choices as the dessert you intend to eat, and then replace it with your dessert.

EXAMPLE:

You usually have a slice of bread with a teaspoon (5 mL) margarine at dinner. Tonight, you would like to have a cookie that contains 1 Other Carbohydrate Exchange or Carbohydrate Choice and 1 Fat Exchange or Choice. If you replace the bread and margarine with the cookie, you'll be on budget.

WHY IS IT IMPORTANT TO MEASURE INGREDIENTS ACCURATELY?

Careful measuring is important for several reasons:

- The Exchange and Choice values accompanying the recipes are based on the ingredient quantities and number of servings stated. If you change ingredient amounts (or the portion size), the stated Exchanges and Choices will no longer be correct.
- Baked goods may not rise properly if ingredient amounts are inaccurate.

For information about measuring cups and other measures, see page 165. You will find tips for accurate measuring on page 65.

What do I need to know about serving size?

We live in an age of ever-larger dinner plates and food packages, and therefore serving sizes. It's often hard to remember what the more reasonable sizes of 10 or 20 years ago looked like. As a result, some of the portions specified in this book may be smaller than you're accustomed to. Be sure to use the serving sizes on the recipes and don't be led astray by the "portion distortion" that is all around us.

You can also use the cookie calculator for other baked goods, such as muffins. For example, you might get 16 muffins from a recipe that says it makes 12. Using the calculator, you can work out how many of your muffins match the nutrients, Exchanges and Choices on the recipe.

Cookie calculator to the rescue

If you're making a batch of cookies and you end up with a different number of cookies than stated in the yield on the recipe, the ingredient quantities in each cookie will be different, as will the number of cookies that correspond to the Exchanges or Choices listed with the recipe.

Using Oatmeal Raisin Cookies (page 89) as an example, here's how you can calculate a new portion size:

EXAMPLE:

Raisin Oatmeal Cookies

This recipe has a yield of 18 cookies, and the serving size is 2 cookies. But when you prepare the recipe, you make smaller cookies and end up with 24. In the table below, enter

- in box *t1*, the stated yield of the recipe (18 cookies);
- in box *s1*, the number of cookies per serving according to the recipe (2); and
- in box *t2*, your yield from the recipe (24 cookies).

Cookies	Total	Per serving
Recipe	t1	s1
You get	t2	s2

So, once the table is filled in, it will look like this:

Cookies	Total	Per serving
Recipe	18	2
You get	24	?

To calculate the number of cookies in your serving (box *s2*), you will:

- Divide the total number of cookies you get (*t2*) by the total number on the recipe (*t1*), then
- Multiply by the number of cookies per serving stated in the recipe (*s1*).

That is, $s2 = (t2 \div t1) \times s1$. In this example, $s2 = (24 \div 18) \times 2 = 2.7$ cookies per serving (for box $s2$).

If your result includes a fraction, round it off to the nearest half-cookie, referring to the ranges in the table below. In this example, the result is 2.7, which should be rounded to $2\frac{1}{2}$. So, if you get 24 cookies from the Raisin Oatmeal Cookie recipe, your serving size will be $2\frac{1}{2}$ cookies.

Cookie calculator rounding table	
If your result for $s2$ equals	Round to
0.3–0.7	$\frac{1}{2}$
0.8–1.2	1
1.3–1.7	$1\frac{1}{2}$
1.8–2.2	2
2.3–2.7	$2\frac{1}{2}$
2.8–3.2	3
3.3–3.7	$3\frac{1}{2}$
3.8–4.2	4

Here's an example for you to work out:

EXAMPLE:
Best-Ever Chocolate Cookies
You've made a batch of Best-Ever Chocolate Cookies (page 106). The recipe says it makes 21 cookies and the serving size is 2 cookies. But you only have 15 cookies (yours are larger). What should your serving size be?

Cookies	Total	Per serving
Recipe	$t1$	$s1$
You get	$t2$	$s2$
Rounded to ____		

You'll find the answer at the bottom of page 32.

More information

For additional information about meal planning and all aspects of managing diabetes, contact:

The American Diabetes Association
www.diabetes.org

The Canadian Diabetes Association
www.diabetes.ca

Estimating Exchanges or Choices for Your Favorite Recipes

The recipe information in this book can help you fit your own recipes into your meal plan. Look for a recipe that has similar quantities of the main ingredients and the same number of servings as your recipe. Because they are similar in these ways, your recipe will have approximately the same number of America's Exchanges and Canada's Choices as the similar recipe in the book.

You can also use the worksheets on the following pages to help you get a more precise estimate of America's Exchanges or Canada's Choices for your recipes. Choose either the America's Exchanges worksheet (page 18) or Canada's Choices worksheet (page 24), and follow the instructions.

Each worksheet is accompanied by an ingredient list that can also be used separately. Here's an example. To find out the number of Carbohydrate Exchanges in 1 cup (250 mL) of granulated sugar, you would look in the "Sugar and Syrups" section on page 21 and see that it contains 13$\frac{1}{2}$ Carbohydrate Exchanges. For Canada's Choices, you would look it up on page 27.

America's Exchanges Recipe Worksheet:
How To Use

a. In column A enter names of recipe ingredients that are called for by volume (i.e., measured in cups, tablespoons or teaspoons)

b. Enter quantities of these ingredients in columns Q1 or Q2.

>*Enter in Q1 if amount is not in cups; otherwise, enter in Q2.*

>*Omit salt, baking powder, baking soda, spices and any other ingredients where the quantity is less than 1 tsp.*

c. Using the equivalent measures below, convert quantities in column Q1 to cups and enter in Q2.

1 tsp = 0.02 cups . . . . 2 tsp = 0.04 cups . . . . 3 tsp = 1 tbsp = 0.06 cups

1 tbsp = 0.06 cups . . . . 2 tbsp = 0.13 cups. . . . . . . 3 tbsp = 0.19 cups

d. For each ingredient, find Carbohydrate, Fat and Meat Sub Exchanges per cup (see pages 20–23) and enter in the corresponding columns (C1, F1, M1).

e. Multiply exchanges per cup in C1 by number of cups in Q2; enter result in C2. Repeat for F1 and M1, entering results in F2 and M2 respectively.

f. Calculate and enter C2, F2 and M2 totals and copy to row k.

Note

Calculations on this worksheet yield approximate exchange counts.
America's Exchanges calculated here may not
agree exactly with those based on a complete
nutrient calculation of the recipe.

g. In Q2 enter number of eggs, egg yolks and/or egg whites in recipe.

Multiply corresponding values in column M1 by these numbers and enter results in column M2.

Enter pie shells and crusts, phyllo sheets and squares of chocolate here.

h. Enter name of ingredient and the number used in the recipe in columns A and Q2.

i. Enter Carbohydrate and Fat Exchanges per unit (see page 23) in columns C1 and F1.

j. Multiply choices in C1 and F1 by value in Q2 and enter results in C2 and F2.

k. See row f.

l. Calculate and enter C2, F2 and M2 totals for rows g. to k.

m. Enter number of servings that recipe makes.

n. Divide C2, F2 and M2 totals in row l. by number of servings and enter. *These are the unrounded Exchange values per serving.*

o. Round values in row n. to nearest 0.5.

Exception: Round 0.4 or fewer Meat Sub Exchanges to zero.

America's Exchanges Recipe Worksheet

Section A

Ingredient	Measures per RECIPE		Carbohydrate Exchanges per		Fat Exchanges per		Meat Sub Exchanges per	
	NOT cups	cups	cup	recipe	cup	recipe	cup	recipe
A	Q1	Q2	C1	C2	F1	F2	M1	M2

Measured ingredients (cups, tablespoons, etc.)

		Convert non-cup amounts to cups							
a. to e.		>							
		>							
		>							
		>							
		>							
		>							
		>							
		>							
		>							
		>							
		>							
		>							

f.   Section A subtotals [   ] - - - - - [   ] - - - - - [   ]

Section B

Ingredient	# units per recipe	Carbohydrate Exchanges per		Fat Exchanges per		Meat Exchanges per	
		1 unit	recipe	1 unit	recipe	1 unit	recipe
A	Q2	C1	C2	F1	F2	M1	M2

"Counted" ingredients

g.	whole egg		....				1	
	egg white		....				0.5	
	egg yolk		....				0.5	
h. to j.								

k.   Section A subtotals from row f. [   ]   [   ]   [   ]

l.   Total exchanges per recipe - - - - - - - - - - - - - - - - - [   ]   [   ]   [   ]

m.   Recipe makes [   ] servings

n.   Total exchanges per serving, unrounded [   ] = = = = [   ] = = = = [   ]

o.   **Exchanges per serving, final** [   ]   [   ]   [   ]

                                           Carbohydrate   **Fat**   **Meat Sub**

America's Exchanges for Recipe Ingredients

(Use with America's Exchanges Recipe Worksheet on page 19.)

Ingredient	America's Exchanges		
	CARB*	FAT	MEAT
See corresponding columns on worksheet	C1	F1	M1
For use in dessert exchange calculator, all carbohydrate is classified as "Other Carbohydrates."			
Enter measured items in section A of worksheet			

Flour
1 cup
  whole wheat flour
  rye flour
  all-purpose flour
  rice flour
  cake flour
	
	6
	$5\frac{1}{2}$
	$6\frac{1}{2}$
	$8\frac{1}{2}$
	7		

Other Dry Grain Ingredients
1 cup
  wheat bran, raw unprocessed
  wheat bran cereal (about 12 g fiber per $\frac{1}{2}$ cup)
  bran flakes (ready-to-eat cereal)
  oat bran, raw unprocessed
  rolled oats (not instant)
  granola (12 g fat per cup)
  cornmeal
  cornstarch
	
	$2\frac{1}{2}$
	$3\frac{1}{2}$
	$1\frac{1}{2}$
	4
	4
	5
	$8\frac{1}{2}$
	8		

Fruit and Fruit Juice
1 cup
  apple juice
  apples, raw, chopped or sliced (about 1 medium)
  applesauce, unsweetened
  banana, mashed (about 2 medium)
  blueberries, raw or frozen without sugar
  cantaloupe, balls or diced
  honeydew melon, balls or diced
  kiwifruit, sliced (about 3 medium)
  mango, raw, sliced
  orange juice, frozen concentrate, not diluted
  peaches, raw, sliced (about 2 medium)
  pears, raw, sliced (about 1 large)
	
	2
	1
	2
	$3\frac{1}{2}$
	$1\frac{1}{2}$
	1
	1
	$1\frac{1}{2}$
	2
	7
	$1\frac{1}{2}$
	$1\frac{1}{2}$		

Ingredient	America's Exchanges		
	CARB	FAT	MEAT
See corresponding columns on worksheet	C1	F1	M1
Fruit and Fruit Juice (continued)			
pineapple, raw or canned, diced	1½		
raspberries, raw or frozen (no sugar added)	1		
rhubarb, raw, diced (about 8 oz)	½		
strawberries, whole or sliced	½		
fresh strawberry purée, no sugar added	1		
Vegetables 1 cup			
carrot, raw, grated (about 2 medium)	½		
zucchini, raw, grated or shredded (about 1 medium)	½		
pumpkin, canned	1½		
Dried Fruit 1 cup			
dates, chopped	8½		
apricots, chopped	8		
prunes	7		
cranberries	6½		
seedless raisins	8½		
golden raisins	7½		
Milk and Yogurt 1 cup			
skim milk	1		
buttermilk	1		
1% milk	1		
2% milk	1		
whole milk	1		
2% evaporated milk, undiluted	2½		
yogurt, plain low-fat (1%–2%)	1½		
Sugar and Syrups 1 cup			
white (granulated) sugar	13½		
brown sugar, packed	14½		
brown sugar, lightly packed	12		
confectioner's sugar (also called icing or powdered sugar)	8		
fructose (powdered form)	13½		
corn syrup	16½		
honey	18½		

Ingredient	America's Exchanges		
	CARB	FAT	MEAT
See corresponding columns on worksheet	C1	F1	M1
Sugar and Syrups (continued)			
maple syrup	14		
molasses	17		
rice syrup	17		
Fats and Oils 1 cup			
vegetable oil (canola, soybean)		$43\frac{1}{2}$	
margarine, soft hydrogenated		$36\frac{1}{2}$	
butter (2 sticks)		37	
hydrogenated vegetable oil shortening		$43\frac{1}{2}$	
Sour Cream and Cream Cheese 1 cup			
sour cream, light, US (10%)		$4\frac{1}{2}$	
sour cream, regular, US (20%)		$9\frac{1}{2}$	
cream cheese, light (about 20% fat), 8 oz		9	
cream cheese, regular (30% fat), 8 oz		16	
Nuts and Seeds 1 cup			
almonds, chopped or slivered ($3\frac{1}{2}$ oz)		$11\frac{1}{2}$	
coconut, dried unsweetened		$9\frac{1}{2}$	
coconut, shredded sweetened		$6\frac{1}{2}$	
flaxseeds, crushed/ground		9	
hazelnuts/filberts, chopped ($3\frac{1}{2}$ oz)		14	
peanut butter		$26\frac{1}{2}$	
pecans, chopped ($3\frac{1}{2}$ oz)		16	
pistachios, shelled ($3\frac{1}{2}$ oz)		$11\frac{1}{2}$	
sunflower seed kernels, unsalted		$14\frac{1}{2}$	
walnuts, small pieces or chopped ($3\frac{1}{2}$ oz)		15	
Meat Substitutes **Egg** 1 cup			
liquid egg product, yolks replaced			$3\frac{1}{2}$
liquid egg white			$3\frac{1}{2}$
liquid whole egg			4
For individual eggs, egg yolks and egg whites, see end of list.			

Ingredient	America's Exchanges		
	CARB	FAT	MEAT
See corresponding columns on worksheet	C1	F1	M1

Cheese
1 cup
    2% cottage cheese
    ricotta cheese, light (5%)
    ricotta cheese, regular (10%)
			$4\frac{1}{2}$
			4
			4

Be sure to copy both Carbohydrate and Fat Exchanges to worksheet for all items below			

Miscellaneous Ingredients
1 cup
    cocoa powder, unsweetened
    semisweet chocolate chips (6 oz)
    white chocolate chips (6 oz)
    butterscotch chips (6 oz)
    chocolate wafer crumbs
    graham wafer crumbs
	3
	7
	$6\frac{1}{2}$
	$7\frac{1}{2}$
	$5\frac{1}{2}$
	$4\frac{1}{2}$
		2
		10
		11
		10
		3
		$1\frac{1}{2}$	

Enter these "counted" items in section B of worksheet			

Pie Shells and Crusts, Phyllo Sheets and Chocolate
1 cup
    chocolate crumb pie shell, ready-to-use: 170 g, 8-inch
    graham wafer pie shell, ready-to-use: 170 g, 8-inch
    pie crust, frozen, ready-to-bake: 175 g, 9-inch
    phyllo dough sheets ($16\frac{1}{2}$- by 12-inch), 1 sheet
    chocolate, bittersweet/semisweet, 1 square (1 oz)
	$7\frac{1}{2}$
	$7\frac{1}{2}$
	5
	$\frac{1}{2}$
	$1\frac{1}{2}$
		7
		8
		10
		0
		5	

Eggs
    egg, whole
    egg white
    egg yolk
For measured quantities of eggs, see page 22.
			1
			$\frac{1}{2}$
			$\frac{1}{2}$

Canada's Food Choices Recipe Worksheet: How To Use

N.B.
If your recipe is written in metric quantities, you first need to convert these amounts to their imperial measure equivalents using the following standard conversion factors.

5 mL = 0.02 cup	15 mL = 0.06 cup	25 mL = 0.13 cup
50 mL = 0.25 cup	75 mL = 0.33 cup	125 mL = 0.5 cup
150 mL = 0.67 cup	175 mL = 0.75 cup	250 mL = 1 cup

---

a. In column A enter names of recipe ingredients that are called for by volume (i.e., measured in cups, tablespoons or teaspoons, or millilitres).

b. Enter quantities of these ingredients in columns Q1 or Q2.

>*Enter in Q1 if amount is not in cups; otherwise, enter in Q2.*

>*Omit salt, baking powder, baking soda, spices and any other ingredients where the quantity is less than 1 tsp (5 mL).*

c. Using the equivalent measures below, convert quantities in column Q1 to cups and enter in Q2.

   If recipe contains metric quantities, refer to conversion chart at top of page.

   1 tsp = 0.02 cups .... 2 tsp = 0.04 cups .... 3 tsp = 1 tbsp = 0.06 cups

   1 tbsp = 0.06 cups .... 2 tbsp = 0.13 cups .... 3 tbsp = 0.19 cups

d. For each ingredient, find Carbohydrate, Fat, and Meat & Alternative Choices per cup (see pages 26–29) and enter in the corresponding columns (C1, F1, M1).

e. Multiply choices per cup in C1 by number of cups in Q2; enter result in C2. Repeat for F1 and M1, entering results in F2 and M2 respectively.

---

f. Calculate and enter C2, F2 and M2 totals and copy to row k.

Note
Calculations on this worksheet yield approximate food choice counts.
Canada's Choices calculated here may not
agree exactly with those based on a complete
nutrient calculation of the recipe.

---

g. In Q2 enter number of eggs, egg yolks and/or egg whites in recipe.

   Multiply corresponding values in column M1 by these numbers and enter results in column M2.

Enter pie shells and crusts, phyllo sheets and squares of chocolate here.

h. Enter name of ingredient and the number used in the recipe in columns A and Q2.

i. Enter Carbohydrate and Fat Choices per unit (see page 29) in columns C1 and F1.

j. Multiply choices in C1 and F1 by value in Q2 and enter results in C2 and F2.

---

k. See row f.

---

l. Calculate and enter C2, F2 and M2 totals for rows g. to k.

m. Enter number of servings that recipe makes.

n. Divide C2, F2 and M2 totals in row l. by number of servings and enter. *These are the unrounded Choice values per serving.*

---

o. Round values in row n. to nearest 0.5.

   Exception: Round 0.4 or fewer Meat & Alt Choices to zero.

There are various ways to determine how a recipe can fit into your meal plan.
For more information, see page 17.

Canada's Food Choices Recipe Worksheet

Section A

Ingredient	Measures per RECIPE		Carbohydrate Choices per		Fat Choices per		Meat & Alt Choices per	
	NOT cups	cups	cup	recipe	cup	recipe	cup	recipe
A	Q1	Q2	C1	C2	F1	F2	M1	M2

Measured ingredients (cups, tablespoons, etc.)

		Convert non-cup amounts to cups							
a. to e.		>							
		>							
		>							
		>							
		>							
		>							
		>							
		>							
		>							
		>							
		>							
		>							
		>							

f.   Section A subtotals [   ] - - - - - [   ] - - - - - [   ]

Section B

Ingredient	# units per recipe	Carbohydrate Choices per		Fat Choices per		Meat Choices per	
A	Q2	1 unit	recipe	1 unit	recipe	1 unit	recipe
		C1	C2	F1	F2	M1	M2

"Counted" ingredients

	Ingredient		Carbohydrate	Fat	Meat
g.	whole egg		....		1
	egg white		....		0.5
	egg yolk		....		0.5
h. to j.					

k.   Section A subtotals from row f. [   ] [   ] [   ]

l.   Total choices per recipe - - - - - - - - - - - - - - - - - - [   ] [   ] [   ]

m.   Recipe makes [   ] servings

n.   Total choices per serving, unrounded [   ] = = = = [   ] = = = = [   ]

o.   **Choices per serving, final** [   ] [   ] [   ]

Carbohydrate   **Fat**   **Meat & Alt**

Canada's Choices for Recipe Ingredients

(Use with Canada's Food Choices Recipe Worksheet on page 25.)

Ingredient	Canada's Choices		
	CARB	FAT	MEAT
See corresponding columns on worksheet	C1	F1	M1
Enter measured items in section A of worksheet			
Flour 1 cup 　whole wheat flour 　rye flour 　all-purpose flour 　rice flour 　cake flour	 5 4½ 6 8 7		
Other Dry Grain Ingredients 1 cup 　wheat bran, raw unprocessed 　wheat bran cereal (about 12 g fiber per ½ cup/125 mL) 　bran flakes (ready-to-eat cereal) 　oat bran, raw unprocessed 　rolled oats (not instant) 　granola (12 g fat per cup) 　cornmeal 　cornstarch	 1 2 1½ 3½ 3½ 4½ 7½ 7½		
Fruit and Fruit Juice 1 cup 　apple juice 　apples, raw, chopped or sliced (about 1 medium) 　applesauce, unsweetened 　banana, mashed (about 2 medium) 　blueberries, raw or frozen without sugar 　cantaloupe, balls or diced 　honeydew melon, balls or diced 　kiwifruit, sliced (about 3 medium) 　mango, raw, sliced 　orange juice, frozen concentrate, not diluted 　peaches, raw, sliced (about 2 medium) 　pears, raw, sliced (about 1 large) 　pineapple, raw or canned, diced 　raspberries, raw or frozen (no sugar added) 　rhubarb, raw, diced (about 8 oz/250 g)	 2 1 1½ 3½ 1 1 1 1½ 2 7 1 1½ 1 ½ 0		

Ingredient	Canada's Choices		
	CARB	FAT	MEAT
See corresponding columns on worksheet	C1	F1	M1
Fruit and Fruit Juice (continued)			
strawberries, whole or sliced	½		
fresh strawberry purée, no sugar added	1		
Vegetables			
1 cup			
carrot, raw, grated (about 2 medium)	½		
zucchini, raw, grated or shredded (about 1 medium)	0		
pumpkin, canned	1		
Dried Fruit			
1 cup			
dates, chopped	7½		
apricots, chopped	7		
prunes	6½		
cranberries	6		
seedless raisins	8½		
golden raisins	7½		
Milk and Yogurt			
1 cup			
skim milk	1		
buttermilk	1		
1% milk	1		
2% milk	1		
whole milk	½		
2% evaporated milk, undiluted	2		
yogurt, plain low-fat (1%–2%)	1		
Sugar and Syrups			
1 cup			
white (granulated) sugar	13½		
brown sugar, packed	14½		
brown sugar, lightly packed	12		
confectioner's sugar (also called icing or powdered sugar)	8		
fructose (powdered form)	13½		
corn syrup	16½		
honey	18½		
maple syrup	14		
molasses	17		
rice syrup	17		

Ingredient	Canada's Choices		
	CARB	FAT	MEAT
See corresponding columns on worksheet	C1	F1	M1

Fats and Oils
 1 cup
     vegetable oil (canola, soybean)
     margarine, soft hydrogenated
     butter (2 sticks)
     hydrogenated vegetable oil shortening
		$43\frac{1}{2}$
		 $36\frac{1}{2}$
		 37
		 $43\frac{1}{2}$	

Sour Cream and Cream Cheese
 1 cup
     sour cream, light, Canada (5%)
     sour cream, regular, Canada (14%)
     cream cheese, light (about 20% fat), 8 oz/250 g
     cream cheese, regular (30% fat), 8 oz/250 g
		$2\frac{1}{2}$
		 $6\frac{1}{2}$
		 9
		 16	

Nuts and Seeds
 1 cup
     almonds, chopped or slivered ($3\frac{1}{2}$ oz/100 g)
     coconut, dried unsweetened
     coconut, shredded sweetened
     flaxseeds, crushed/ground
     hazelnuts/filberts, chopped ($3\frac{1}{2}$ oz/100 g)
     peanut butter
     pecans, chopped ($3\frac{1}{2}$ oz/100 g)
     pistachios, shelled ($3\frac{1}{2}$ oz/100 g)
     sunflower seed kernels, unsalted
     walnuts, small pieces or chopped ($3\frac{1}{2}$ oz/100 g)
		$11\frac{1}{2}$
		 $9\frac{1}{2}$
		 $6\frac{1}{2}$
		 9
		 14
		 $26\frac{1}{2}$
		 16
		 $11\frac{1}{2}$
		 $14\frac{1}{2}$
		 15	

Meat Alternatives
 Egg
 1 cup
     liquid egg product, yolks replaced
     liquid egg white
     liquid whole egg
 For individual eggs, egg yolks and egg whites, see end of list.
			$3\frac{1}{2}$
			 $3\frac{1}{2}$
			 4

Cheese
 1 cup
     2% cottage cheese
     ricotta cheese, light (5%)
     ricotta cheese, regular (10%)
			$4\frac{1}{2}$
			 4
			 4

Ingredient	Canada's Choices		
	CARB	FAT	MEAT
See corresponding columns on worksheet	C1	F1	M1
Be sure to copy both Carbohydrate and Fat Choices to worksheet for all items below			
Miscellaneous Ingredients 1 cup			
cocoa powder, unsweetened	$1\frac{1}{2}$	2	
semisweet chocolate chips (6 oz/170 g)	$6\frac{1}{2}$	10	
white chocolate chips (6 oz/170 g)	$6\frac{1}{2}$	11	
butterscotch chips (6 oz/170 g)	$7\frac{1}{2}$	10	
chocolate wafer crumbs	5	3	
graham wafer crumbs	4	$1\frac{1}{2}$	
Enter these "counted" items in section B of worksheet			
Pie Shells and Crusts, Phyllo Sheets and Chocolate 1 cup			
chocolate crumb pie shell, ready-to-use: 170 g, 8-inch/20 cm	7	7	
graham wafer pie shell, ready-to-use: 170 g, 8-inch/20 cm	7	8	
pie crust frozen, ready-to-bake: 175 g, 9-inch/23 cm	5	10	
phyllo dough sheets ($16\frac{1}{2}$- by 12-inch/42 by 30 cm), 1 sheet	$\frac{1}{2}$	0	
chocolate, bittersweet/semisweet, 1 square (1 oz/30 g)	$1\frac{1}{2}$	5	
Eggs			
egg, whole			1
egg white			$\frac{1}{2}$
egg yolk			$\frac{1}{2}$
For measured quantities of eggs, see page 28.			

About the Nutrient Analysis and Exchange or Choice Values

Food Intelligence (Toronto, Ontario) calculated the nutrient values for the recipes in this book and assigned America's Exchanges and Canada's Choices (see pages 31–32).

Calculations were carried out with the assistance of Genesis® R&D SQL software, using current versions of the Canadian Nutrient File and USDA Nutrient Database for Standard Reference and reviewed data from other sources when required. All nutrient values were rounded to the nearest whole number; Canada's Choices and America's Exchanges were rounded to the nearest half.

The calculations were based on:

- imperial weights and measures (cup, tsp, lb, etc.), unless a metric package would typically be purchased and a specified proportion of it used in the recipe;
- the first ingredient listed where there is a choice;
- the exclusion of "optional" ingredients; and
- the exclusion of ingredients with non-specified or "to taste" amounts.

America's Exchanges calculations were based on the American Diabetes Association food exchange values in the table below. Carbohydrate choices are based on total carbohydrate, including fiber.

America's Exchanges

Group/Lists	Carbohydrate (g)	Protein (g)	Fat (g)
Carbohydrate Group			
Starches	15	0–3	0–1
Fruit	15	–	–
Milk			
Fat-Free, Low-Fat (1%)	12	8	0.3
Reduced-Fat (2%)	12	8	5
Whole	12	8	8
Other Carbohydrates	15	v*	v*
Vegetables	5	2	–
Meat and Meat Substitutes Group			
Lean	–	7	0–3
Medium-Fat	–	7	4–7
High-Fat	–	7	8
Plant-Based Proteins	v*	7	v*
Fat Group	–	–	5

* v = variable

Adapted from *Choose Your Foods — Exchange Lists for Diabetes*. American Diabetes Association and American Dietetic Association, 2008.

Canada's Choices calculations were based on the Canadian Diabetes Association food choice values in the table below. Carbohydrate choices are based on available carbohydrate (total carbohydrate minus fiber).

Canada's Choices

Canada's Choice	Carbohydrate (g)	Protein (g)	Fat (g)
Carbohydrate			
Grains & Starches	15	3	0
Fruits	15	0	0
Milk & Alternatives	15	8	2.5
Other Choices	15	v*	v*
Vegetables	<5 (most)	2	0
Meat & Alternatives	0	7	3
Fats	0	0	5
Extras	<5	0	0

* v = variable

Adapted from *Beyond the Basics: Meal Planning for Healthy Eating, Diabetes Prevention and Management.* Canadian Diabetes Association, 2007.

Answer to cookie calculator problem on page 16

(15 ÷ 21) x 2 = 1.4, rounded according to the table on page 16 = 1½

If your batch makes only 15 cookies, a serving will be 1½ cookies (not 2).

Muffins, Loaves and Scones

Streusel Apple Muffins

**MAKES 12 MUFFINS
(1 MUFFIN PER
SERVING)**

TIP

When using margarine, choose a soft (non-hydrogenated) version to limit consumption of trans fats.

MAKE AHEAD

Prepare up to a day before. Freeze for up to 6 weeks.

BARB'S NUTRITION NOTE

These muffins can also be made without the topping. It contributes about 2 g carbohydrate per muffin.

- Preheat oven to 375°F (190°C)
- 12-cup muffin tin, sprayed with nonstick vegetable spray

½ cup	packed brown sugar	125 mL
½ cup	applesauce	125 mL
¼ cup	vegetable oil	50 mL
1	egg	1
1 tsp	vanilla	5 mL
1 cup	all-purpose flour	250 mL
1 tsp	baking soda	5 mL
1 tsp	baking powder	5 mL
½ tsp	cinnamon	2 mL
¾ cup	diced peeled apple	175 mL

Topping

2 tbsp	packed brown sugar	25 mL
2 tsp	all-purpose flour	10 mL
½ tsp	cinnamon	2 mL
1 tsp	margarine	5 mL

1. In a large bowl, combine brown sugar, applesauce, oil, egg and vanilla until well mixed. Combine flour, baking soda, baking powder and cinnamon; stir into bowl just until incorporated. Stir in apple. Pour into muffin cups, filling two-thirds full.

2. *Topping:* In a small bowl, combine sugar, flour and cinnamon; cut in margarine until crumbly. Sprinkle evenly over muffins. Bake for 20 minutes or until tops are firm to the touch.

NUTRIENTS PER SERVING	
Calories	142
Carbohydrate	22 g
Fiber	1 g
Protein	2 g
Fat, total	5 g
Fat, saturated	1 g
Cholesterol	16 mg
Sodium	141 mg

AMERICA'S EXCHANGES	
½	Starch
1	Other Carbohydrates
1	Fat

CANADA'S CHOICES	
1½	Carbohydrate
1	Fat

Orange Cranberry Muffins

MAKES 12 MUFFINS (1 MUFFIN PER SERVING)

These delicious fruit muffins are perfect with a cup of tea when you need a mid-afternoon boost — and they're a festive choice for the holiday season. It's hard to believe that you mix in the whole orange, but it makes the muffins so moist!

VARIATION

Substitute fresh or frozen blueberries for the cranberries.

■ Preheat oven to 375°F (190°C)
■ 12-cup muffin tin, lightly greased or lined with paper cups

1½ cups	all-purpose flour	375 mL
¾ cup	granulated sugar	175 mL
2 tsp	baking powder	10 mL
1 tsp	baking soda	5 mL
1	whole navel orange	1
1	egg	1
½ cup	milk	125 mL
⅓ cup	vegetable oil	75 mL
1 cup	fresh cranberries (or frozen, thawed)	250 mL

1. In a large bowl, combine flour, sugar, baking powder and baking soda.
2. Cut off ends of orange, then cut into quarters, without peeling. Remove seeds.
3. In food processor, process orange (including peel), egg, milk and oil until blended. Stir into flour mixture until just moistened. Gently stir in cranberries.
4. Divide batter evenly among prepared muffin cups.
5. Bake in preheated oven for 20 to 25 minutes or until tops are firm to the touch and a tester inserted in the center of a muffin comes out clean. Let cool in tin for 10 minutes, then remove to a wire rack to cool completely.

NUTRIENTS PER SERVING	
Calories	179
Carbohydrate	27 g
Fiber	1 g
Protein	3 g
Fat, total	7 g
Fat, saturated	1 g
Cholesterol	16 mg
Sodium	159 mg

AMERICA'S EXCHANGES	
1	Starch
1	Other Carbohydrates
1½	Fat

CANADA'S CHOICES	
2	Carbohydrate
1½	Fat

Banana Date Muffins

MAKES 12 MUFFINS (1 MUFFIN PER SERVING)

TIPS

These muffins will be fairly flat due to the weight of the dates.

When using margarine, choose a soft (non-hydrogenated) version.

MAKE AHEAD

Prepare up to a day ahead, or freeze for up to 3 weeks.

- Preheat oven to 375°F (190°C)
- 12-cup muffin tin, sprayed with vegetable spray

¼ cup	margarine or butter	50 mL
1	medium banana, mashed	1
¾ cup	granulated sugar	175 mL
1	egg	1
1 tsp	vanilla	5 mL
¾ cup	all-purpose flour	175 mL
½ cup	bran or corn flakes cereal	125 mL
1 tsp	baking powder	5 mL
1 tsp	baking soda	5 mL
¾ cup	chopped pitted dates	175 mL
½ cup	2% yogurt	125 mL

1. In a large bowl, combine margarine, banana, sugar, egg and vanilla; mix well.

2. In a bowl, combine flour, bran flakes cereal, baking powder and baking soda. Add to wet ingredients and stir just until mixed. Stir in dates and yogurt, just until smooth.

3. Spoon batter into prepared muffin cups and bake for 15 to 20 minutes or until tops are firm and tester inserted in center comes out clean.

NUTRIENTS PER SERVING	
Calories	168
Carbohydrate	31 g
Fiber	2 g
Protein	2 g
Fat, total	5 g
Fat, saturated	1 g
Cholesterol	16 mg
Sodium	202 mg

AMERICA'S EXCHANGES	
½	Starch
½	Fruit
1	Other Carbohydrates
1	Fat

CANADA'S CHOICES	
2	Carbohydrate
1	Fat

Big-Batch Banana Blueberry Muffins

MAKES 36 MUFFINS (1 MUFFIN PER SERVING)

These tasty muffins are a great way to use up ripe bananas.

TIP

Ripe bananas can be thrown in the freezer, peel and all. To use, just thaw, peel and mash. You can also mash bananas and freeze in amounts appropriate for your recipes.

■ Preheat oven to 350°F (180°C)
■ Two 12-cup muffin tins, lightly greased or lined with paper cups

3 cups	whole wheat flour	750 mL
3 cups	ground flaxseed	750 mL
2 cups	lightly packed brown sugar	500 mL
1 tbsp	baking powder	15 mL
1 tbsp	baking soda	15 mL
Pinch	salt	Pinch
3	eggs	3
3	ripe bananas, mashed (about 1⅓ cups/325 mL)	3
1	jar (4½ oz/128 mL) baby food prunes or unsweetened applesauce	1
⅔ cup	vegetable oil	150 mL
2 tsp	vanilla	10 mL
2 cups	fresh or frozen blueberries	500 mL

1. In a large bowl, combine flour, flaxseed, brown sugar, baking powder, baking soda and salt.

2. In a very large bowl, combine eggs, bananas, prunes, oil and vanilla. Fold in flour mixture until just combined. Fold in blueberries.

3. Divide batter evenly among prepared muffin cups.

4. Bake in preheated oven for 20 minutes, rotating pans halfway through, or until tops are firm to the touch and a tester inserted in the center of a muffin comes out clean. Let cool in tin for 10 minutes, then remove to a wire rack to cool completely.

NUTRIENTS PER SERVING	
Calories	185
Carbohydrate	25 g
Fiber	5 g
Protein	4 g
Fat, total	8 g
Fat, saturated	1 g
Cholesterol	16 mg
Sodium	141 mg

AMERICA'S EXCHANGES	
½	Starch
½	Fruit
½	Other Carbohydrates
1½	Fat

CANADA'S CHOICES	
1½	Carbohydrate
1½	Fat

Banana Applesauce Muffins

**MAKES 12 MUFFINS
(1 MUFFIN PER
SERVING)**

*This recipe uses whole
wheat flour and less oil
than other recipes.*

- Preheat oven to 400°F (200°C)
- 12-cup muffin tin, lightly greased or lined with paper cups

2 cups	whole wheat flour	500 mL
1 tbsp	baking powder	15 mL
1 tsp	baking soda	5 mL
½ tsp	salt	2 mL
3	ripe bananas, mashed (about 1⅓ cups/325 mL)	3
1	egg, lightly beaten	1
1 cup	unsweetened applesauce	250 mL
½ cup	granulated sugar	125 mL
¼ cup	vegetable oil	50 mL

1. In a large bowl, combine flour, baking powder, baking soda and salt.

2. In a medium bowl, combine bananas, egg, applesauce, sugar and oil. Stir into flour mixture until just combined.

3. Divide batter evenly among prepared muffin cups.

4. Bake in preheated oven for 15 to 20 minutes or until tops are firm to the touch and a tester inserted in the center of a muffin comes out clean. Let cool in tin for 10 minutes, then remove to a wire rack to cool completely.

NUTRIENTS PER SERVING	
Calories	183
Carbohydrate	32 g
Fiber	3 g
Protein	4 g
Fat, total	5 g
Fat, saturated	1 g
Cholesterol	16 mg
Sodium	274 mg

AMERICA'S EXCHANGES	
1	Starch
½	Fruit
½	Other Carbohydrates
1	Fat

CANADA'S CHOICES	
2	Carbohydrate
1	Fat

Blueberry Lemon Cornmeal Muffins

MAKES 12 MUFFINS (1 MUFFIN PER SERVING)

TIPS

Fresh blueberries are always best tasting, especially the small ones available in the summer. If using frozen berries, do not thaw. The flour will help to absorb the excess liquid.

When using margarine, choose a soft (non-hydrogenated) version.

MAKE AHEAD

Bake up to 2 days in advance; store in an airtight container.

Freeze for up to 6 weeks.

- Preheat oven to 350°F (180°C)
- 12-cup muffin tin, sprayed with vegetable spray

¾ cup	granulated sugar	175 mL
¼ cup	margarine or butter	50 mL
1	egg	1
3 tbsp	freshly squeezed lemon juice	45 mL
3 tbsp	2% milk	45 mL
1½ tsp	grated lemon zest	7 mL
1 cup	all-purpose flour	250 mL
¼ cup	cornmeal	50 mL
1½ tsp	baking powder	7 mL
1 tsp	baking soda	5 mL
½ cup	2% plain yogurt	125 mL
1¼ cups	fresh or frozen blueberries	300 mL
2 tsp	all-purpose flour	10 mL

1. In a large bowl, with an electric mixer, beat sugar, margarine, egg, lemon juice, milk and lemon zest until well blended. (Mixture may appear curdled.)

2. In another bowl, stir together flour, cornmeal, baking powder and baking soda. Add flour mixture and yogurt alternately to creamed mixture. In a small bowl, toss blueberries with flour; fold into batter. Divide batter among prepared muffin cups.

3. Bake for 20 to 25 minutes or until tops are firm to the touch and tester inserted in center comes out clean.

NUTRIENTS PER SERVING	
Calories	156
Carbohydrate	27 g
Fiber	1 g
Protein	2 g
Fat, total	5 g
Fat, saturated	1 g
Cholesterol	16 mg
Sodium	201 mg

AMERICA'S EXCHANGES	
1	Starch
½	Fruit
½	Other Carbohydrates
1	Fat

CANADA'S CHOICES	
2	Carbohydrate
1	Fat

Chocolate Chip Oatmeal Muffins

MAKES 12 MUFFINS (1 MUFFIN PER SERVING)

The kids on our tasting panel loved these muffins made with chocolate chips, but adults may prefer them with dried fruit.

TIPS

If you choose to use dried fruit instead of chocolate chips, you will add nutrition and fiber to your muffins.

For the nuts, try walnuts, pecans or almonds.

BARB'S NUTRITION NOTE

Substituting dried fruit, such as raisins, for the chocolate chips will trim ½ Fat Exchange or Choice from the total. Adding the optional chopped nuts will add ½ Fat Exchange or Choice.

- Preheat oven to 400°F (200°C)
- 12-cup muffin tin, lightly greased or lined with paper cups

1½ cups	whole wheat flour	375 mL
½ cup	quick-cooking rolled oats	125 mL
¼ cup	ground flaxseed	50 mL
¼ cup	granulated sugar	50 mL
2 tsp	baking powder	10 mL
½ tsp	baking soda	2 mL
½ tsp	salt	2 mL
1	egg	1
1 cup	milk	250 mL
¼ cup	vegetable oil	50 mL
¼ cup	liquid honey	50 mL
½ cup	semisweet chocolate chips or dried fruit	125 mL
½ cup	chopped nuts (optional)	125 mL

1. In a large bowl, combine flour, oats, flaxseed, sugar, baking powder, baking soda and salt.
2. In a small bowl, whisk together egg, milk, oil and honey. Stir into flour mixture until just combined. Fold in chocolate chips and nuts (if using).
3. Divide batter evenly among prepared muffin cups.
4. Bake in preheated oven for 15 to 20 minutes or until tops are firm to the touch and a tester inserted in the center of a muffin comes out clean. Let cool in tin for 10 minutes, then remove to a wire rack to cool completely.

NUTRIENTS PER SERVING	
Calories	239
Carbohydrate	31 g
Fiber	4 g
Protein	5 g
Fat, total	12 g
Fat, saturated	2 g
Cholesterol	17 mg
Sodium	211 mg

AMERICA'S EXCHANGES	
1	Starch
1	Other Carbohydrates
2½	Fat

CANADA'S CHOICES	
2	Carbohydrate
2½	Fat

Banana Chocolate Chunk Muffins

**MAKES 12 MUFFINS
($\frac{1}{2}$ MUFFIN PER
SERVING)**

MAKE AHEAD
Store tightly wrapped
in foil in the freezer for
up to 2 weeks.

**BARB'S
NUTRITION NOTE**
*Half of this muffin is a
serving*, so share this one
with a friend.

- Preheat oven to 375°F (190°C), with rack in lower middle position
- Stand mixer
- 12-cup muffin tin, lightly greased

2$\frac{1}{4}$ cups	unbleached all-purpose flour	550 mL
2 tsp	baking powder	10 mL
1 tsp	salt	5 mL
$\frac{1}{2}$ tsp	baking soda	2 mL
1 cup	granulated sugar	250 mL
$\frac{1}{2}$ cup	unsalted butter, softened	125 mL
2	eggs	2
1 cup	mashed bananas (about 2)	250 mL
1 cup	lower-fat plain yogurt	250 mL
1 cup	semisweet chocolate chunks or chips	250 mL

1. In a medium bowl, combine flour, baking powder, salt and baking soda. Set aside.

2. Place sugar and butter in the mixer bowl. Attach the flat beater and mixer bowl to the mixer. Set to Speed 4 and beat until light and fluffy, about 2 minutes. Stop mixer to scrape down bowl. Set to Speed 4 and add eggs, one at a time, beating well after each addition. Add bananas and beat well. Stop mixer to scrape down bowl. Set to Speed 2 and beat in flour mixture alternately with yogurt, making 3 additions of dry and 2 of wet. Stop mixer to scrape down bowl. Set to Stir and mix in chocolate chunks.

3. Divide batter evenly among muffin cups. Bake in middle of preheated oven for 25 to 30 minutes or until golden brown. Let cool in tin on a wire rack for 5 minutes. Serve warm or let cool completely.

NUTRIENTS PER SERVING	
Calories	163
Carbohydrate	25 g
Fiber	1 g
Protein	3 g
Fat, total	7 g
Fat, saturated	4 g
Cholesterol	26 mg
Sodium	159 mg

AMERICA'S EXCHANGES	
$\frac{1}{2}$	Starch
1	Other Carbohydrates
1$\frac{1}{2}$	Fat

CANADA'S CHOICES	
2	Carbohydrate
1$\frac{1}{2}$	Fat

Perfect Bran Muffins

MAKES 12 MUFFINS (1 MUFFIN PER SERVING)

A great source of fiber and nutrients.

TIP

Make sure you wait the entire 5 minutes for bran to soak up buttermilk or the muffins will be very dry.

VARIATION

You can add ½ cup (125 mL) of fresh berries such as raspberries, blackberries, etc. with the raisins.

■ Preheat oven to 375°F (190°C)
■ 12-cup muffin tin, lined with paper liners or sprayed with nonstick spray

1½ cups	natural wheat bran	375 mL
1 cup	buttermilk	250 mL
1 cup	all-purpose flour	250 mL
1 tsp	baking soda	5 mL
1 tsp	baking powder	5 mL
½ tsp	salt	2 mL
1	egg	1
⅔ cup	packed brown sugar	150 mL
⅓ cup	vegetable oil	75 mL
½ tsp	vanilla	2 mL
½ cup	golden raisins	125 mL

1. In a bowl, soak bran with buttermilk for 5 minutes. In another bowl, whisk together flour, baking soda, baking powder and salt. Set aside.

2. In a large bowl, whisk together egg, brown sugar, oil and vanilla until blended. Add bran mixture and flour mixture and, using a wooden spoon, stir just until moistened. Fold in raisins.

3. Scoop into prepared muffin tin. Bake in preheated oven until firm to the touch and a toothpick inserted into center comes out clean, 15 to 20 minutes. Let cool in tin on a wire rack for 10 minutes. Transfer to rack to cool completely.

NUTRIENTS PER SERVING	
Calories	188
Carbohydrate	31 g
Fiber	4 g
Protein	4 g
Fat, total	7 g
Fat, saturated	1 g
Cholesterol	16 mg
Sodium	257 mg

AMERICA'S EXCHANGES	
1	Starch
1	Other Carbohydrates
1½	Fat

CANADA'S CHOICES	
2	Carbohydrate
1½	Fat

Yogurt Bran Muffins

BARB'S NUTRITION NOTES

For added fiber, use whole wheat flour whenever you can. In most recipes, you can replace up to half the all-purpose flour with whole wheat without affecting the finished product.

Because whole wheat flour contains the germ of the wheat, it can become rancid if kept for a long time. Buy it in small quantities and store in a cool place.

- Preheat oven to 375°F (190°C)
- 12-cup muffin tin, sprayed with nonstick vegetable spray

½ cup	brown sugar	125 mL
¼ cup	margarine	50 mL
1 tbsp	molasses	15 mL
1	egg	1
1 tsp	vanilla	5 mL
¾ cup	bran cereal*	175 mL
½ cup	all-purpose flour	125 mL
⅓ cup	whole wheat flour	75 mL
¾ tsp	baking powder	4 mL
½ tsp	baking soda	2 mL
½ cup	2% yogurt	125 mL
⅓ cup	raisins	75 mL

* Use a wheat bran breakfast cereal

1. In a large bowl, combine brown sugar, margarine, molasses, egg and vanilla until well blended.

2. Combine cereal, all-purpose and whole wheat flours, baking powder and baking soda; add to bowl alternately with yogurt. Stir in raisins. Pour into prepared muffin cups; bake for 15 to 18 minutes or until tops are firm to the touch.

NUTRIENTS PER SERVING	
Calories	142
Carbohydrate	24 g
Fiber	2 g
Protein	3 g
Fat, total	5 g
Fat, saturated	1 g
Cholesterol	16 mg
Sodium	173 mg

AMERICA'S EXCHANGES	
½	Starch
1	Other Carbohydrates
1	Fat

CANADA'S CHOICES	
1½	Carbohydrate
1	Fat

Pumpkin Bran Muffins

**MAKES 24 MUFFINS
(1 MUFFIN PER
SERVING)**

*Since the batter is made
ahead, it takes no time
at all to bake these fresh
for a special breakfast or
coffee break. You can bake
them all at once or scoop
the batter as you need it.*

TIPS

If you don't have buttermilk
for a baking recipe, sour
milk is a great substitute.
Simply add 1 tbsp (15 mL)
lemon juice or vinegar to
each cup (250 mL) of
regular milk. Let stand for
10 minutes before using.

You can substitute 1 cup
(250 mL) natural bran for
the bran cereal.

The batter will keep in the
refrigerator for up to 1 week,
so there's no need to bake
the muffins all at once.

■ Two 12-cup muffin tins, lightly greased or lined
with paper cups

2 cups	bran cereal	500 mL
1¼ cups	all-purpose flour	300 mL
1¼ cups	whole wheat flour	300 mL
1 cup	raisins	250 mL
½ cup	sesame seeds	125 mL
½ cup	ground flaxseed	125 mL
¼ cup	wheat germ	50 mL
2½ tsp	baking soda	12 mL
½ tsp	salt	2 mL
2	eggs, lightly beaten	2
2 cups	buttermilk or sour milk	500 mL
1½ cups	lightly packed brown sugar	375 mL
1 cup	mashed cooked pumpkin	250 mL
½ cup	vegetable oil	125 mL

1. In a large bowl, combine bran cereal, all-purpose flour,
   whole wheat flour, raisins, sesame seeds, flaxseed, wheat
   germ, baking soda and salt.
2. In a very large bowl, combine eggs, buttermilk,
   brown sugar, pumpkin and oil. Gradually fold in bran
   mixture until well combined. Bake immediately or
   cover and refrigerate for up to 1 week. Preheat oven
   to 400°F (200°C).

NUTRIENTS PER SERVING	
Calories	216
Carbohydrate	34 g
Fiber	5 g
Protein	5 g
Fat, total	8 g
Fat, saturated	1 g
Cholesterol	16 mg
Sodium	262 mg

AMERICA'S EXCHANGES	
1	Starch
½	Fruit
1	Other Carbohydrates
1½	Fat

CANADA'S CHOICES	
2	Carbohydrate
1½	Fat

TIP
If you don't have leftover cooked pumpkin, you can use canned pumpkin purée (not pie filling).

BARB'S NUTRITION NOTE
When purchasing canned pumpkin, read the label carefully and make sure you're not buying pumpkin pie filling by mistake. Canned pumpkin may also contain squash but has nothing else added to it. Pumpkin pie filling contains sugar, salt and other ingredients.

3. Scoop about $\frac{1}{3}$ cup (75 mL) batter per muffin into prepared muffin cups.

4. Bake for 15 to 20 minutes or until tops are firm to the touch and a tester inserted in the center of a muffin comes out clean. Let cool in tins for 10 minutes, then remove to a wire rack to cool completely.

BARB'S NUTRITION NOTE
We've seen a lot of "**portion distortion**" in muffins in recent years. It's not hard to find coffee-shop muffins that are three to four times the size of the ones in this book. When you make a muffin recipe (or any other recipe) from this book, take the opportunity to remember the size, and the nutrients and Exchanges/Choices it contains. This will help you make better choices when you're eating away from home.

Triple B Health Muffins

**MAKES 12 MUFFINS
(1 MUFFIN PER
SERVING)**

*These healthy muffins
are a good choice
for breakfast or a
mid-morning snack.*

■ Preheat oven to 400°F (200°C)
■ 12-cup muffin tin, lightly greased or lined with paper cups

1 cup	whole wheat flour	250 mL
1 cup	natural wheat bran or oat bran	250 mL
1 cup	fresh or frozen blueberries	250 mL
1 tsp	baking soda	5 mL
1 tsp	baking powder	5 mL
2	ripe bananas, mashed (about 1 cup/250 mL)	2
1	egg, lightly beaten	1
½ cup	granulated sugar	125 mL
½ cup	milk	125 mL
¼ cup	vegetable oil	50 mL
1 tsp	vanilla	5 mL

1. In a medium bowl, combine flour, wheat bran, blueberries, baking soda and baking powder.

2. In a large bowl, combine bananas, egg, sugar, milk, oil and vanilla. Fold in flour mixture until just combined.

3. Divide batter evenly among prepared muffin cups, filling each two-thirds full.

4. Bake in preheated oven for 20 to 25 minutes or until tops are firm to the touch and a tester inserted in the center of a muffin comes out clean. Let cool in tin for 10 minutes, then remove to a wire rack to cool completely.

NUTRIENTS PER SERVING	
Calories	153
Carbohydrate	25 g
Fiber	4 g
Protein	3 g
Fat, total	6 g
Fat, saturated	1 g
Cholesterol	16 mg
Sodium	139 mg

AMERICA'S EXCHANGES	
½	Starch
½	Fruit
½	Other Carbohydrates
1	Fat

CANADA'S CHOICES	
1½	Carbohydrate
1	Fat

Oat Berry Muffins

MAKES 12 MUFFINS (1 MUFFIN PER SERVING)

The sweetness of berries complements the nutty flavor of oats.

TIP

If using frozen berries, keep them frozen until you are ready to add them to the batter to prevent the color from tinting the batter.

VARIATION

You can use one type of berry, but I enjoy a multi-colored muffin you get with using a mixture of varieties.

- Preheat oven to 400°F (200°C)
- 12-cup muffin tin, lined with paper liners or sprayed with nonstick spray

1 cup	all-purpose flour	250 mL
1 cup	old-fashioned rolled oats	250 mL
1 tbsp	baking powder	15 mL
½ tsp	salt	2 mL
¼ cup	unsalted butter, softened	50 mL
¾ cup	packed brown sugar	175 mL
1	egg	1
1 cup	buttermilk	250 mL
1 cup	mixed berries, frozen or fresh	250 mL

1. In a bowl, whisk together flour, oats, baking powder and salt. Set aside.

2. In a mixer bowl fitted with paddle attachment, cream butter and brown sugar until fluffy, for 2 minutes. Beat in egg and buttermilk. Using a wooden spoon, stir in flour mixture just until moistened. Fold in berries.

3. Scoop into prepared muffin tin. Bake in preheated oven until light brown and a toothpick inserted into center comes out clean, 20 to 24 minutes. Let cool in tin on a wire rack for 10 minutes. Transfer to rack to cool completely.

NUTRIENTS PER SERVING	
Calories	176
Carbohydrate	30 g
Fiber	2 g
Protein	3 g
Fat, total	5 g
Fat, saturated	3 g
Cholesterol	27 mg
Sodium	195 mg

AMERICA'S EXCHANGES	
1	Starch
1	Other Carbohydrate
1	Fat

CANADA'S CHOICES	
2	Carbohydrate
1	Fat

Pineapple Carrot Date Muffins

MAKES 12 MUFFINS (1 MUFFIN PER SERVING)

MAKE AHEAD
Prepare up to a day ahead. Freeze for up to 6 weeks.

BARB'S NUTRITION NOTE
For baking, always use plain, unflavored oats. Fifty grams of plain rolled oats of any type contains about 33 grams of total carbohydrate, including 5 grams of fiber. In 50 grams of flavored sweetened instant oats, however, you will find only 2 to 3 grams of fiber. This is because only two-thirds of the sweetened variety is actually oats — the rest is sugar.

■ Preheat oven to 375°F (190°C)
■ 12-cup muffin tin, sprayed with vegetable spray

¾ cup	granulated sugar	175 mL
⅓ cup	vegetable oil	75 mL
1	egg	1
1 tsp	vanilla	5 mL
½ cup	grated carrots	75 mL
½ cup	canned pineapple, drained and crushed	75 mL
⅓ cup	finely chopped dates	75 mL
⅓ cup	light sour cream or 2% yogurt	75 mL
1 cup	all-purpose flour	250 mL
⅔ cup	rolled oats	150 mL
1 tsp	baking powder	5 mL
1 tsp	baking soda	5 mL
1 tsp	cinnamon	5 mL
¼ tsp	nutmeg	1 mL

1. In a large bowl, combine sugar, oil, egg and vanilla; mix well.
2. Stir in carrots, pineapple, dates and sour cream.
3. In a bowl, combine flour, oats, baking powder, baking soda, cinnamon and nutmeg. Add to wet ingredients and mix just until combined. Spoon into prepared muffin cups and bake for 15 to 18 minutes or until tops are firm to the touch and tester inserted in center comes out clean.

NUTRIENTS PER SERVING	
Calories	195
Carbohydrate	30 g
Fiber	1 g
Protein	3 g
Fat, total	7 g
Fat, saturated	1 g
Cholesterol	16 mg
Sodium	143 mg

AMERICA'S EXCHANGES	
1	Starch
1	Other Carbohydrates
1½	Fat

CANADA'S CHOICES	
2	Carbohydrate
1½	Fat

Sunrise Zucchini Muffins

**MAKES 12 MUFFINS
(1 MUFFIN PER
SERVING)**

- Preheat oven to 400°F (200°C), with rack in lower middle position
- Stand mixer
- 12-cup muffin tin, greased and floured

2 cups	unbleached all-purpose flour	500 mL
1 cup	shredded zucchini	250 mL
$\frac{1}{2}$ cup	whole wheat flour	125 mL
$\frac{1}{2}$ cup	raisins	125 mL
$\frac{1}{2}$ cup	granulated sugar	125 mL
1 tbsp	baking powder	15 mL
1 tbsp	grated orange zest	15 mL
1 tsp	baking soda	5 mL
$\frac{3}{4}$ tsp	salt	4 mL
$\frac{1}{2}$ tsp	ground cinnamon	2 mL
$\frac{1}{4}$ tsp	ground nutmeg	1 mL
2	eggs, beaten	2
$\frac{1}{2}$ cup	homogenized (whole) milk	125 mL
$\frac{1}{3}$ cup	vegetable oil	75 mL
$\frac{1}{4}$ cup	freshly squeezed orange juice	50 mL

1. Place all-purpose flour, zucchini, whole wheat flour, raisins, sugar, baking powder, orange zest, baking soda, salt, cinnamon and nutmeg in the mixer bowl. Attach the flat beater and mixer bowl to the mixer. Set to Stir and mix until combined.

2. In a small bowl, combine eggs, milk, oil and orange juice. Add to the mixer bowl and mix until just combined.

3. Divide batter evenly among muffin cups. Bake in middle of preheated oven for 10 minutes, then reduce temperature to 375°F (190°C) and bake until golden, about 10 minutes. Remove muffins from tins and let cool on a wire rack. Serve warm or let cool completely.

NUTRIENTS PER SERVING	
Calories	224
Carbohydrate	35 g
Fiber	2 g
Protein	5 g
Fat, total	8 g
Fat, saturated	1 g
Cholesterol	32 mg
Sodium	333 mg

AMERICA'S EXCHANGES	
$1\frac{1}{2}$	Starch
$\frac{1}{2}$	Fruit
$\frac{1}{2}$	Other Carbohydrates
$1\frac{1}{2}$	Fat

CANADA'S CHOICES	
2	Carbohydrate
$1\frac{1}{2}$	Fat

Sweet Potato Muffins

**MAKES 12 MUFFINS
(1 MUFFIN PER
SERVING)**

TIP
For the mixed dried fruit,
try raisins, blueberries,
cherries and cranberries.

**BARB'S
NUTRITION NOTES**
This recipe contains ¼ cup
(50 mL) oil. In recipes for
12 muffins that call for
more than this amount,
you can often reduce it.
Use ¼ cup (50 mL) oil
and add unsweetened
applesauce or mashed
banana to make up the
difference in volume.

Cut dried fruit into small
pieces to spread its flavor
through a batter or dough.

■ Preheat oven to 400°F (200°C)
■ 12-cup muffin tin, lightly greased or lined with paper cups

1 cup	quick-cooking rolled oats	250 mL
1 cup	buttermilk (approx.)	250 mL
½ cup	all-purpose flour	125 mL
½ cup	whole wheat flour	125 mL
¼ cup	granulated sugar	50 mL
1 tbsp	wheat germ	15 mL
1 tbsp	baking powder	15 mL
1 tsp	salt	5 mL
½ tsp	baking soda	2 mL
1 cup	mixed dried fruit	250 mL
1	egg, beaten	1
½ cup	grated sweet potato	125 mL
¼ cup	lightly packed brown sugar	50 mL
¼ cup	vegetable oil	50 mL
1 tsp	grated orange zest	5 mL

1. Place oatmeal in a large bowl and pour in buttermilk;
   stir to combine. Cover and let stand for 10 minutes.

2. Meanwhile, in a small bowl, combine all-purpose flour,
   whole wheat flour, granulated sugar, wheat germ, baking
   powder, salt and baking soda. Stir in dried fruit.

3. In another small bowl, combine egg, sweet potato,
   brown sugar, oil and orange zest. Stir into oatmeal
   mixture. Gradually fold in flour mixture until just
   moistened. If too stiff, add a little more buttermilk.

NUTRIENTS PER SERVING	
Calories	185
Carbohydrate	31 g
Fiber	3 g
Protein	4 g
Fat, total	6 g
Fat, saturated	1 g
Cholesterol	16 mg
Sodium	342 mg

AMERICA'S EXCHANGES	
1	Starch
½	Fruit
½	Other Carbohydrates
1	Fat

CANADA'S CHOICES	
2	Carbohydrate
1	Fat

**BARB'S
NUTRITION NOTE**

These muffins contain
more salt than most
homemade muffins, so
they are higher in sodium.
To lower sodium by 100 mg
per muffin, reduce the salt
to $\frac{1}{2}$ teaspoon (2 mL).
At the same time, you
may want to increase the
quantity of orange zest.

4. Divide batter evenly among prepared muffin cups, filling almost to the top (these muffins do not rise much).

5. Bake for 20 minutes or until a tester inserted in the center of a muffin comes out clean. Let cool in tin for 10 minutes, then remove to a wire rack to cool completely.

BARB'S NUTRITION NOTE

When you look for new recipes, keep your eye out for ones with nutritious ingredients. This one contains rolled oats, whole wheat flour and wheat germ, all of which boost fiber. Wheat germ is also rich in B vitamins and vitamin E. The dried fruit and sweet potato add vitamins and bursts of flavor and sweetness, but they don't contain much sugar — there's only 1 tsp (5 mL) per muffin.

Lemon Poppy Seed Loaf

MAKES 20 HALF-SLICES (1 HALF-SLICE PER SERVING)

TIP
When using margarine, choose a soft (non-hydrogenated) version to limit consumption of trans fats.

MAKE AHEAD
Bake a day before or freeze for up to 6 weeks.

BARB'S NUTRITION NOTE
The lemon glaze on this loaf adds a lot of flavor but only a small amount of carbohydrate. The small quantity of icing sugar contributes about 2 grams of carbohydrate per serving.

- Preheat oven to 350°F (180°C)
- 9- by 5- inch (2 L) loaf pan, sprayed with nonstick vegetable spray

¾ cup	granulated sugar	175 mL
⅓ cup	soft margarine	75 mL
1	egg	1
2 tsp	grated lemon zest	10 mL
3 tbsp	freshly squeezed lemon juice	45 mL
⅓ cup	2% milk	75 mL
1¼ cups	all-purpose flour	300 mL
1 tbsp	poppy seeds	15 mL
1 tsp	baking powder	5 mL
½ tsp	baking soda	2 mL
⅓ cup	2% yogurt or light sour cream	75 mL
Glaze		
¼ cup	icing sugar	50 mL
2 tbsp	freshly squeezed lemon juice	25 mL

1. In a large bowl or food processor, beat together sugar, margarine, egg, lemon zest and juice, mixing well. Add milk, mixing well.

2. Combine flour, poppy seeds, baking powder and baking soda; add to bowl alternately with yogurt, mixing just until incorporated. Do not overmix. Pour into pan and bake for 35 to 40 minutes or until a tester inserted into center comes out dry.

3. *Glaze:* Prick holes in top of loaf with fork. Combine icing sugar with lemon juice; pour over loaf.

NUTRIENTS PER SERVING	
Calories	102
Carbohydrate	16 g
Fiber	0 g
Protein	2 g
Fat, total	4 g
Fat, saturated	1 g
Cholesterol	10 mg
Sodium	94 mg

AMERICA'S EXCHANGES	
½	Starch
½	Other Carbohydrates
1	Fat

CANADA'S CHOICES	
1	Carbohydrate
1	Fat

Banana Nut Raisin Loaf

MAKES 20 HALF-SLICES (1 HALF-SLICE PER SERVING)

TIP
When using margarine, choose a soft (non-hydrogenated) version to limit consumption of trans fats.

MAKE AHEAD
Bake up to 2 days in advance or freeze for up to 6 weeks.

- Preheat oven to 375°F (190°C)
- 9- by 5-inch (2 L) loaf pan, sprayed with nonstick vegetable spray

2	large ripe bananas	2
1/3 cup	soft margarine	75 mL
1/2 cup	granulated sugar	125 mL
1	egg	1
1	egg white	1
1/4 cup	hot water	50 mL
1 1/3 cups	whole wheat flour	325 mL
3/4 tsp	baking soda	4 mL
1/4 cup	raisins	50 mL
1/3 cup	chopped pecans or walnuts	75 mL

1. In a bowl or food processor, beat bananas and margarine; beat in sugar, egg, egg white and water until smooth.

2. Combine flour and baking soda; stir into batter along with raisins and all but a few of the pecans, mixing just until blended. Do not overmix. Pour into pan; arrange reserved nuts down middle of mixture. Bake for 35 to 45 minutes or until a tester inserted into center comes out dry.

BARB'S NUTRITION NOTE
Serving the correct portion size is important. This recipe makes 20 servings, but it's often difficult to cut a loaf of this size into 20 slices. Instead, cut it into 10 slices and then cut each slice in half to make 20 servings.

NUTRIENTS PER SERVING	
Calories	110
Carbohydrate	16 g
Fiber	1 g
Protein	2 g
Fat, total	5 g
Fat, saturated	1 g
Cholesterol	9 mg
Sodium	95 mg

AMERICA'S EXCHANGES	
1/2	Starch
1/2	Other Carbohydrates
1	Fat

CANADA'S CHOICES	
1	Carbohydrate
1	Fat

Pumpkin Molasses Raisin Loaf

MAKES 20 HALF-SLICES (1 HALF-SLICE PER SERVING)

TIP

When using margarine, choose a soft (non-hydrogenated) version to limit consumption of trans fats.

MAKE AHEAD

Can be prepared up to 2 days ahead.

BARB'S NUTRITION NOTE

Serving the correct portion size is important. This recipe makes 20 servings, but it's often difficult to cut a loaf of this size into 20 slices. Instead, cut it into 10 slices and then cut each slice in half to make 20 servings.

- Preheat oven to 350°F (180°C)
- 9- by 5-inch (2 L) loaf pan, sprayed with vegetable spray

1¼ cups	brown sugar	300 mL
⅓ cup	margarine or butter	75 mL
2	eggs	2
2 tbsp	molasses	25 mL
1 tsp	vanilla	5 mL
1 cup	canned pumpkin purée (not pie filling)	250 mL
1 cup	raisins	250 mL
1⅓ cups	all-purpose flour	325 mL
⅔ cup	whole wheat flour	150 mL
2¼ tsp	cinnamon	11 mL
1½ tsp	baking powder	7 mL
½ tsp	baking soda	2 mL
¼ tsp	ginger	1 mL
½ cup	2% yogurt	125 mL

1. In a large bowl, beat sugar and margarine together until crumbly. Add eggs and mix until smooth. Beat in molasses, vanilla and pumpkin. (Mixture may appear curdled.) Stir in raisins.

2. In a bowl, combine flour, whole wheat flour, cinnamon, baking powder, baking soda and ginger. Add to wet ingredients alternately with the yogurt; stir just until combined. Pour into pan and bake for 55 to 60 minutes or until a cake tester inserted in center comes out clean.

NUTRIENTS PER SERVING	
Calories	170
Carbohydrate	32 g
Fiber	1 g
Protein	3 g
Fat, total	4 g
Fat, saturated	1 g
Cholesterol	19 mg
Sodium	110 mg

AMERICA'S EXCHANGES	
½	Starch
½	Fruit
1	Other Carbohydrates
1	Fat

CANADA'S CHOICES	
2	Carbohydrate
1	Fat

Carrot Pineapple Zucchini Loaf

**MAKES 20 HALF-SLICES
(1 HALF-SLICE PER
SERVING)**

TIP
If you like muffins, fill
12 muffin cups and bake
for 20 minutes or until
tops are firm to the touch.

MAKE AHEAD
Make up to 2 days in
advance or freeze for
up to 2 months.

■ Preheat oven to 350°F (180°C)
■ 9- by 5-inch (2 L) loaf pan, sprayed with nonstick
vegetable spray

¼ cup	margarine	50 mL
1 cup	granulated sugar	250 mL
1	egg	1
1	egg white	1
2 tsp	cinnamon	10 mL
1½ tsp	vanilla	7 mL
¼ tsp	nutmeg	1 mL
¾ cup	grated carrot	175 mL
¾ cup	grated zucchini	175 mL
½ cup	drained crushed pineapple	125 mL
⅓ cup	raisins	75 mL
1¼ cups	all-purpose flour	300 mL
½ cup	whole wheat flour	125 mL
1 tsp	baking powder	5 mL
1 tsp	baking soda	5 mL

1. In a large bowl or food processor, cream margarine with
   sugar. Add egg, egg white, cinnamon, vanilla and nutmeg;
   beat well. Stir in carrot, zucchini, pineapple and raisins,
   blending until well combined.

2. Combine all-purpose and whole wheat flours,
   baking powder and soda; add to bowl and mix just
   until combined. Pour into loaf pan and bake for
   35 to 45 minutes or until a tester inserted into center
   comes out dry.

NUTRIENTS PER SERVING	
Calories	118
Carbohydrate	22 g
Fiber	1 g
Protein	2 g
Fat, total	3 g
Fat, saturated	0 g
Cholesterol	9 mg
Sodium	116 mg

AMERICA'S EXCHANGES	
½	Starch
½	Fruit
½	Other Carbohydrates
½	Fat

CANADA'S CHOICES	
1½	Carbohydrate
½	Fat

Oat Bran Banana Bread

MAKES 12 SLICES (1 SLICE PER SERVING)

TIP

When using margarine, choose a non-hydrogenated version to limit consumption of trans fats.

BARB'S NUTRITION NOTES

This recipe contains ground flaxseed, a source of omega-3 fatty acids. There is also an optional quantity of whole flaxseed, but the tough coat on it prevents absorption of its nutrients.

Ground flaxseed goes rancid quickly. Prepare it only as needed or purchase in small quantities and store in the freezer.

- Preheat oven to 325°F (160°C)
- 9- by 5-inch (2 L) loaf pan, lightly greased

1½ cups	whole wheat flour	375 mL
½ cup	oat bran	125 mL
⅓ cup	ground flaxseed	75 mL
1 tsp	baking powder	5 mL
1 tsp	baking soda	5 mL
2	egg whites	2
1	egg	1
½ cup	granulated sugar	125 mL
¼ cup	vegetable oil or margarine	50 mL
1 tsp	vanilla	5 mL
¾ cup	low-fat plain yogurt	175 mL
3	ripe bananas, mashed (about 1⅓ cups/325 mL)	3
2 tbsp	whole flaxseed (optional)	25 mL

1. In a medium bowl, combine flour, oat bran, ground flaxseed, baking powder and baking soda.

2. In a large bowl, beat egg whites, whole egg, sugar, oil and vanilla for 3 to 4 minutes or until creamy. Stir in yogurt until well combined. Stir in bananas. Gradually fold in flour mixture.

3. Spoon batter into prepared loaf pan and smooth top. Sprinkle with whole flaxseed (if using).

4. Bake in preheated oven for 50 to 60 minutes or until top is firm to the touch and a tester inserted in the center comes out clean. Let cool in pan for 10 minutes, then remove to a wire rack to cool completely.

NUTRIENTS PER SERVING	
Calories	197
Carbohydrate	31 g
Fiber	4 g
Protein	6 g
Fat, total	7 g
Fat, saturated	1 g
Cholesterol	16 mg
Sodium	154 mg

AMERICA'S EXCHANGES	
1	Starch
½	Fruit
½	Other Carbohydrates
1½	Fat

CANADA'S CHOICES	
2	Carbohydrate
1½	Fat

Banana Walnut Bread

MAKES 20 HALF-SLICES (1 HALF-SLICE PER SERVING)

BARB'S NUTRITION NOTE
Sesame seeds and additional walnuts are optional in this recipe. One-third cup (75 mL) chopped walnuts or sesame seeds will increase the fat per serving by less than 2 grams.

■ Preheat oven to 375°F (190°C)
■ 9- by 5-inch (2 L) loaf pan, sprayed with baking spray

2	ripe bananas, mashed	2
½ cup	butter, softened	125 mL
½ cup	granulated sugar	125 mL
1	egg	1
1	egg white	1
1⅓ cups	whole wheat flour	325 mL
⅓ cup	chopped walnuts	75 mL
1 tsp	baking soda	5 mL
¼ tsp	salt	1 mL
¼ cup	hot water	50 mL
	Sesame seeds or extra chopped walnuts (optional)	

1. In a bowl, beat bananas with butter until well mixed. Beat in sugar, whole egg and egg white until fluffy.

2. In another bowl, stir together flour, walnuts, baking soda and salt. Stir into banana mixture along with hot water just until blended. Pour into prepared loaf pan. If desired, sprinkle with sesame seeds or extra chopped walnuts.

3. Bake for 35 to 45 minutes or until a cake tester inserted in center comes out clean. Cool in pan for 5 minutes. Remove from pan and cool on wire rack.

NUTRIENTS PER SERVING	
Calories	115
Carbohydrate	14 g
Fiber	1 g
Protein	2 g
Fat, total	6 g
Fat, saturated	3 g
Cholesterol	22 mg
Sodium	146 mg

AMERICA'S EXCHANGES	
½	Starch
½	Other Carbohydrates
1	Fat

CANADA'S CHOICES	
1	Carbohydrate
1	Fat

Pumpkin Spice Nut Bread

**MAKES 12 SLICES
(1 SLICE PER SERVING)**

*This terrific recipe offers
the benefits of pumpkin,
as well as whole grains
and nuts.*

**BARB'S
NUTRITION NOTE**

Nuts are high in calories
because they are high in
fat. This fat, however, is
primarily the desirable
monounsaturated type.
The ½ cup (125 mL) of
pecans in this recipe
contributes about 3 grams
of fat per serving, or about
½ Fat Exchange or Choice.
To reduce the amount
of fat, you can decrease
the amount of nuts in this
recipe. To get the most
flavor from nuts, toast
them on a rimmed baking
sheet at 350°F (180°C)
for about 5 minutes.

■ Preheat oven to 350°F (180°C)
■ 9- by 5-inch (2 L) loaf pan, lightly greased

1 cup	all-purpose flour	250 mL
¾ cup	whole wheat flour	175 mL
2 tsp	ground allspice	10 mL
1½ tsp	baking powder	7 mL
1 tsp	baking soda	5 mL
½ tsp	salt	2 mL
1 tsp	ground cinnamon	5 mL
½ tsp	ground nutmeg	2 mL
½ tsp	ground ginger	2 mL
1 cup	canned pumpkin purée (not pie filling)	250 mL
¾ cup	packed brown sugar	175 mL
½ cup	vegetable oil	125 mL
2	eggs, lightly beaten	2
1 tsp	vanilla	5 mL
⅓ cup	water (approx.), divided	75 mL
½ cup	chopped pecans or walnuts	125 mL

1. In a small bowl, combine all-purpose flour, whole wheat flour, allspice, baking powder, baking soda, salt, cinnamon, nutmeg and ginger.

2. In a large bowl, whisk together pumpkin, brown sugar and oil. Whisk in eggs, vanilla and half of the water. Fold in flour mixture (do not overmix). If batter is too thick, stir in the remaining water, a little at a time. Fold in pecans.

NUTRIENTS PER SERVING	
Calories	251
Carbohydrate	30 g
Fiber	2 g
Protein	4 g
Fat, total	14 g
Fat, saturated	1 g
Cholesterol	31 mg
Sodium	252 mg

AMERICA'S EXCHANGES	
1	Starch
1	Other Carbohydrates
3	Fat

CANADA'S CHOICES	
2	Carbohydrate
3	Fat

VARIATION

Use mini loaf pans to make 12 mini loaves. Bake at the same temperature for 25 minutes, or until a tester comes out clean.

3. Spoon batter into prepared loaf pan and smooth top.

4. Bake in preheated oven for 50 to 60 minutes or until top is firm to the touch and a tester inserted in the center comes out clean. Let cool in pan for 10 minutes, then remove to a wire rack to cool completely.

BARB'S NUTRITION NOTE

For help in planning your meals, ask your doctor to refer you to a diabetes education center or a dietitian. Your local public health unit and hospitals may also have referral services. On the Internet, look for the "find a dietitian" feature at www.eatright.org (in the U.S.) or www.dietitians.ca (in Canada).

Pumpkin Raisin Scones

MAKES 12 SCONES (1 SCONE PER SERVING)

These scones have a beautiful orange color, just like fall leaves.

BARB'S NUTRITION NOTE

Baking parchment is specially treated paper that does not stick to most foods and can withstand oven temperatures up to 425°F (220°C). Waxed paper cannot be used in the same way; it will smoke.

- Preheat oven to 425°F (220°C)
- Baking sheet, lined with parchment paper or Silpat
- Pizza cutter

1½ cups	all-purpose flour	375 mL
1¼ cups	cake flour	300 mL
3 tbsp	granulated sugar	45 mL
1 tbsp	baking powder	15 mL
1 tsp	salt	5 mL
1 tsp	ground cinnamon	5 mL
½ tsp	ground nutmeg	2 mL
¼ tsp	ground allspice	1 mL
¼ tsp	ground cloves	1 mL
6 tbsp	cold vegetable shortening or unsalted butter, cut into chunks	90 mL
2	eggs, beaten, divided	2
¼ cup	pumpkin purée (not pie filling)	50 mL
½ cup	milk, preferably whole	125 mL
1 tbsp	freshly squeezed lemon juice	15 mL
½ cup	golden raisins	125 mL

Mixer Method

1. In a mixer bowl fitted with paddle attachment, beat all-purpose flour, cake flour, sugar, baking powder, salt, cinnamon, nutmeg, allspice and cloves on low speed until blended, for 2 minutes. With mixer running, drop in chunks of shortening, mixing until it resembles coarse crumbs. Set 1 tbsp (15 mL) of the beaten egg aside. Whisk together remaining egg, pumpkin, milk and lemon juice. Pour over the dry ingredients and, using a fork, stir just until dough starts to bind together.

NUTRIENTS PER SERVING	
Calories	214
Carbohydrate	31 g
Fiber	1 g
Protein	4 g
Fat, total	8 g
Fat, saturated	2 g
Cholesterol	32 mg
Sodium	275 mg

AMERICA'S EXCHANGES	
1½	Starch
½	Fruit
1½	Fat

CANADA'S CHOICES	
2	Carbohydrate
1½	Fat

BARB'S NUTRITION NOTE

In this recipe, salt contributes about 200 mg of sodium per scone. Reducing the salt to $\frac{1}{2}$ teaspoon (2 mL) will lower the sodium in each scone by about 100 mg. Doing so, however, may cause the scones to rise less.

2. Turn dough out onto a lightly floured work surface and knead in raisins. Continue to knead dough just until it holds together, about 6 times. Shape into a ball and pat into a 10-inch (25 cm) circle. Place on prepared baking sheet.

3. Using a pizza cutter or sharp knife, cut into 12 wedges. Do not separate wedges. Brush with reserved egg. Bake in preheated oven until light brown, 18 to 22 minutes. Serve warm.

Food Processor Method

1. In work bowl fitted with metal blade, process all-purpose flour, cake flour, sugar, baking powder, salt, cinnamon, nutmeg, allspice and cloves until combined, about 10 seconds. Add butter chunks around work bowl; pulse until mixture resembles coarse crumbs, about 10 times. Set 1 tbsp (15 mL) of the beaten egg aside. With motor running, add remaining egg, pumpkin, milk and lemon juice through feed tube and process just until mixture starts to gather. If dough is tacky, refrigerate for 5 minutes. Proceed with Step 2, above.

BARB'S NUTRITION NOTE

Vegetable shortening used to be a common baking ingredient. Because of concern about its trans fat content, we now see it much less often. In most recipes, you can substitute vegetable oil or soft non-hydrogenated margarine. Some people, however, still prefer shortening for biscuits, scones and pastry; the dough is easier to handle and the results are lighter. (See more about ingredient substitutions on page 173.)

Pecan Cinnamon Biscuits

**MAKES 18 BISCUITS
(1 BISCUIT PER
SERVING)**

*This flavorful biscuit is
perfect served on the
side with an egg dish
or topped with fresh
fruit or a fruit compote
for a dessert.*

TIP

Silpat is the brand name
of a silicone mat used in
baking. Its nonstick surface
does not require greasing.

■ Preheat oven to 425°F (220°C)
■ Baking sheet, lined with parchment paper or Silpat
■ 2½-inch (6 cm) round biscuit cutter
■ Blending fork

2 cups	all-purpose flour	500 mL
2 tbsp	granulated sugar	25 mL
4 tsp	baking powder	20 mL
1 tsp	ground cinnamon	5 mL
½ tsp	salt	2 mL
½ cup	cold vegetable shortening	125 mL
¾ cup	milk, preferably whole	175 mL
¼ cup	pecans, chopped	50 mL

1. In a large bowl, using a blending fork, combine flour, sugar, baking powder, cinnamon and salt. Add shortening by spoonfuls, blending with fork until well mixed into dry ingredients and it resembles coarse meal. Add milk all at once and stir just until dry ingredients are moistened.

2. Turn dough out onto a floured surface and knead, adding pecans, a few times just until dough gathers. Pat down. Using a rolling pin, roll dough to about ½-inch (1 cm) thickness. Cut with biscuit cutter, rerolling scraps. Place biscuits close to each other on prepared baking sheet. Bake in preheated oven until biscuits have risen and are light brown, 15 to 22 minutes. Serve warm.

NUTRIENTS PER SERVING	
Calories	128
Carbohydrate	13 g
Fiber	1 g
Protein	2 g
Fat, total	8 g
Fat, saturated	2 g
Cholesterol	1 mg
Sodium	128 mg

AMERICA'S EXCHANGES	
1	Starch
1½	Fat

CANADA'S CHOICES	
1	Carbohydrate
1½	Fat

Biscotti and Shortbread

Fiber-Power Biscotti

MAKES 30 BISCOTTI (1 BISCOTTI PER SERVING)

Biscotti are twice-baked cookies that are usually very crunchy and work well dipped in your favorite coffee beverage. These ones taste even better than the coffee-shop version.

■ Preheat oven to 350°F (180°C)
■ Baking sheets, lightly greased or lined with parchment paper

2 cups	bran cereal, crushed	500 mL
1½ cups	all-purpose flour	375 mL
1 cup	granulated sugar	250 mL
¾ cup	quick-cooking rolled oats	175 mL
½ cup	sliced almonds	125 mL
½ cup	finely chopped dried apricots	125 mL
2 tsp	baking powder	10 mL
3	eggs, lightly beaten	3
1 tbsp	vegetable oil	15 mL
2 tsp	almond extract	10 mL
1 tsp	vanilla	5 mL

1. In a large bowl, combine bran cereal, flour, sugar, oats, almonds, apricots and baking powder.

2. In a small bowl, beat eggs, oil, almond extract and vanilla. Stir into bran cereal mixture until well blended (dough will be dry and crumbly).

3. Turn dough out onto a lightly floured surface and knead 10 to 15 times, until dough holds together. Divide dough in half and shape each half into a log about 8 inches (20 cm) long and 3 inches (7.5 cm) wide. Place on prepared baking sheets.

NUTRIENTS PER SERVING	
Calories	94
Carbohydrate	17 g
Fiber	1 g
Protein	2 g
Fat, total	2 g
Fat, saturated	0 g
Cholesterol	19 mg
Sodium	41 mg

AMERICA'S EXCHANGES	
½	Starch
½	Other Carbohydrates
½	Fat

CANADA'S CHOICES	
1	Carbohydrate
½	Fat

4. Bake in preheated oven for 30 minutes. Remove from oven and reduce oven temperature to 325°F (160°C). Remove logs from baking sheets and let cool on a wire rack for 10 minutes.

5. Using a serrated knife, cut each log into $\frac{1}{2}$-inch (1 cm) thick slices. Return slices, cut side down, to baking sheets.

6. Bake for 15 minutes. Turn biscotti over and bake for 15 to 20 minutes or until light brown and crisp. Let cool on baking sheets on a wire rack for 5 minutes, then remove to rack to cool completely.

Apricot Date Biscotti

MAKES 48 BISCOTTI (1 BISCOTTI PER SERVING)

When using margarine, choose a soft (non-hydrogenated) version to limit consumption of trans fats.

TIPS

Use a serrated knife to cut the logs into slices.

Dried prunes or raisins can replace, or be used in combination with, the apricots and dates.

Orange juice concentrate gives a more intense flavor than just orange juice. Use frozen concentrate, then refreeze the remainder.

MAKE AHEAD

Bake cookies up to 2 days ahead for best flavor, keeping tightly covered in cookie tin.

Freeze cookie dough for up to 2 weeks.

■ Preheat oven to 350°F (180°C)
■ Baking sheet, sprayed with vegetable spray

⅓ cup	margarine or butter	75 mL
¾ cup	granulated sugar	175 mL
2	eggs	2
2 tbsp	orange juice concentrate, thawed	25 mL
2 tbsp	water	25 mL
2 tsp	grated orange zest	10 mL
1 tsp	vanilla	5 mL
2⅔ cups	all-purpose flour	650 mL
2¼ tsp	baking powder	11 mL
1 tsp	cinnamon	5 mL
⅔ cup	chopped pitted dates	150 mL
⅔ cup	chopped dried apricots	150 mL

1. In a large bowl, cream together margarine and sugar; add eggs, orange juice concentrate, water, orange zest and vanilla and mix well.

2. In a bowl, combine flour, baking powder, cinnamon, dates and apricots; add to wet ingredients and stir just until mixed. Divide dough into 3 portions; shape each portion into a 12-inch (30 cm) long log, 2 inches wide (5 cm), and put on prepared baking sheet. Bake for 20 minutes. Let cool for 10 minutes.

3. Cut logs on an angle into ½-inch (1 cm) thick slices. Put slices flat on baking sheet and bake for another 20 minutes or until lightly browned.

NUTRIENTS PER SERVING	
Calories	67
Carbohydrate	12 g
Fiber	1 g
Protein	1 g
Fat, total	2 g
Fat, saturated	0 g
Cholesterol	8 mg
Sodium	32 mg

AMERICA'S EXCHANGES	
½	Starch
½	Fruit
½	Fat

CANADA'S CHOICES	
1	Carbohydrate
½	Fat

Lemon and Lime
Poppy Seed Biscotti

MAKES 40 BISCOTTI (1 BISCOTTI PER SERVING)

When using margarine, choose a soft (non-hydrogenated) version to limit consumption of trans fats.

TIPS

If desired, omit lime and use double the quantity of lemon juice and zest.

If dough is sticky when forming into logs, try wetting your fingers.

MAKE AHEAD

Store cookies in airtight containers for up to 1 week.

Freeze in airtight containers up to 6 weeks.

■ Preheat oven to 350°F (180°C)
■ Baking sheet, sprayed with vegetable spray

1 cup	granulated sugar	250 mL
1/4 cup	margarine or butter	50 mL
2	eggs	2
1 1/2 tsp	grated lime zest	7 mL
1 1/2 tsp	grated lemon zest	7 mL
2 tbsp	freshly squeezed lime juice	25 mL
2 tbsp	freshly squeezed lemon juice	25 mL
1 tsp	vanilla	5 mL
2 1/2 cups	all-purpose flour	625 mL
2 1/4 tsp	baking powder	11 mL
2 tsp	poppy seeds	10 mL

1. In a food processor or in a bowl with an electric mixer, beat sugar, margarine and eggs until smooth. Beat in lime zest, lemon zest, lime juice, lemon juice and vanilla.

2. In a separate bowl, stir together flour, baking powder and poppy seeds. Add wet ingredients to dry ingredients, mixing just until combined. Dough will be stiff.

3. Divide dough in half. Form each half into a log 12 inches (30 cm) long and 1 1/2 inches (4 cm) around; transfer to prepared baking sheet. Bake 20 minutes. Cool 10 minutes.

4. Cut logs on an angle into 1/2-inch (1 cm) slices. Bake 20 minutes.

NUTRIENTS PER SERVING	
Calories	63
Carbohydrate	11 g
Fiber	0 g
Protein	1 g
Fat, total	2 g
Fat, saturated	0 g
Cholesterol	9 mg
Sodium	33 mg

AMERICA'S EXCHANGES	
1/2	Starch
1/2	Other Carbohydrates
1/2	Fat

CANADA'S CHOICES	
1	Carbohydrate
1/2	Fat

Mini Hazelnut Biscotti

**MAKES 60 BISCOTTI
(1 BISCOTTI PER
SERVING)**

*The honey flavor is
especially nice in these
small crisp biscotti.
They are perfect to
dip in coffee or tea.*

TIPS

Be prepared — this dough
is very stiff, so you will
need to work it with your
hands to get it smooth.
Use a sharp serrated knife
to cut biscotti.

Although recipes usually
call for an electric mixer
to blend ingredients, you
can almost always use a
wooden spoon when
making cookies. It just takes
more physical effort. With
either method, it usually
takes about 3 minutes to
get a butter-and-sugar
mixture light and creamy.

VARIATION

Substitute almonds or Brazil
nuts for the hazelnuts.

NUTRIENTS PER SERVING	
Calories	45
Carbohydrate	8 g
Fiber	0 g
Protein	1 g
Fat, total	1 g
Fat, saturated	0 g
Cholesterol	0 mg
Sodium	23 mg

- Preheat oven to 350°F (180°C)
- Baking sheet, greased or lined with parchment paper

2 cups	unbleached all-purpose flour	500 mL
2/3 cup	granulated sugar	150 mL
1/2 cup	ground hazelnuts	125 mL
1/2 tsp	baking powder	2 mL
1/2 tsp	baking soda	2 mL
1/4 tsp	salt	1 mL
1 tsp	ground cinnamon	5 mL
3/4 cup	whole hazelnuts	175 mL
1/3 cup	liquid honey	75 mL
2 tsp	grated orange zest	10 mL
1/3 cup	orange juice	75 mL

1. In a large bowl, combine flour, sugar, ground hazelnuts, baking powder, baking soda, salt, cinnamon and whole hazelnuts. Mix to blend.

2. Add honey and orange zest and juice. With a wooden spoon, stir until blended, then, using your hands, knead to form a smooth, stiff dough.

3. Divide dough into halves. Shape each into a roll 15 inches (37.5 cm) long. Place about 2 inches (5 cm) apart on prepared baking sheet. Bake in preheated oven for 25 to 30 minutes or until set and golden. Cool for 15 minutes on sheet, then transfer to a cutting board. Cut diagonally into $1/2$-inch (1 cm) slices. Place upright about 1 inch (2.5 cm) apart on baking sheet. Bake for 15 minutes until crisp and golden. Cool for 5 minutes on sheet, then transfer to a rack and cool completely.

AMERICA'S EXCHANGES	
1/2	Other Carbohydrates

CANADA'S CHOICES	
1/2	Carbohydrate

Pecan Biscotti

**MAKES 45 BISCOTTI
(1 BISCOTTI PER
SERVING)**

TIPS

Instead of pecans, you can use almonds, hazelnuts, pine nuts or a combination.

When using margarine, choose a soft (non-hydrogenated) version to limit consumption of trans fats.

BARB'S NUTRITION NOTE

Sometimes you will get more or fewer biscotti than stated in the recipe. When this happens, see the cookie calculator on page 15 for help in determining how many cookies make up a serving.

■ Preheat oven to 350°F (180°C)
■ Baking sheet, sprayed with nonstick vegetable spray

2	eggs	2
¾ cup	granulated sugar	175 mL
⅓ cup	margarine	75 mL
¼ cup	water	50 mL
2 tsp	vanilla	10 mL
1 tsp	almond extract	5 mL
2¾ cups	all-purpose flour	675 mL
½ cup	chopped pecans	125 mL
2¼ tsp	baking powder	11 mL

1. In a large bowl, blend eggs with sugar; beat in margarine, water, vanilla and almond extract until smooth.

2. Add flour, pecans and baking powder; mix until dough forms ball. Divide dough in half; shape each portion into 12-inch (30 cm) long log and place on baking sheet. Bake for 20 minutes. Let cool for 5 minutes.

3. Cut logs on angle into ½-inch (1 cm) thick slices. Place slices on sides on baking sheet; bake for 20 minutes or until lightly browned.

NUTRIENTS PER SERVING	
Calories	79
Carbohydrate	13 g
Fiber	0 g
Protein	1 g
Fat, total	3 g
Fat, saturated	0 g
Cholesterol	8 mg
Sodium	644 mg

AMERICA'S EXCHANGES	
½	Starch
½	Other Carbohydrates
½	Fat

CANADA'S CHOICES	
1	Carbohydrate
½	Fat

Maple Walnut Biscotti

MAKES 30 BISCOTTI (1 BISCOTTI PER SERVING)

Maple extract has a wonderful real maple flavor that is ideal for baking. Because cookies don't require much liquid, you can't use maple syrup to provide that taste.

TIP

When grinding nuts in a food processor, add a little flour or sugar from your recipe to keep them from clumping.

BARB'S NUTRITION NOTE

Did you get a different number of cookies than the recipe states? Use the cookie calculator on page 15 to help you determine how many of your cookies match the nutrients, America's Exchanges and Canada's Choices displayed on the recipe.

- Preheat oven to 350°F (180°C)
- Baking sheet, greased or lined with parchment paper

2 cups	all-purpose flour	500 mL
1/3 cup	ground walnuts	75 mL
1 1/4 tsp	baking powder	6 mL
1/4 tsp	salt	1 mL
2	eggs	2
1/2 cup	packed brown sugar	125 mL
1/4 cup	granulated sugar	50 mL
1/2 cup	vegetable oil	125 mL
1 tsp	maple extract	5 mL
1 cup	coarsely chopped walnuts	250 mL

1. On a sheet of waxed paper or in a bowl, combine flour, ground walnuts, baking powder and salt. Set aside.

2. In a large bowl, using a wooden spoon, beat eggs, brown and granulated sugars, oil and maple extract until smoothly blended. Add flour mixture, stirring until smooth. Add walnuts. Using your hands, knead to form a smooth dough.

NUTRIENTS PER SERVING	
Calories	120
Carbohydrate	13 g
Fiber	1 g
Protein	2 g
Fat, total	7 g
Fat, saturated	1 g
Cholesterol	12 mg
Sodium	37 mg

AMERICA'S EXCHANGES	
1/2	Starch
1/2	Other Carbohydrates
1 1/2	Fat

CANADA'S CHOICES	
1	Carbohydrate
1 1/2	Fat

TIP

Be sure biscotti are thoroughly dry and cool before packing or they will soften during storage.

VARIATIONS

Replace walnuts with pecans.

Omit maple extract. Add 1 tbsp (15 mL) instant espresso coffee powder along with the flour mixture.

3. Divide dough into halves. Shape each into a roll 8 inches (20 cm) long. Place about 4 inches (10 cm) apart on prepared baking sheet. Flatten rolls to 3 inches (7.5 cm) wide, leaving top slightly rounded. Bake in preheated oven for 25 to 30 minutes or until light golden. Cool for 15 minutes on sheet, then transfer to a cutting board. Cut into $1/2$-inch (1 cm) slices. Place cut side down on baking sheet. Bake for 10 minutes. Turn slices over and bake for 5 to 10 minutes or until crisp and golden. Cool for 5 minutes on sheet, then transfer to a rack and cool completely.

BARB'S NUTRITION NOTE

Parchment paper is a great invention. When you line a baking sheet with it, the cookies do not stick — and the baking sheet stays clean. You can use the same sheet of parchment paper several times when you're baking a large batch. If it starts to curl up, sprinkle or spray water on the baking sheet, then smooth the parchment over it.

Chocolate Cherry Biscotti

MAKES 40 BISCOTTI (1 BISCOTTI PER SERVING)

Over the years, I have developed many recipes for biscotti (there are no bad biscotti), but this is one of my favorites.

VARIATION

If you don't have dried cherries, dried cranberries work really well.

- Preheat oven to 350°F (180°C)
- Baking sheets, lined with parchment paper

3 cups	all-purpose flour	750 mL
2 tsp	baking powder	10 mL
¼ tsp	salt	1 mL
1 cup	granulated sugar	250 mL
3	eggs	3
2 tbsp	vegetable oil	25 mL
2 tsp	vanilla	10 mL
1½ tsp	almond extract	7 mL
1 cup	semisweet chocolate chips	250 mL
⅔ cup	dried sour cherries	150 mL

1. In a medium bowl, combine flour, baking powder and salt.

2. In a large bowl, using an electric mixer, beat sugar and eggs until thickened and pale, about 4 minutes. Add oil, vanilla and almond extract, beating just until blended. Add flour mixture, beating on low speed just until blended. Stir in chocolate chips and cherries.

3. Divide dough in half. Turn out dough onto prepared baking sheets. Shape each half into a 10-inch (25 cm) long log and flatten to 1-inch (2.5 cm) thickness. Bake in preheated oven for 25 to 30 minutes or until lightly browned. Transfer logs to a rack. Let cool for 10 minutes. Reduce oven temperature to 325°F (160°C).

4. Transfer logs to a cutting board. Cut each log diagonally into ½-inch (1 cm) slices. Place slices, cut side down, on baking sheet. Bake for 15 to 20 minutes longer or until golden and toasted. The biscotti will be slightly soft in center but will harden as they cool. Transfer to racks and let cool completely.

NUTRIENTS PER SERVING	
Calories	93
Carbohydrate	17 g
Fiber	1 g
Protein	2 g
Fat, total	2 g
Fat, saturated	1 g
Cholesterol	14 mg
Sodium	33 mg

AMERICA'S EXCHANGES	
½	Starch
½	Other Carbohydrates
½	Fat

CANADA'S CHOICES	
1	Carbohydrate
½	Fat

Chocolate Chip Orange Biscotti

MAKES 30 BISCOTTI (1 BISCOTTI PER SERVING)

These biscotti are a very popular item in our gift baskets. Orange and chocolate leave an everlasting impression on the taste buds. My buds are partial to this combo. Properly stored in an airtight container, they will last for 2 months.

BARB'S NUTRITION NOTE

Unless otherwise stated, recipes are tested with large eggs. You may not get the same results if you use another size, especially in recipes, such as these biscotti, that contain a very small amount of liquid.

■ Preheat oven to 350°F (180°C)
■ Baking sheets, lined with parchment paper

2¾ cups	all-purpose flour	675 mL
1 cup	granulated sugar	250 mL
2 tsp	baking powder	10 mL
1 tbsp	vegetable oil	15 mL
1 tbsp	orange extract	15 mL
2 tsp	grated orange zest	10 mL
1 tsp	vanilla	5 mL
3	eggs	3
1 cup	semisweet chocolate chips	250 mL

1. In a medium bowl, combine flour, sugar and baking powder.

2. In a large bowl, using an electric mixer, beat oil, orange extract, orange zest, vanilla and eggs until blended. Add flour mixture, beating until well blended. Stir in chocolate chips.

3. Divide dough in half. Turn out dough onto prepared baking sheets. Shape each half into a 10-inch (25 cm) long log and flatten to 1-inch (2.5 cm) thickness. Bake in preheated oven for 25 to 30 minutes or until lightly browned. Transfer logs to a rack. Let cool for 10 minutes. Reduce oven temperature to 325°F (160°C).

4. Transfer logs to cutting board. Cut each log diagonally into ½-inch (1 cm) slices. Place slices, cut side down, on baking sheet. Bake for 15 to 20 minutes longer or until golden and toasted. The biscotti will be soft in center but will harden as they cool. Transfer to racks and let cool completely.

NUTRIENTS PER SERVING	
Calories	108
Carbohydrate	19 g
Fiber	1 g
Protein	2 g
Fat, total	3 g
Fat, saturated	1 g
Cholesterol	19 mg
Sodium	24 mg

AMERICA'S EXCHANGES	
½	Starch
½	Other Carbohydrates
½	Fat

CANADA'S CHOICES	
1	Carbohydrate
½	Fat

Two-Tone Chocolate Orange Biscotti

MAKES 40 BISCOTTI (1 BISCOTTI PER SERVING)

TIPS

If dough is sticky when forming into logs, try wetting your fingers.

Two colors of dough make these cookies very attractive.

When using margarine, choose a soft (non-hydrogenated) version to limit consumption of trans fats.

MAKE AHEAD

Freeze in containers for up to 6 weeks.

■ Preheat oven to 350°F (180°C)
■ Baking sheet, sprayed with vegetable spray

1 1/4 cups	granulated sugar	300 mL
1/3 cup	margarine or butter	75 mL
2	eggs	2
2 tbsp	orange juice concentrate	25 mL
1 tbsp	grated orange zest	15 mL
2 2/3 cups	all-purpose flour	650 mL
2 1/2 tsp	baking powder	12 mL
3 tbsp	unsweetened cocoa powder	45 mL

1. In a food processor or in a bowl with an electric mixer, beat together sugar, margarine, eggs, orange juice concentrate and orange zest until smooth. Add flour and baking powder; mix just until combined.

2. Divide dough in half; to one half, add cocoa and mix well. Divide chocolate and plain doughs in half to produce 4 doughs. Roll each piece into a long, thin rope approximately 12 inches (30 cm) long and 1 inch (2.5 cm) wide. Use extra flour if too sticky. Place 1 cocoa dough on top of (or beside) each plain dough. (Ensure the plain and cocoa doughs touch one another.)

3. Bake for 20 minutes. Cool 10 minutes. Cut logs on an angle into 1/2-inch (1 cm) slices. Bake another 20 minutes.

NUTRIENTS PER SERVING	
Calories	74
Carbohydrate	13 g
Fiber	0 g
Protein	1 g
Fat, total	2 g
Fat, saturated	0 g
Cholesterol	9 mg
Sodium	40 mg

AMERICA'S EXCHANGES	
1/2	Starch
1/2	Other Carbohydrates
1/2	Fat

CANADA'S CHOICES	
1	Carbohydrate
1/2	Fat

Gingerbread Biscotti

MAKES 40 BISCOTTI (2 BISCOTTI PER SERVING)

TIPS

To add fiber, use ⅔ cup (150 mL) whole wheat flour and 1⅔ cups (400 mL) all-purpose flour.

For a decadent treat, melt 2 oz (50 g) semisweet chocolate and dip ends of cookies. Let harden.

BARB'S NUTRITION NOTE

If you choose to dip these biscotti in chocolate, each cookie will pick up about 1 gram of chocolate, which you don't need to count.

■ Preheat oven to 350°F (180°C)
■ Baking sheet, sprayed with vegetable spray

¾ cup	packed brown sugar	175 mL
¼ cup	margarine or butter	50 mL
¼ cup	molasses	50 mL
2	eggs	2
1 tsp	vanilla	5 mL
2⅓ cups	all-purpose flour	575 mL
2¼ tsp	baking powder	11 mL
1 tsp	ground cinnamon	5 mL
1 tsp	ground ginger	5 mL
½ tsp	ground allspice	2 mL
¼ tsp	ground nutmeg	1 mL

1. In a food processor or in a bowl with an electric mixer, beat together brown sugar, margarine, molasses, eggs and vanilla until smooth. In a separate bowl, stir together flour, baking powder, cinnamon, ginger, allspice and nutmeg. Add wet ingredients to dry ingredients, mixing just until combined.

2. Divide dough in half. Form each half into a log 12 inches (30 cm) long and 2 inches (5 cm) around; transfer to prepared baking sheet. Bake 20 minutes. Cool 10 minutes.

3. Cut logs on an angle into ½-inch (1 cm) slices. Bake for 20 minutes or until lightly browned.

NUTRIENTS PER SERVING	
Calories	63
Carbohydrate	11 g
Fiber	0 g
Protein	1 g
Fat, total	1 g
Fat, saturated	0 g
Cholesterol	9 mg
Sodium	36 mg

AMERICA'S EXCHANGES	
½	Starch
½	Other Carbohydrates

CANADA'S CHOICES	
1	Carbohydrate

Chocolate-Wrapped Ginger Biscotti

MAKES 30 BISCOTTI (1 BISCOTTI PER SERVING)

A dark chocolate dough wraps around a lighter ginger dough to form attractive two-toned biscotti.

TIPS

To distribute cocoa evenly and avoid streaks in a dough, knead the dough with your hands on a lightly floured surface.

Cocoa tends to lump during storage. Before mixing, even the smallest amount should be sifted to remove the lumps, as they won't disappear during baking.

A sharp serrated knife works best for cutting biscotti.

- Preheat oven to 375°F (190°C)
- Baking sheet, greased or lined with parchment paper

2 cups	all-purpose flour	500 mL
2 tsp	baking powder	10 mL
¼ tsp	salt	1 mL
⅓ cup	butter, softened	75 mL
⅔ cup	granulated sugar	150 mL
2	eggs	2
2 tbsp	unsweetened cocoa powder, sifted	25 mL
¼ cup	finely chopped crystallized ginger	50 mL
½ cup	miniature semisweet chocolate chips	125 mL
¼ tsp	ground ginger	1 mL

1. On a sheet of waxed paper or in a bowl, combine flour, baking powder and salt. Set aside.

2. In a large bowl, using an electric mixer on medium speed, beat butter and sugar until light and creamy, about 3 minutes. Add eggs, one at a time, beating well after each addition. On low speed, gradually add flour mixture, beating until blended. Divide dough into halves. With a wooden spoon, stir cocoa powder and crystallized ginger into 1 portion and, using your hands, knead until thoroughly integrated. Add mini chocolate chips and ground ginger to the other portion and, using your hands, knead until thoroughly integrated.

NUTRIENTS PER SERVING	
Calories	98
Carbohydrate	15 g
Fiber	0 g
Protein	2 g
Fat, total	4 g
Fat, saturated	2 g
Cholesterol	18 mg
Sodium	63 mg

AMERICA'S EXCHANGES	
½	Starch
½	Other Carbohydrates
1	Fat

CANADA'S CHOICES	
1	Carbohydrate
1	Fat

3. Divide each portion into halves to make 4 portions. Between two sheets of waxed paper, roll 1 portion of chocolate dough into an 8- by 6-inch (20 by 15 cm) rectangle. Remove top sheet of waxed paper. Shape 1 portion of light dough into a roll 8 inches (20 cm) long. Place roll in the center of chocolate dough and wrap chocolate dough around it. Repeat with remaining dough and place the 2 rolls about 4 inches (10 cm) apart on prepared baking sheet. Flatten slightly, leaving top slightly rounded.

4. Bake in preheated oven for 35 to 40 minutes or until set. Cool for 15 minutes on sheet, then transfer to a cutting board. Reduce oven temperature to 325°F (160°C). Cut rolls into $\frac{1}{2}$-inch (1 cm) slices. Place upright on baking sheet. Bake for 10 to 15 minutes or until crisp and center is light golden. Cool for 5 minutes on sheet, then transfer to a rack and cool completely.

BARB'S NUTRITION NOTE

The name of a food can tell us a lot, sometimes in a single word. "Biscotti" is an Italian word meaning "twice cooked" (*bis cotti*). To make these hard, dry cookies, the dough is first baked in a loaf, then it is sliced and baked again.

Holiday Biscotti

MAKES 40 BISCOTTI (1 BISCOTTI PER SERVING)

These biscotti are a favorite at Christmastime.

TIP
When using margarine, choose a non-hydrogenated version to limit consumption of trans fats.

VARIATION
You can replace the orange zest with 1½ tbsp (22 mL) ground cardamom or 2 tbsp (25 mL) roasted fennel seeds. To roast seeds, place on a baking sheet and bake in preheated 350°F (180°C) oven until they become aromatic but not brown, about 3 minutes.

■ Preheat oven to 325°F (160°C)
■ Baking sheets, lined with parchment paper

2½ cups	all-purpose flour	625 mL
1 cup	slivered almonds or pistachios	250 mL
1 tbsp	grated orange zest	15 mL
1 tsp	baking powder	5 mL
½ tsp	salt	2 mL
2	eggs	2
¾ cup	granulated sugar	175 mL
½ cup	margarine	125 mL
2 tsp	vanilla or almond extract	10 mL

1. In a medium bowl, combine flour, almonds, orange zest, baking powder and salt.

2. In a large bowl, beat eggs, sugar, margarine and vanilla until slightly foamy. Fold in flour mixture.

3. Divide dough in half and shape each half into a log about 14 inches (35 cm) long and 2 inches (5 cm) wide. Place on prepared baking sheets. Smooth top and sides with clean hands.

4. Bake in preheated oven for 30 minutes. Remove from oven and reduce oven temperature to 275°F (140°C). Remove logs from baking sheets and let cool on a wire rack for 10 minutes.

5. Using a serrated knife, cut each log into ½-inch (1 cm) thick slices. Place slices upright on baking sheets.

6. Bake for 20 to 25 minutes or until golden and crisp. Let cool on baking sheets on a wire rack for 5 minutes, then remove to rack to cool completely.

NUTRIENTS PER SERVING	
Calories	82
Carbohydrate	10 g
Fiber	1 g
Protein	2 g
Fat, total	4 g
Fat, saturated	1 g
Cholesterol	9 mg
Sodium	70 mg

AMERICA'S EXCHANGES	
½	Starch
1	Fat

CANADA'S CHOICES	
½	Carbohydrate
1	Fat

Oatmeal Shortbread

MAKES 54 BARS (1 BAR PER SERVING)

The large-flake oats give this shortbread a wonderful nutty flavor and an appealingly rustic appearance.

BARB'S NUTRITION TIP

Most bars and squares should be cut after they've cooled, but shortbread and crisp bars should be cut while they're still warm to avoid shattering them. They may not, however, stay completely separated, which is why this recipe includes the instruction to "recut."

- Preheat oven to 350°F (180°C)
- 13- by 9-inch (3 L) cake pan, ungreased

1 cup	butter, softened	250 mL
⅔ cup	packed brown sugar	150 mL
1½ cups	all-purpose flour	375 mL
1 tsp	cinnamon	5 mL
1¼ cups	old-fashioned (large-flake) rolled oats	300 mL

1. In a bowl, using an electric mixer on medium speed, beat butter and brown sugar until light and creamy, about 3 minutes. Stir in flour, cinnamon and oats, mixing well. Using your hands, knead to form a smooth dough. Press evenly into pan. Prick surface all over with a fork.

2. Bake in preheated oven until light golden, 25 to 30 minutes. Cut into bars or squares just as the pan comes out of the oven, then let cool completely in pan on rack. Recut.

BARB'S NUTRITION NOTE

In the past, one of the meanings of the word "short" was "crumbly," hence what we know as "shortbread." Its crumbly texture is a result of the high amount of fat (usually butter) in the recipe — two parts butter to one part sugar and three parts flour. Shortbread originated in Scotland, where it was first made with oat flour.

NUTRIENTS PER SERVING	
Calories	61
Carbohydrate	7 g
Fiber	0 g
Protein	1 g
Fat, total	4 g
Fat, saturated	2 g
Cholesterol	9 mg
Sodium	36 mg

AMERICA'S EXCHANGES	
½	Starch
1	Fat

CANADA'S CHOICES	
½	Carbohydrate
1	Fat

Almond Spice Shortbread

**MAKES 54 BARS
(1 BAR PER SERVING)**

A hint of spice in the dough and a crunchy almond topping gives these bars a wonderful flavor and a texture that's quite different from plain shortbread.

TIPS

When creaming butter and sugar, it's important to have the butter at the right temperature. It should be a spreadable consistency. If it's too hard, it won't mix to a creamy, light texture, and if it's too soft, the dough will be too soft.

Due to the addition of an egg yolk, this dough is a little softer than regular shortbread dough. That's the advantage of bars — the pan holds the shape. Softer dough in cookies will spread out and flatten, resulting in crisp, potentially overbaked cookies.

- Preheat oven to 300°F (150°C)
- 13- by 9-inch (3 L) cake pan, ungreased

1 cup	butter, softened	250 mL
3/4 cup	granulated sugar	175 mL
1	egg, separated	1
1/2 tsp	almond extract	2 mL
2 cups	all-purpose flour	500 mL
1 tsp	cinnamon	5 mL
1/4 tsp	ground nutmeg	1 mL
3/4 cup	sliced almonds	175 mL

1. In a bowl, using an electric mixer on medium speed, beat butter, sugar, egg yolk and almond extract until smooth and creamy. Stir in flour, cinnamon and nutmeg, mixing well. Using your hands, knead to form a smooth dough. Press evenly into pan.

2. In a bowl, whisk egg white lightly (you don't want it to be frothy). Brush lightly over dough. Sprinkle almonds evenly over top.

3. Bake in preheated oven until light golden all over, 30 to 35 minutes. Cut into bars or squares just as the pan comes out of the oven, then let cool completely in pan on rack. Recut.

NUTRIENTS PER SERVING	
Calories	67
Carbohydrate	7 g
Fiber	0 g
Protein	1 g
Fat, total	4 g
Fat, saturated	2 g
Cholesterol	13 mg
Sodium	36 mg

AMERICA'S EXCHANGES	
1/2	Starch
1	Fat

CANADA'S CHOICES	
1/2	Carbohydrate
1	Fat

Oatmeal Pecan Shortbread

**MAKES 24 PIECES
(2 PIECES PER SERVING)**

Brown sugar gives this shortbread a nice caramel flavor and crisp texture.

TIPS

Use quick-cooking oats, not instant or old-fashioned large-flake oats, in this recipe.

Use an offset spatula to transfer cookies that are more fragile, such as these, to and from baking sheets.

BARB'S NUTRITION NOTE

The bend in the blade near the handle of an offset spatula helps you slide it more easily under what you are lifting.

- Preheat oven to 300°F (150°C)
- 2-inch (5 cm) cookie cutters
- Baking sheet, ungreased

1½ cups	all-purpose flour	375 mL
⅔ cup	quick-cooking rolled oats	150 mL
½ cup	packed brown sugar	125 mL
¼ cup	finely chopped pecans	50 mL
½ tsp	ground cinnamon	2 mL
¾ cup	butter, softened	175 mL

1. In a large bowl, combine flour, oats, brown sugar, pecans and cinnamon. Mix well. With a wooden spoon, blend in butter until mixture is crumbly. Using your hands, knead to form a soft, smooth dough. If necessary, cover and chill for 30 minutes for easy rolling.

2. Divide dough into halves. On floured surface, roll out one portion at a time to $\frac{1}{4}$-inch (0.5 cm) thickness. Dip cutters in flour and cut into desired shapes. Place on baking sheet about 1 inch (2.5 cm) apart. Bake in preheated oven for 15 to 20 minutes or until light golden. Cool for 5 minutes on sheet, then transfer to a rack and cool completely.

NUTRIENTS PER SERVING	
Calories	115
Carbohydrate	12 g
Fiber	1 g
Protein	1 g
Fat, total	7 g
Fat, saturated	4 g
Cholesterol	16 mg
Sodium	61 mg

AMERICA'S EXCHANGES	
½	Starch
½	Other Carbohydrates
1½	Fat

CANADA'S CHOICES	
1	Carbohydrate
1½	Fat

Rice Flour Shortbread

This thick, melt-in-your-mouth shortbread is similar to the Scottish shortbread usually baked in rounds or shortbread molds and cut in wedges.

■ Preheat oven to 300°F (150°C)
■ 8-inch (2 L) square cake pan, ungreased

1½ cups	all-purpose flour	375 mL
⅓ cup	superfine granulated sugar	75 mL
⅓ cup	rice flour	75 mL
¼ tsp	salt	1 mL
¾ cup	cold butter, cubed	175 mL

1. In a bowl, combine all-purpose flour, sugar, rice flour and salt. Using a pastry blender, 2 knives or your fingers, work in butter until mixture resembles coarse crumbs. Knead dough on a lightly floured surface until very smooth, about 5 minutes. Press evenly into pan. Prick surface all over with a fork.

2. Bake in preheated oven until lightly browned around edges, 30 to 35 minutes. Cut into bars or squares just as the pan comes out of the oven, then let cool completely in pan on rack. Recut.

NUTRIENTS PER SERVING	
Calories	65
Carbohydrate	7 g
Fiber	0 g
Protein	1 g
Fat, total	4 g
Fat, saturated	2 g
Cholesterol	10 mg
Sodium	55 mg

AMERICA'S EXCHANGES	
½	Starch
1	Fat

CANADA'S CHOICES	
½	Carbohydrate
1	Fat

Cornmeal Shortbread

**MAKES 48 BARS
(1 BAR PER SERVING)**

*This Italian favorite gets
an extra-crunchy texture
from cornmeal and
almonds. The cornmeal
also provides a wonderful
yellow color. This is a
particularly nice cookie
to serve with fresh or
stewed fruit.*

■ Preheat oven to 350°F (180°C)
■ 9-inch (2.5 L) square cake pan, ungreased

¾ cup	whole unblanched almonds	175 mL
½ cup	yellow cornmeal	125 mL
1¾ cups	all-purpose flour	425 mL
¾ cup	granulated sugar	175 mL
1 cup	cold butter, cubed	250 mL

1. In a food processor, pulse almonds until coarsely chopped. Add cornmeal, flour, sugar and butter. Pulse until mixture resembles coarse crumbs. Press three-quarters of the dough evenly into pan. Using your fingers, scatter remainder on top.

2. Bake in preheated oven until light golden, 25 to 30 minutes. Cut into bars or squares just as the pan comes out of the oven, then let cool completely in pan on rack. Recut.

NUTRIENTS PER SERVING	
Calories	82
Carbohydrate	8 g
Fiber	0 g
Protein	1 g
Fat, total	5 g
Fat, saturated	3 g
Cholesterol	10 mg
Sodium	40 mg

AMERICA'S EXCHANGES	
½	Starch
1	Fat

CANADA'S CHOICES	
½	Carbohydrate
1	Fat

Chunky Chocolate Shortbread

**MAKES 54 BARS
(1 BAR PER SERVING)**

This crisp shortbread cookie has lots of crunch from the nuts and a great chocolate flavor from the chopped chocolate.

BARB'S NUTRITION NOTE

This recipe calls for superfine sugar, but it's not necessary to buy it. You can make it by processing granulated sugar in a blender or food processor until fine.

■ Preheat oven to 350°F (180°C)
■ 13- by 9-inch (3 L) cake pan, ungreased

1 cup	butter, softened	250 mL
½ cup	superfine granulated sugar	125 mL
1¾ cups	all-purpose flour	425 mL
¼ cup	cornstarch	50 mL
4	squares (1 oz/28 g each) bittersweet chocolate, coarsely chopped	4
⅔ cup	coarsely chopped pecans, toasted	150 mL

1. In a bowl, beat butter and sugar until light and creamy. Combine flour and cornstarch. Stir into butter mixture, mixing well. Stir in chocolate and pecans. Press evenly into pan.

2. Bake in preheated oven until lightly browned around edges, 30 to 35 minutes. Let cool completely in pan on rack. Cut into bars or squares.

NUTRIENTS PER SERVING	
Calories	76
Carbohydrate	7 g
Fiber	0 g
Protein	1 g
Fat, total	5 g
Fat, saturated	3 g
Cholesterol	9 mg
Sodium	35 mg

AMERICA'S EXCHANGES	
½	Other Carbohydrates
1	Fat

CANADA'S CHOICES	
½	Carbohydrate
1	Fat

Cookies

Crispy Oatmeal Cookies

MAKES 72 COOKIES (1 COOKIE PER SERVING)

VARIATION

Substitute pecans or slivered almonds for the walnuts.

MAKE AHEAD

Store in an airtight container in the freezer for up to 4 weeks.

BARB'S NUTRITION NOTE

You can use salted butter in this recipe, but you should then omit the salt. One-quarter cup (50 mL) salted butter contains about $1/4$ tsp (1 mL) salt.

- Preheat oven to 350°F (180°C)
- Stand mixer
- Baking sheets, lined with parchment paper

1¼ cups	unbleached all-purpose flour	300 mL
1 tsp	salt	5 mL
1 tsp	baking soda	5 mL
1 tsp	ground cinnamon	5 mL
1½ cups	unsalted butter, softened	375 mL
1 cup	lightly packed light brown sugar	250 mL
½ cup	granulated sugar	125 mL
1	egg	1
1 tsp	vanilla	5 mL
3 cups	old-fashioned rolled oats	750 mL
2 cups	walnut halves, chopped	500 mL
1 cup	dried cranberries	250 mL

1. In a small bowl, whisk together flour, salt, baking soda and cinnamon.

2. Place butter in the mixer bowl. Attach the flat beater and mixer bowl to the mixer. Set to Speed 4 and beat until soft and creamy. Beat in brown sugar and granulated sugar until light and fluffy. Beat in egg and vanilla. Reduce speed to Stir and mix in flour mixture, in 3 additions. Mix in oats, walnuts and cranberries until evenly incorporated.

3. Drop by rounded teaspoonfuls (5 mL), 2 inches (5 cm) apart, onto prepared baking sheets. Bake in middle of preheated oven for 8 to 10 minutes, or until lightly browned. Let cool on sheets for 5 minutes, then transfer to wire racks to cool completely.

NUTRIENTS PER SERVING	
Calories	96
Carbohydrate	10 g
Fiber	1 g
Protein	1 g
Fat, total	6 g
Fat, saturated	3 g
Cholesterol	13 mg
Sodium	53 mg

AMERICA'S EXCHANGES	
½	Other Carbohydrates
1	Fat

CANADA'S CHOICES	
½	Carbohydrate
1	Fat

Oatmeal Orange Coconut Cookies

MAKES 40 COOKIES (2 COOKIES PER SERVING)

TIP

When using margarine, choose a soft (non-hydrogenated) version to limit consumption of trans fats.

MAKE AHEAD

Bake cookies up to a day ahead, keeping tightly covered in a cookie tin. Freeze cookie dough for up to 2 weeks.

BARB'S NUTRITION NOTE

The cookies will have more fiber if you use bran flakes. Flaked cereals can generally be substituted for one another, but bran flakes are not interchangeable with raw bran or the very high-fiber bran cereals.

▪ Preheat oven to 350°F (180°C)
▪ Baking sheets, sprayed with vegetable spray

¼ cup	margarine or butter	50 mL
¼ cup	brown sugar	50 mL
½ cup	granulated sugar	125 mL
1	egg	1
1 tsp	vanilla	5 mL
2 tbsp	orange juice concentrate, thawed	25 mL
½ tsp	grated orange zest	2 mL
⅔ cup	all-purpose flour	150 mL
½ tsp	baking powder	2 mL
½ tsp	baking soda	2 mL
½ tsp	cinnamon	2 mL
1 cup	corn flakes or bran flakes cereal	250 mL
⅔ cup	raisins	150 mL
½ cup	rolled oats	125 mL
¼ cup	coconut	50 mL

1. In large bowl, cream together margarine, brown sugar and granulated sugar. Add egg, vanilla, orange juice concentrate and orange zest and mix well.

2. In another bowl, combine flour, baking powder, baking soda, cinnamon, corn flakes, raisins, rolled oats and coconut just until combined. Add to sugar mixture and mix until just combined

3. Drop by heaping teaspoons (5 mL) onto prepared baking sheets, 2 inches (5 cm) apart, and press down with back of fork; bake for approximately 10 minutes or until browned.

NUTRIENTS PER SERVING	
Calories	109
Carbohydrate	19 g
Fiber	1 g
Protein	1 g
Fat, total	3 g
Fat, saturated	1 g
Cholesterol	9 mg
Sodium	86 mg

AMERICA'S EXCHANGES	
½	Starch
½	Other Carbohydrates
½	Fat

CANADA'S CHOICES	
1	Carbohydrate
½	Fat

Cranberry Pecan Oatmeal Cookies

MAKES 48 COOKIES (1 COOKIE PER SERVING)

Depending upon how you bake them, these cookies can be soft and chewy or crispy. They are delicious either way, so the choice is yours.

TIP

Bake the minimum time for chewy cookies. They will look like they are not quite done when you take them out of the oven, but they will continue to cook on the sheet. Bake longer, until golden, if you prefer crisp cookies.

VARIATION

Omit cinnamon. Replace milk with orange juice and 1 tbsp (15 mL) grated orange zest.

■ Preheat oven to 350°F (180°C)
■ Baking sheet, greased or lined with parchment paper

¾ cup	all-purpose flour	175 mL
¾ tsp	baking soda	3 mL
¼ tsp	salt	1 mL
1 tsp	ground cinnamon	5 mL
¾ cup	butter, softened	175 mL
¾ cup	packed brown sugar	175 mL
½ cup	granulated sugar	125 mL
1	egg	1
2 tbsp	milk	25 mL
3 cups	quick-cooking rolled oats	750 mL
1 cup	dried cranberries	250 mL
¾ cup	chopped pecans	175 mL
⅓ cup	sunflower seeds	75 mL

1. On a sheet of waxed paper or in a bowl, combine flour, baking soda, salt and cinnamon. Set aside.

2. In a large bowl, using an electric mixer on medium speed, beat butter, brown and granulated sugars, egg and milk until light and creamy, about 3 minutes. On low speed, gradually add flour mixture, beating until blended. With a wooden spoon, stir in oats, cranberries, pecans and sunflower seeds.

3. Drop dough by tablespoonfuls (15 mL), about 2 inches (5 cm) apart, on prepared baking sheet. Press flat with a fork dipped in flour. Bake in preheated oven for 11 to 15 minutes (see Tip). Cool for 5 minutes on sheet, then transfer to a rack and cool completely.

NUTRIENTS PER SERVING	
Calories	104
Carbohydrate	14 g
Fiber	1 g
Protein	2 g
Fat, total	5 g
Fat, saturated	2 g
Cholesterol	12 mg
Sodium	65 mg

AMERICA'S EXCHANGES	
1	Other Carbohydrates
1	Fat

CANADA'S CHOICES	
1	Carbohydrate
1	Fat

Oatmeal Raisin Cookies

MAKES 18 COOKIES (2 COOKIES PER SERVING)

BARB'S NUTRITION NOTE

Wheat germ is the nutritious heart of a wheat kernel. Together with fiber-containing bran, it is removed when white flour is manufactured. To avoid rancidity, buy wheat germ in small quantities and keep it in the refrigerator.

■ Preheat oven to 375°F (190°C)
■ Baking sheet, sprayed with baking spray

6 tbsp	packed brown sugar	90 mL
1/4 cup	butter, softened	50 mL
1	egg	1
1 tsp	vanilla	5 mL
1/2 cup	rolled oats	125 mL
1/2 cup	raisins	125 mL
1/4 cup	whole wheat flour	50 mL
1/4 cup	wheat germ	50 mL
1/2 tsp	baking powder	2 mL

1. In a bowl, cream brown sugar with butter. Beat in egg and vanilla. In another bowl, stir together oats, raisins, whole wheat flour, wheat germ and baking powder. Stir into creamed mixture just until blended.

2. Drop batter by teaspoonfuls (5 mL) onto prepared baking sheet, leaving 2 inches (5 cm) between cookies. Bake for 10 to 12 minutes or until golden. Cool on wire racks.

NUTRIENTS PER SERVING	
Calories	160
Carbohydrate	24 g
Fiber	2 g
Protein	3 g
Fat, total	6 g
Fat, saturated	4 g
Cholesterol	34 mg
Sodium	79 mg

AMERICA'S EXCHANGES	
1/2	Fruit
1	Other Carbohydrates
1	Fat

CANADA'S CHOICES	
1 1/2	Carbohydrate
1	Fat

Oatmeal Raisin Pecan Cookies

MAKES 30 COOKIES (2 COOKIES PER SERVING)

TIPS

These cookies are soft and chewy if baked for a shorter time; crisp if baked longer.

If wheat germ is not available, substitute another 1/4 cup (50 mL) rolled oats.

When using margarine, choose a soft (non-hydrogenated) version.

MAKE AHEAD

Dough can be frozen for up to 2 weeks.

- Preheat oven to 350°F (180°C)
- Baking sheets, sprayed with nonstick vegetable spray

1/2 cup	brown sugar	125 mL
1/4 cup	soft margarine	50 mL
1	egg	1
1 tsp	vanilla	5 mL
1/2 cup	rolled oats	125 mL
1/4 cup	whole wheat flour	50 mL
1/4 cup	wheat germ	50 mL
1/4 cup	pecan pieces	50 mL
1/4 cup	raisins	50 mL
1/2 tsp	baking powder	2 mL

1. In a large bowl or food processor, beat together brown sugar, margarine, egg and vanilla until well blended.

2. Add rolled oats, flour, wheat germ, pecans, raisins and baking powder; mix just until incorporated.

3. Drop by heaping teaspoonfuls (5 mL), 2 inches (5 cm) apart, onto prepared baking sheets. Bake for 12 to 15 minutes or until browned.

NUTRIENTS PER SERVING	
Calories	106
Carbohydrate	14 g
Fiber	1 g
Protein	2 g
Fat, total	5 g
Fat, saturated	1 g
Cholesterol	12 mg
Sodium	57 mg

AMERICA'S EXCHANGES	
1	Other Carbohydrates
1	Fat

CANADA'S CHOICES	
1	Carbohydrate
1	Fat

Fruity Oatmeal Cookies

MAKES 36 COOKIES (1 COOKIE PER SERVING)

These make a tasty, healthy snack any time of the day.

TIPS

When using margarine, choose a non-hydrogenated version to limit consumption of trans fats.

We tested these cookies with different dried fruits (raisins, chopped apricots, cranberries). All versions worked out well. A mixture would also work.

VARIATIONS

Replace the semisweet chocolate chips with white chocolate or butterscotch chips, or leave them out entirely for a fruitier cookie.

Try rice syrup or fancy molasses instead of honey.

- ▪ Preheat oven to 350°F (180°C)
- ▪ Baking sheets, lightly greased or lined with parchment paper

2 cups	old-fashioned rolled oats	500 mL
1¼ cups	whole wheat flour	300 mL
1 cup	semisweet chocolate chips	250 mL
1 cup	dried fruit	250 mL
¾ cup	ground flaxseed	175 mL
1 tsp	baking soda	5 mL
½ tsp	salt	2 mL
2	large bananas, mashed	2
¾ cup	liquid honey	175 mL
½ cup	margarine	125 mL

1. In a large bowl, combine oats, flour, chocolate chips, dried fruit, flaxseed, baking soda and salt.

2. In another large bowl, combine bananas, honey and margarine. Fold in oats mixture.

3. Drop dough by tablespoonfuls (15 mL), about 2 inches (5 cm) apart, onto prepared baking sheets. Flatten with a fork.

4. Bake in preheated oven for about 10 minutes or until lightly browned. Let cool on baking sheets on a wire rack for 5 minutes, then remove to rack to cool completely.

NUTRIENTS PER SERVING	
Calories	130
Carbohydrate	20 g
Fiber	2 g
Protein	2 g
Fat, total	5 g
Fat, saturated	1 g
Cholesterol	0 mg
Sodium	104 mg

AMERICA'S EXCHANGES	
½	Starch
1	Other Carbohydrates
1	Fat

CANADA'S CHOICES	
1	Carbohydrate
1	Fat

Oatmeal Date Cookies

BARB'S NUTRITION NOTES

For baking, use a soft, non-hydrogenated margarine. They contain 55% to 80% less saturated fat than butter and no trans fat. Do not use margarines that come in a stick or block; they are high in saturated and trans fat.

Flaked cereals can generally be substituted for one another, but bran flakes are not interchangeable with raw bran or the very high-fiber bran cereals. For maximum fiber, use bran flakes in this recipe.

■ Preheat oven to 350°F (180°C)
■ Baking sheets, sprayed with vegetable spray

⅓ cup	margarine or butter	75 mL
⅓ cup	granulated sugar	75 mL
1	egg	1
1 tsp	vanilla	5 mL
⅔ cup	all-purpose flour	150 mL
1 tsp	baking powder	5 mL
¾ tsp	cinnamon	4 mL
¾ cup	rolled oats	175 mL
¾ cup	bran flakes or corn flakes cereal	175 mL
⅔ cup	chopped pitted dates	150 mL

1. In a large bowl, cream together margarine and sugar. Add egg and vanilla and mix well.

2. In another bowl, combine flour, baking powder, cinnamon, rolled oats, cereal and dates. Add to sugar mixture and mix until just combined.

3. Drop by heaping teaspoonfuls (5 mL) onto prepared baking sheets, 2 inches (5 cm) apart, and press down with back of fork; bake for approximately 10 minutes or until browned.

NUTRIENTS PER SERVING	
Calories	117
Carbohydrate	18 g
Fiber	1 g
Protein	2 g
Fat, total	5 g
Fat, saturated	1 g
Cholesterol	12 mg
Sodium	84 mg

AMERICA'S EXCHANGES	
½	Starch
½	Fruit
1	Fat

CANADA'S CHOICES	
1	Carbohydrate
1	Fat

Crunchy Apricot Oat Drops

**MAKES 36 COOKIES
(2 COOKIES PER
SERVING)**

TIPS

Do not use light or
whipped margarine when
baking. These products
are lower in fat and often
contain water, which may
result in baked goods that
aren't acceptable.

When baking, always
place cookie dough on
a cool sheet. Cookies
will spread too much if
the sheet is warm.

Always set your timer for the
minimum time suggested.
You can always bake longer,
if necessary.

VARIATION

Replace apricots with
dried cranberries, raisins
or chopped dates.

- Preheat oven to 350°F (180°C)
- Baking sheet, greased or lined with parchment paper

¾ cup	unbleached all-purpose flour	175 mL
½ tsp	baking soda	2 mL
¼ tsp	salt	1 mL
½ tsp	ground cinnamon	2 mL
½ cup	butter, softened	125 mL
¾ cup	packed brown sugar	175 mL
1	egg	1
¾ cup	quick-cooking rolled oats	175 mL
⅓ cup	wheat germ	75 mL
1 cup	crisp rice cereal	250 mL
¾ cup	chopped dried apricots	175 mL
⅓ cup	unsweetened flaked coconut	75 mL
¼ cup	sunflower seeds	50 mL

1. On a sheet of waxed paper or in a bowl, combine flour, baking soda, salt and cinnamon. Set aside.

2. In a large bowl, using an electric mixer on medium speed, beat butter, brown sugar and egg until light and creamy, about 3 minutes. On low speed, gradually add flour mixture, beating until blended. With a wooden spoon, stir in oats and wheat germ. Add cereal, apricots, coconut and sunflower seeds. Mix well.

3. Drop dough by tablespoonfuls (15 mL), about 2 inches (5 cm) apart, onto prepared baking sheet. Bake in preheated oven for 8 to 12 minutes or until golden. Cool for 5 minutes on sheet, then transfer to a rack and cool completely.

NUTRIENTS PER SERVING	
Calories	171
Carbohydrate	24 g
Fiber	2 g
Protein	3 g
Fat, total	8 g
Fat, saturated	4 g
Cholesterol	24 mg
Sodium	145 mg

AMERICA'S EXCHANGES	
½	Starch
1	Other Carbohydrates
1½	Fat

CANADA'S CHOICES	
1½	Carbohydrate
1½	Fat

Date Roll-Up Cookies

**MAKES 32 COOKIES
(1 COOKIE PER
SERVING)**

TIPS

For maximum freshness,
store cookies in airtight
containers in the freezer;
remove as needed.

Try this recipe with dried
figs or apricots.

When using margarine,
choose a soft (non-
hydrogenated) version
to limit consumption
of trans fats.

- Preheat oven to 350°F (180°C)
- Large baking sheet, sprayed with vegetable spray

Filling

8 oz	pitted dates	250 g
1 cup	orange juice	250 mL
¼ tsp	ground cinnamon	1 mL

Dough

2¼ cups	all-purpose flour	550 mL
⅔ cup	granulated sugar	150 mL
¼ cup	margarine or butter	50 mL
¼ cup	vegetable oil	50 mL
¼ cup	2% plain yogurt	50 mL
3 tbsp	water	45 mL
1 tsp	vanilla	5 mL
1 tsp	grated orange zest	5 mL

1. *Filling:* In a saucepan, bring dates, orange juice and cinnamon to a boil; reduce heat to medium-low and cook 10 minutes or until soft. Mash with a fork until liquid is absorbed. Refrigerate.

2. *Dough:* In a food processor, combine flour, sugar, margarine, oil, yogurt, water, vanilla and orange zest; process until dough forms. Add up to 1 tbsp (15 mL) more water, if necessary. Divide dough in half; form each half into a ball, wrap and refrigerate for 15 minutes or until chilled.

NUTRIENTS PER SERVING	
Calories	101
Carbohydrate	17 g
Fiber	1 g
Protein	1 g
Fat, total	3 g
Fat, saturated	0 g
Cholesterol	0 mg
Sodium	21 mg

AMERICA'S EXCHANGES	
½	Fruit
½	Other Carbohydrates
½	Fat

CANADA'S CHOICES	
1	Carbohydrate
½	Fat

MAKE AHEAD
Prepare date mixture and
freeze until needed.

3. Between 2 sheets of waxed paper sprinkled with flour, roll one of the dough balls into a rectangle, approximately 12 by 10 inches (30 by 25 cm) and $1/8$ inch (0.25 cm) thick. Remove top sheet of waxed paper. Spread half of date mixture over rolled dough. Starting at short end and using the waxed paper as an aid, roll up tightly. Cut into $1/2$-inch (1 cm) slices and place on prepared baking sheet. Repeat with remaining dough and filling.

4. Bake 25 minutes or until lightly browned.

BARB'S NUTRITION NOTE
We are all familiar with peanut butter, but "butter" can also be made from other nuts, including cashews and almonds. Regardless of the type of nut, or whether it's smooth or chunky, all nut butters contain 8 to 10 grams of fat per tablespoon (15 mL). The unsalted varieties contain almost no sodium, but salted varieties have around 80 milligrams of sodium per tablespoon (15 mL).

Soft Apple Cinnamon Cookies

**MAKES 48 COOKIES
(1 COOKIE PER
SERVING)**

*These cookies, which
stay nice and soft, make
a great-tasting, healthy
treat for a packed lunch
or after-school snack.*

**BARB'S
NUTRITION NOTES**

You can lower the saturated
fat in this recipe by using
soft, non-hydrogenated
margarine instead of butter.

To make ½ cup (125 mL)
sour milk, place 1½ tsp
(7 mL) vinegar or lemon
juice in a measuring cup
and add milk to make up
the full amount. Let stand
for 5 minutes before using.

■ Preheat oven to 400°F (200°C)
■ Baking sheets, lightly greased or lined with parchment
paper

2 cups	all-purpose flour	500 mL
1 tbsp	ground cinnamon	15 mL
1 tsp	baking powder	5 mL
½ tsp	baking soda	2 mL
½ tsp	salt	2 mL
3	large apples (unpeeled), grated	3
1 cup	packed brown sugar	250 mL
⅔ cup	butter	150 mL
2	eggs	2
½ cup	sour milk or buttermilk	125 mL
2 cups	quick-cooking rolled oats	500 mL

1. In a small bowl, sift together flour, cinnamon, baking
   powder, baking soda and salt.

2. Sprinkle grated apples with ½ cup (125 mL) of the
   flour mixture.

3. In a large bowl, cream brown sugar and butter. Add
   eggs, one at a time, beating well after each addition.
   Add milk, then oats, and blend well. Fold in remaining
   flour mixture. Stir in apples.

4. Drop dough by tablespoonfuls (15 mL), about 2 inches
   (5 cm) apart, onto prepared baking sheets.

5. Bake in preheated oven for 8 to 10 minutes or until
   lightly browned. Let cool on baking sheets on a wire rack
   for 5 minutes, then remove to rack to cool completely.

NUTRIENTS PER SERVING	
Calories	86
Carbohydrate	13 g
Fiber	1 g
Protein	1 g
Fat, total	3 g
Fat, saturated	2 g
Cholesterol	15 mg
Sodium	76 mg

AMERICA'S EXCHANGES	
1	Other Carbohydrates
½	Fat

CANADA'S CHOICES	
1	Carbohydrate
½	Fat

Lemon Lime Cookies

MAKES 72 COOKIES (2 COOKIES PER SERVING)

A strong hit of lemon makes these tender, crisp cookies particularly delicious.

TIPS

I prefer combining the dry ingredients on a piece of waxed paper instead of dirtying a bowl. Then I use the paper as a funnel when adding them to the butter mixture.

Try not to use too much flour when rolling. It will toughen any dough. You need just enough on the surface of the dough, your hands and the rolling pin to prevent sticking. If you use a pastry cloth and rolling pin cover, you'll have no problems with the dough sticking.

- Preheat oven to 350°F (180°C)
- 2-inch (5 cm) round cookie cutter
- Baking sheet, ungreased

3½ cups	all-purpose flour	875 mL
2 tsp	baking powder	10 mL
½ tsp	salt	2 mL
1 cup	butter, softened	250 mL
1¼ cups	granulated sugar	300 mL
2	eggs	2
2 tbsp	grated lemon zest	25 mL
2 tbsp	grated lime zest	25 mL
½ tsp	lemon extract	2 mL

1. On a sheet of waxed paper or in a bowl, combine flour, baking powder and salt. Set aside.

2. In a large bowl, using an electric mixer on medium speed, beat butter and sugar until light and creamy, about 3 minutes. Add eggs, one at a time, beating well after each addition. Add lemon zest, lime zest and lemon extract. On low speed, gradually add flour mixture, beating until dough becomes too stiff for the mixer, then finish mixing with a wooden spoon. Using your hands, knead to form a smooth dough.

3. On a floured surface, roll out dough to $\frac{1}{8}$-inch (0.25 cm) thickness. Using cutter dipped in flour, cut into rounds. Place about 1 inch (2.5 cm) apart on baking sheet. Bake in preheated oven for 7 to 11 minutes or until lightly browned around edges. Cool for 5 minutes on sheet, then transfer to a rack and cool completely.

NUTRIENTS PER SERVING	
Calories	121
Carbohydrate	16 g
Fiber	0 g
Protein	2 g
Fat, total	6 g
Fat, saturated	3 g
Cholesterol	24 mg
Sodium	103 mg

AMERICA'S EXCHANGES	
½	Starch
½	Other Carbohydrates
1	Fat

CANADA'S CHOICES	
1	Carbohydrate
1	Fat

Lemon Poppy Seed Balls

MAKES 48 COOKIES (2 COOKIES PER SERVING)

Lemon and poppy seeds are a popular combination. It works well in these cookies.

VARIATION

For a plain cookie, omit the poppy seeds and lemon zest. Add 1 tsp (5 mL) vanilla or ½ tsp (2 mL) almond extract.

■ Preheat oven to 325°F (160°C)
■ Baking sheet, ungreased

2½ cups	all-purpose flour	625 mL
2 tbsp	poppy seeds	25 mL
¼ tsp	salt	1 mL
1 cup	butter, softened	250 mL
⅔ cup	granulated sugar	150 mL
1	egg	1
1 tbsp	grated lemon zest	15 mL

1. On a sheet of waxed paper or in a bowl, combine flour, poppy seeds and salt. Set aside.

2. In a large bowl, using an electric mixer on medium speed, beat butter, sugar, egg and lemon zest until light and creamy, about 3 minutes. On low speed, gradually add flour mixture, beating until dough becomes too stiff for the mixer, then finish mixing with a wooden spoon until smooth. Using your hands, knead to form a smooth dough.

3. Shape dough into 1-inch (2.5 cm) balls. Place about 1 inch (2.5 cm) apart on baking sheet. Bake in preheated oven for 15 to 19 minutes or until golden around edges. Cool for 5 minutes on sheet, then transfer to a rack and cool completely.

NUTRIENTS PER SERVING	
Calories	144
Carbohydrate	16 g
Fiber	1 g
Protein	2 g
Fat, total	8 g
Fat, saturated	5 g
Cholesterol	28 mg
Sodium	105 mg

AMERICA'S EXCHANGES	
½	Starch
½	Other Carbohydrates
1½	Fat

CANADA'S CHOICES	
1	Carbohydrate
1½	Fat

Lemon Cranberry Pistachio Wafers

MAKES 48 COOKIES (3 COOKIES PER SERVING)

This cookie has a tender, buttery, shortbread-like texture and colorful red and green flecks scattered throughout.

TIPS

In refrigerator rolls, ingredients like nuts and fruit are much easier to slice if they are chopped fairly fine.

When cutting dough, always ensure that your knife is sharp. I prefer to use a serrated knife for this dough as it contains nuts.

VARIATIONS

Replace lemon zest with orange zest.

Replace dried cranberries with dried cherries.

■ Baking sheet, ungreased

1¾ cups	all-purpose flour	425 mL
¼ tsp	baking powder	1 mL
¼ tsp	salt	1 mL
¾ cup	butter, softened	175 mL
½ cup	confectioner's (icing) sugar, sifted	125 mL
1	egg	1
1 tbsp	grated lemon zest	15 mL
⅓ cup	finely chopped pistachios	75 mL
¼ cup	chopped dried cranberries	50 mL

1. On a sheet of waxed paper or in a bowl, combine flour, baking powder and salt. Set aside.

2. In a large bowl, using an electric mixer on medium speed, beat butter, confectioner's sugar, egg and lemon zest until light and creamy, about 3 minutes. On low speed, gradually add flour mixture, beating until blended. With a wooden spoon, stir in pistachios and cranberries. Shape into a roll 12 inches (30 cm) long. Wrap and chill until firm, at least 3 hours.

3. Fifteen minutes before you're ready to bake, preheat oven to 375°F (190°C). Cut roll into ¼-inch (0.5 cm) slices. Place about 1 inch (2.5 cm) apart on baking sheet. Bake in preheated oven for 8 to 12 minutes or until golden. Cool for 5 minutes on sheet, then transfer to a rack and cool completely.

NUTRIENTS PER SERVING	
Calories	166
Carbohydrate	17 g
Fiber	1 g
Protein	2 g
Fat, total	10 g
Fat, saturated	6 g
Cholesterol	35 mg
Sodium	133 mg

AMERICA'S EXCHANGES	
1	Other Carbohydrates
2	Fat

CANADA'S CHOICES	
1	Carbohydrate
2	Fat

Orange Coffee Pecan Slices

TIPS

Be sure to remove the
zest from oranges and
lemons before you cut
them to squeeze out the
juice. Oranges with a thick,
rough skin will give you
more zest, but less juice.

One orange should give
you about 1/3 cup (75 mL)
juice and 4 tsp (20 mL)
grated zest.

A thin knife is usually the
best choice for cutting
dough, but if it contains
chunky ingredients, you
may find a serrated knife
works better. Just make
sure your knife is sharp.

■ Baking sheet, greased or lined with parchment paper

2¾ cups	all-purpose flour	675 mL
1 tbsp	instant espresso coffee powder	15 mL
2 tsp	baking powder	10 mL
¼ tsp	salt	1 mL
¾ cup	butter, softened	175 mL
1 cup	packed brown sugar	250 mL
1 tbsp	grated orange zest	15 mL
¼ cup	orange juice	50 mL
1 cup	chopped pecans	250 mL

1. On a sheet of waxed paper or in a bowl, combine flour, coffee powder, baking powder and salt. Set aside.

2. In a large bowl, using an electric mixer on medium speed, beat butter, brown sugar, and orange zest and juice until smooth. On low speed, gradually add flour mixture, beating until blended. With a wooden spoon, stir in pecans. Divide dough into halves. Shape each into a roll 12 inches (30 cm) long. Wrap and chill until firm, at least 2 hours.

3. Fifteen minutes before you're ready to bake, preheat oven to 375°F (190°C). Cut rolls into 1/4-inch (0.5 cm) slices. Place about 1 inch (2.5 cm) apart on prepared baking sheet. Bake in preheated oven for 7 to 11 minutes or until golden around edges. Cool for 5 minutes on sheet, then transfer to a rack and cool completely.

NUTRIENTS PER SERVING	
Calories	129
Carbohydrate	16 g
Fiber	1 g
Protein	1 g
Fat, total	7 g
Fat, saturated	3 g
Cholesterol	12 mg
Sodium	81 mg

AMERICA'S EXCHANGES	
1	Other Carbohydrates
1½	Fat

CANADA'S CHOICES	
1	Carbohydrate
1½	Fat

Crisp Nut Cookies

**MAKES 45 COOKIES
(3 COOKIES PER
SERVING)**

*These resemble the
classic Jewish cookie,
mandelbrot.*

TIP
Use almonds, pecans, pine
nuts or a combination.

■ Preheat oven to 350°F (180°C)
■ Baking sheet, sprayed with baking spray

2	eggs	2
¾ cup	granulated sugar	175 mL
6 tbsp	melted butter	90 mL
¼ cup	water	50 mL
2 tsp	vanilla	10 mL
1 tsp	almond extract	5 mL
2½ cups	all-purpose flour	625 mL
½ cup	chopped nuts	125 mL
2¼ tsp	baking powder	11 mL

1. In a bowl, beat eggs with sugar until well mixed. Beat in butter, water, vanilla and almond extract.

2. In another bowl, stir together flour, nuts and baking powder. Stir into egg-sugar mixture until dough forms a ball. Divide dough in half. Form each half into a log 12 inches (30 cm) long. Put on prepared baking sheet.

3. Bake for 20 minutes. Cool for 5 minutes. Cut on the diagonal into ½-inch (1 cm) thick slices. Bake for 20 minutes or until golden.

NUTRIENTS PER SERVING	
Calories	129
Carbohydrate	18 g
Fiber	1 g
Protein	2 g
Fat, total	5 g
Fat, saturated	2 g
Cholesterol	25 mg
Sodium	63 mg

AMERICA'S EXCHANGES	
1	Other Carbohydrates
1	Fat

CANADA'S CHOICES	
1	Carbohydrate
1	Fat

Maple Walnut Slice 'n' Bake Cookies

MAKES 96 COOKIES (3 COOKIES PER SERVING)

TIPS

Although it's not as common as some other extracts, maple extract is an excellent product with a true maple flavor. It's sold in grocery stores where you find vanilla.

To get perfectly round cookies, pack the dough into an appropriate-size used roll from waxed paper, plastic wrap or aluminum foil. Once chilled, simply cut the tube open. When using frozen rolls of dough, let them thaw in the refrigerator overnight or for about 1 hour at room temperature, until they can be sliced easily.

VARIATION

Replace maple extract with vanilla and walnuts with pecans.

■ Baking sheet, ungreased

2²⁄₃ cups	all-purpose flour	650 mL
1 tsp	baking powder	5 mL
½ tsp	baking soda	2 mL
¼ tsp	salt	1 mL
1 cup	butter, softened	250 mL
½ cup	granulated sugar	125 mL
½ cup	packed brown sugar	125 mL
2	eggs	2
1½ tsp	maple extract	7 mL
1½ cups	chopped walnuts	375 mL

1. On a sheet of waxed paper or in a bowl, combine flour, baking powder, baking soda and salt. Set aside.

2. In a large bowl, using an electric mixer on medium speed, beat butter, granulated and brown sugars, eggs and maple extract until light and creamy, about 3 minutes. On low speed, gradually add flour mixture, beating until blended. With a wooden spoon, stir in walnuts. Divide dough into halves. Shape each into a roll 12 inches (30 cm) long. Wrap and chill until firm, at least 4 hours.

3. Fifteen minutes before you're ready to bake, preheat oven to 375°F (190°C). Cut rolls into ¼-inch (0.5 cm) slices. Place about 1 inch (2.5 cm) apart on baking sheet. Bake in preheated oven for 8 to 12 minutes or until lightly browned. Cool for 5 minutes on sheet, then transfer to a rack and cool completely.

NUTRIENTS PER SERVING	
Calories	155
Carbohydrate	16 g
Fiber	1 g
Protein	2 g
Fat, total	10 g
Fat, saturated	4 g
Cholesterol	27 mg
Sodium	111 mg

AMERICA'S EXCHANGES	
½	Starch
½	Other Carbohydrates
2	Fat

CANADA'S CHOICES	
1	Carbohydrate
2	Fat

Peanut Butter Cookies

**MAKES 40 COOKIES
(2 COOKIES PER
SERVING)**

TIPS
Use a natural, all-peanut
type of peanut butter.

When using margarine,
choose a soft (non-
hydrogenated) version
to limit consumption
of trans fats.

■ Preheat oven to 350°F (180°C)
■ Baking sheet, sprayed with baking spray

½ cup	peanut butter	125 mL
½ cup	packed brown sugar	125 mL
⅓ cup	margarine	75 mL
1	egg	1
1 tsp	vanilla	5 mL
½ cup	all-purpose flour	125 mL
2 tbsp	sesame seeds	25 mL
¾ tsp	baking soda	4 mL
½ tsp	nutmeg	2 mL

Coating (optional)

1	egg white, beaten	1
½ cup	wheat germ	125 mL

1. In a bowl, beat peanut butter, brown sugar, margarine, egg and vanilla until light and fluffy. In another bowl, stir together flour, sesame seeds, baking soda and nutmeg. Stir flour mixture into peanut butter mixture just until combined. Form into 1-inch (2.5 cm) balls. If desired, dip balls in egg white, then roll in wheat germ. Put on prepared baking sheet.

2. Bake for 10 to 12 minutes or until golden.

BARB'S NUTRITION NOTE
Many types of nuts (not just peanuts) can be made
into nut butter. For more information about nut
butters, see page 95.

NUTRIENTS PER SERVING	
Calories	107
Carbohydrate	9 g
Fiber	1 g
Protein	2 g
Fat, total	7 g
Fat, saturated	1 g
Cholesterol	9 mg
Sodium	124 mg

AMERICA'S EXCHANGES	
½	Other Carbohydrates
1½	Fat

CANADA'S CHOICES	
½	Carbohydrate
1½	Fat

Peanut Butter Flaxseed Cookies

MAKES 28 COOKIES (1 COOKIE PER SERVING)

Although these cookies appear rich, they contain wholesome ingredients and beat traditional coffee-shop fare by a long shot! Our taste panel said these were the best peanut butter cookies they had ever tasted.

BARB'S NUTRITION NOTE

Sometimes you will get more or fewer cookies than stated in the recipe. When this happens, see the cookie calculator on page 15 for help in determining how many cookies make up a serving.

■ Preheat oven to 350°F (180°C)
■ Baking sheets, lightly greased or lined with parchment paper

1¼ cups	all-purpose flour	300 mL
½ cup	ground flaxseed	125 mL
1 tsp	baking soda	5 mL
Pinch	salt	Pinch
½ cup	granulated sugar	125 mL
½ cup	packed brown sugar	125 mL
½ cup	butter, softened	125 mL
1	egg	1
1 tsp	vanilla	5 mL
½ cup	creamy peanut butter	125 mL

1. In a small bowl, combine flour, flaxseed, baking soda and salt.

2. In a large bowl, cream granulated sugar, brown sugar and butter. Beat in egg and vanilla. Beat in peanut butter until smooth. Fold in flour mixture.

3. Shape dough into balls, using about 1 tbsp (15 mL) dough per cookie, and place 2 inches (5 cm) apart on prepared baking sheets. Using a fork, flatten cookies in a criss-cross pattern.

4. Bake in preheated oven for 8 to 10 minutes or until lightly browned. Let cool on baking sheets on a wire rack for 5 minutes, then remove to rack to cool completely.

NUTRIENTS PER SERVING	
Calories	120
Carbohydrate	13 g
Fiber	1 g
Protein	2 g
Fat, total	7 g
Fat, saturated	3 g
Cholesterol	16 mg
Sodium	105 mg

AMERICA'S EXCHANGES	
1	Other Carbohydrates
1½	Fat

CANADA'S CHOICES	
1	Carbohydrate
1½	Fat

Peanut Butter Fudge Cookies

**MAKES 40 COOKIES
(2 COOKIES PER
SERVING)**

TIPS
Chopped dates can
replace raisins.

Use a natural peanut
butter, smooth or chunky.

When using margarine,
choose a soft (non-
hydrogenated) version
to limit consumption
of trans fats.

MAKE AHEAD
Cookies never last long,
but these can be made
up to a day ahead, kept
tightly covered in a cookie
jar or tin.

Prepare cookie dough
and freeze for up to
2 weeks, then bake.

- Preheat oven to 350°F (180°C)
- Baking sheets, sprayed with vegetable spray

1/4 cup	softened margarine or butter	50 mL
1/3 cup	peanut butter	75 mL
3/4 cup	granulated sugar	175 mL
1/4 cup	brown sugar	50 mL
1	egg	1
1 tsp	vanilla	5 mL
1 cup	all-purpose flour	250 mL
1/4 cup	unsweetened cocoa powder	50 mL
1 tsp	baking powder	5 mL
1/4 cup	2% yogurt	50 mL
3/4 cup	raisins	175 mL
3 tbsp	chocolate chips	45 mL

1. In a large bowl, cream together margarine, peanut butter, sugar and brown sugar. Add egg and vanilla and beat well.

2. In another bowl, combine flour, cocoa and baking powder; add to peanut butter mixture and stir just until combined. Stir in yogurt, raisins and chocolate chips. Drop by heaping teaspoonfuls (5 mL) onto prepared sheets, 2 inches (5 cm) apart, and press down slightly with back of fork. Bake approximately 12 minutes or until firm to the touch and slightly browned.

NUTRIENTS PER SERVING	
Calories	143
Carbohydrate	23 g
Fiber	1 g
Protein	3 g
Fat, total	5 g
Fat, saturated	1 g
Cholesterol	10 mg
Sodium	71 mg

AMERICA'S EXCHANGES	
1½	Other Carbohydrates
1	Fat

CANADA'S CHOICES	
1½	Carbohydrate
1	Fat

Best-Ever Chocolate Cookies

MAKES 42 COOKIES (2 COOKIES PER SERVING)

Your family and friends will never know that bran cereal is one of the ingredients in these delicious crunchy cookies.

TIP

When using margarine, choose a non-hydrogenated version to limit consumption of trans fats.

■ Preheat oven to 350°F (180°C)
■ Baking sheets, ungreased

1 cup	all-purpose flour	250 mL
½ cup	unsweetened cocoa powder	125 mL
1 tsp	baking soda	5 mL
¼ tsp	salt	1 mL
2	eggs	2
1 cup	margarine or butter, softened	250 mL
¾ cup	packed brown sugar	175 mL
1½ cups	quick-cooking rolled oats	375 mL
1 cup	bran cereal (not flakes)	250 mL
¾ cup	white chocolate chips	175 mL

1. In a small bowl, sift flour, cocoa powder, baking soda and salt.

2. In a large bowl, beat eggs, margarine and brown sugar. Fold in flour mixture. Stir in oats, bran cereal and white chocolate chips.

3. Drop dough by heaping tablespoonfuls (15 mL), about 2 inches (5 cm) apart, onto baking sheets.

4. Bake in preheated oven for 7 to 9 minutes or until just crisp. Let cool on baking sheets on a wire rack for 5 minutes, then remove to rack to cool completely.

BARB'S NUTRITION NOTE

Two of these cookies contain 247 mg of sodium, and about 120 mg of that comes from the margarine. Salted margarine has about 30 times as much sodium as its salt-free counterpart. But whether you choose salted or unsalted margarine, be sure it's a soft, non-hydrogenated type, which will be free of trans fat and low in saturated fat.

NUTRIENTS PER SERVING	
Calories	207
Carbohydrate	24 g
Fiber	2 g
Protein	3 g
Fat, total	12 g
Fat, saturated	3 g
Cholesterol	18 g
Sodium	247 mg

AMERICA'S EXCHANGES	
½	Starch
1	Other Carbohydrates
2½	Fat

CANADA'S CHOICES	
1½	Carbohydrate
2½	Fat

Double Chocolate Raisin Cookies

MAKES 40 COOKIES (2 COOKIES PER SERVING)

TIPS

Try white chocolate or peanut butter chips for a change.

When using margarine, choose a soft (non-hydrogenated) version to limit consumption of trans fats.

MAKE AHEAD

Dough can be frozen for up to 2 weeks.

- ■ Preheat oven to 350°F (180°C)
- ■ Baking sheets, sprayed with nonstick vegetable spray

¼ cup	soft margarine	50 mL
¾ cup	granulated sugar	175 mL
1	egg	1
1 tsp	vanilla	5 mL
3 tbsp	unsweetened cocoa powder	45 mL
½ tsp	baking soda	2 mL
½ tsp	baking powder	2 mL
½ cup	whole wheat flour	125 mL
¾ cup	all-purpose flour	175 mL
¼ cup	chocolate chips	50 mL
¼ cup	raisins	50 mL

1. In a large bowl or food processor, beat together margarine, sugar, egg and vanilla until well blended.

2. Combine cocoa, baking soda, baking powder, whole wheat and all-purpose flours; add to bowl and mix until just combined. Stir in chocolate chips and raisins.

3. Drop by heaping teaspoonfuls (5 mL), 2 inches (5 cm) apart, onto prepared baking sheets. Bake for 12 to 15 minutes or until browned.

NUTRIENTS PER SERVING	
Calories	99
Carbohydrate	17 g
Fiber	1 g
Protein	2 g
Fat, total	3 g
Fat, saturated	1 g
Cholesterol	9 mg
Sodium	73 mg

AMERICA'S EXCHANGES	
1	Other Carbohydrates
½	Fat

CANADA'S CHOICES	
1	Carbohydrate
½	Fat

Chocolate Chip Refrigerator Cookies

MAKES 96 COOKIES (2 COOKIES PER SERVING)

Once you've tried these, you'll never buy another roll of slice 'n' bake chocolate chip cookies. They are delicious and very easy to make.

TIPS

When chilling, wrap dough in waxed paper or plastic wrap.

The chocolate chips make cutting a bit difficult, but not to worry. If the rounds aren't even, reshape them on the baking sheet with your fingers. The cookies will look great when baked and taste even better.

Rolls of cookie dough can also be frozen. Thaw for about an hour at room temperature or in the refrigerator overnight, until the dough can be sliced easily.

■ Baking sheet, ungreased

2¾ cups	all-purpose flour	675 mL
1 tsp	baking soda	5 mL
¼ tsp	baking powder	1 mL
¼ tsp	salt	1 mL
1 cup	butter, softened	250 mL
1 cup	packed brown sugar	250 mL
½ cup	granulated sugar	125 mL
2	eggs	2
1 tsp	vanilla	5 mL
1 cup	semisweet chocolate chips	250 mL
½ cup	finely chopped pecans	125 mL

1. On a sheet of waxed paper or in a bowl, combine flour, baking soda, baking powder and salt. Set aside.

2. In a large bowl, using an electric mixer on medium speed, beat butter and brown and granulated sugars until light and creamy, about 3 minutes. Add eggs, one at a time, beating well after each addition. Add vanilla. On low speed, gradually add flour mixture, beating until blended. With a wooden spoon, stir in chocolate chips and pecans. Divide dough into halves. Shape each into a roll 12 inches (30 cm) long. Wrap and chill until firm, at least 4 hours.

NUTRIENTS PER SERVING	
Calories	114
Carbohydrate	14 g
Fiber	1 g
Protein	1 g
Fat, total	6 g
Fat, saturated	3 g
Cholesterol	18 mg
Sodium	84 mg

AMERICA'S EXCHANGES	
1	Other Carbohydrate
1	Fat

CANADA'S CHOICES	
1	Carbohydrate
1	Fat

VARIATIONS

Use milk chocolate chips or miniature semisweet chocolate chips.

Omit nuts or replace pecans with your favorite nut.

3. Fifteen minutes before you're ready to bake, preheat oven to 350°F (180°C). Cut rolls into $1/4$-inch (0.5 cm) slices. Place about 2 inches (5 cm) apart on baking sheet. Bake in preheated oven for 8 to 12 minutes or until light golden. Cool for 5 minutes on sheet, then transfer to a rack and cool completely.

BARB'S NUTRITION NOTE

Finely chopping the pecans will make it easier to slice the cookies. It also spreads them more evenly through the batter, giving you more of their delicious flavor with every bite. The same rule holds true for chocolate chips, so use mini chips when you can. One cup (250 mL) of mini chocolate chips has the same weight and nutrients as 1 cup (250 mL) of regular chocolate chips.

Rugelach (Cinnamon Chocolate Twist Cookies)

MAKES 26 COOKIES (1 COOKIE PER SERVING)

TIPS

These traditionally high-fat cookies are lower in fat and calories because we've used yogurt instead of cream cheese, and cocoa instead of chocolate.

These are best eaten the day they are made; any leftover cookies are best eaten biscotti fashion, dipped in coffee.

When using margarine, choose a soft (non-hydrogenated) version to limit consumption of trans fats.

- Preheat oven to 350°F (180°C)
- Baking sheets, sprayed with vegetable spray

2¼ cups	all-purpose flour	550 mL
⅔ cup	granulated sugar	150 mL
½ cup	cold margarine or butter	125 mL
⅓ cup	2% yogurt	75 mL
3 to 4 tbsp	water	45 to 60 mL
½ cup	brown sugar	125 mL
⅓ cup	raisins	75 mL
2 tbsp	semisweet chocolate chips	25 mL
1 tbsp	unsweetened cocoa powder	15 mL
½ tsp	cinnamon	2 mL

1. In a bowl, combine flour and sugar. Cut in margarine until crumbly. Add yogurt and water, and mix until combined. Roll into a smooth ball, wrap and place in refrigerator for 30 minutes.

2. Put brown sugar, raisins, chocolate chips, cocoa and cinnamon in food processor; process until crumbly, approximately 20 seconds.

3. Divide dough in half. Roll one portion into a rectangle of ¼-inch (0.5 cm) thickness on a well-floured surface. Sprinkle half of the filling on top of the dough rectangle. Roll up tightly, long end to long end, jelly-roll fashion; pinch ends together. Cut into 1-inch (2.5 cm) thick pieces; some filling will fall out. Place on baking sheets, cut side up. Repeat with remaining dough and filling.

NUTRIENTS PER SERVING	
Calories	119
Carbohydrate	20 g
Fiber	1 g
Protein	1 g
Fat, total	4 g
Fat, saturated	1 g
Cholesterol	0 mg
Sodium	52 mg

AMERICA'S EXCHANGES	
1	Other Carbohydrates
1	Fat
1	Free Food

CANADA'S CHOICES	
1	Carbohydrate
1	Fat
1	Extra

MAKE AHEAD

Prepare dough and freeze for up to 2 weeks. Bake cookies up to a day ahead, keeping tightly covered.

4. With the back of a spoon or your fingers, gently flatten each cookie. Bake for 25 minutes, turning the cookies over at the halfway mark ($12\frac{1}{2}$ minutes).

BARB'S NUTRITION NOTE

When you will be eating away from home, plan ahead — and bring your meal planning skills with you. How you deal with eating out will depend partly on how you are controlling your diabetes: whether it's through diet and exercise alone or with oral medication and/or insulin. A dietitian or diabetes educator can help you learn to plan for these occasions, whether they are daily occurrences, such as eating at work, or special events.

In a self-serve situation, such as a buffet dinner, survey the buffet first to identify what you would really like to eat and then decide how to "spend" the food Exchanges or Choices you have. If you choose something that turns out not to be as good as expected, don't feel obliged to finish it. Set it aside and search out something you will like better.

Likewise, if you are being served, you don't need to eat everything on your plate. Eat what you know is a healthy portion for you. Most restaurants are happy to provide "doggy bags," so if you really like what you're eating, ask them to pack up the leftovers.

Cocoa Kisses

MAKES 40 COOKIES (3 COOKIES PER SERVING)

TIP

It's easier to separate eggs when they're cold, but egg whites beat to a greater volume when at room temperature.

BARB'S NUTRITION NOTES

The leavening ("lightening") agent in these cookies is the air trapped in the meringue (egg whites beaten with sugar).

Sometimes you will get more or fewer cookies than stated in the recipe. When this happens, see the cookie calculator on page 15 for help in determining how many cookies make up a serving.

- Preheat oven to 250°F (120°C)
- Baking sheet, sprayed with baking spray

3	egg whites, at room temperature	3
1 cup	granulated sugar	250 mL
1/8 tsp	salt	0.5 mL
1 tsp	vanilla	5 mL
3 tbsp	unsweetened cocoa powder	45 mL
1/2 cup	chopped pecans	125 mL

1. In a large bowl, beat egg whites until soft peaks form; gradually add sugar and salt, beating until mixture is glossy and stiff peaks form. Beat in vanilla. Sift cocoa into bowl; fold into meringue along with pecans.

2. Put mixture in a pastry bag fitted with star tip; pipe small kisses onto prepared baking sheet (alternatively, drop mixture by teaspoonfuls (5 mL) onto baking sheet). Bake for 1 hour or until firm and dry.

NUTRIENTS PER SERVING	
Calories	95
Carbohydrate	17 g
Fiber	1 g
Protein	1 g
Fat, total	3 g
Fat, saturated	0 g
Cholesterol	0 mg
Sodium	34 mg

AMERICA'S EXCHANGES	
1	Other Carbohydrates
1/2	Fat

CANADA'S CHOICES	
1	Carbohydrate
1/2	Fat

White Chocolate Cranberry Drops

**MAKES 48 COOKIES
(1 COOKIE PER
SERVING)**

*Sweet, creamy white
chocolate blends
beautifully with tart
cranberries in a rich
shortbread dough.
These are so easy to
make, there's no excuse
for not baking.*

TIPS

If you don't have
superfine sugar, whirl
regular granulated sugar
in a food processor or
blender until fine.

I recommend using
parchment paper when
baking these cookies,
as the white chocolate
is likely to stick.

VARIATIONS

Replace white chocolate
chips with semisweet
chocolate chips.

Replace cranberries
with dried cherries or
dried blueberries.

- Preheat oven to 350°F (180°C)
- Baking sheet, lined with parchment paper

2 cups	all-purpose flour	500 mL
1/4 cup	cornstarch	50 mL
1 cup	butter, softened	250 mL
1/2 cup	superfine granulated sugar (see Tips)	125 mL
1 tsp	vanilla	5 mL
1 cup	chopped dried cranberries	250 mL
3/4 cup	white chocolate chips	175 mL

1. On a sheet of waxed paper or in a bowl, combine flour and cornstarch. Set aside.

2. In a large bowl, using an electric mixer on medium speed, beat butter, sugar and vanilla until light and creamy, about 3 minutes. On low speed, gradually add flour mixture, beating until blended. Using your hands, knead to form a smooth dough. Add cranberries and white chocolate chips. Knead well.

3. Drop dough by tablespoonfuls (15 mL), about 2 inches (5 cm) apart, on prepared baking sheet. Bake in preheated oven for 13 to 18 minutes or until lightly browned around edges. Cool for 5 minutes on sheet, then transfer to a rack and cool completely.

NUTRIENTS PER SERVING	
Calories	86
Carbohydrate	10 g
Fiber	0 g
Protein	1 g
Fat, total	5 g
Fat, saturated	3 g
Cholesterol	10 mg
Sodium	42 mg

AMERICA'S EXCHANGES	
1/2	Other Carbohydrates
1	Fat

CANADA'S CHOICES	
1	Carbohydrate
1	Fat

Gingersnaps

MAKES 78 COOKIES (3 COOKIES PER SERVING)

This spicy cookie has definitely withstood the test of time. This variation is crisp and thin with a pleasantly mild ginger flavor.

TIP

If ground white pepper isn't available, use ¼ tsp (1 mL) freshly ground black pepper. You will notice black specks in the dough.

- ■ Preheat oven to 350°F (180°C)
- ■ Baking sheet, ungreased

3¾ cups	all-purpose flour	925 mL
1¼ tsp	baking powder	6 mL
¼ tsp	salt	1 mL
2 tbsp	ground ginger	25 mL
1 tbsp	ground cinnamon	15 mL
½ tsp	ground white pepper	2 mL
¼ tsp	ground cloves	1 mL
1½ cups	butter, softened	375 mL
1¾ cups	packed brown sugar	425 mL
1	egg	1
1 tbsp	grated gingerroot	15 mL
2 tsp	grated lemon zest	10 mL
¼ cup	turbinado sugar	50 mL

1. On a sheet of waxed paper or in a bowl, combine flour, baking powder, salt, ground ginger, cinnamon, pepper and cloves. Set aside.

2. In a large bowl, using an electric mixer on medium speed, beat butter, brown sugar, egg, gingerroot and lemon zest until smooth and creamy. On low speed, gradually add flour mixture, beating until dough becomes too stiff for the mixer, then finish mixing with a wooden spoon until smooth. Cover and chill dough for 2 hours for easy handling.

NUTRIENTS PER SERVING	
Calories	225
Carbohydrate	30 g
Fiber	1 g
Protein	2 g
Fat, total	11 g
Fat, saturated	7 g
Cholesterol	36 mg
Sodium	152 mg

AMERICA'S EXCHANGES	
1	Starch
1	Other Carbohydrates
2	Fat

CANADA'S CHOICES	
2	Carbohydrate
2	Fat

3. Shape teaspoonfuls (5 mL) of dough into balls. Place about 1 inch (2.5 cm) apart on baking sheet. With the bottom of a glass dipped in flour, press down firmly on each to form thin rounds. Sprinkle turbinado sugar evenly over tops. Bake in preheated oven for 10 to 14 minutes or until crisp and golden. Cool for 5 minutes on sheet, then transfer to a rack and cool completely.

Ginger Cookies

*A crisp, spicy cookie
for those who like the
flavor of gingerbread.*

**BARB'S
NUTRITION NOTE**

This recipe contains both
baking soda and baking
powder. These leavening
agents cause baked goods
to rise by releasing carbon
dioxide. Baking soda must
be combined with an acidic
ingredient (molasses, in this
recipe). Baking powder, on
the other hand, contains
both baking soda and an
acid component.

- Preheat oven to 350°F (180°C)
- Baking sheets, lightly greased or lined with parchment paper

1¾ cups	all-purpose flour	425 mL
1½ tsp	baking powder	7 mL
1 tsp	ground ginger	5 mL
1 tsp	ground cinnamon	5 mL
½ tsp	baking soda	2 mL
½ tsp	salt	2 mL
¼ tsp	ground cloves	1 mL
1	egg	1
½ cup	granulated sugar	125 mL
½ cup	vegetable oil	125 mL
½ cup	fancy molasses	125 mL

1. In a small bowl, combine flour, baking powder, ginger, cinnamon, baking soda, salt and cloves.

2. In a medium bowl, whisk egg, sugar, oil and molasses until blended. Fold in flour mixture until a moist dough forms.

3. Shape dough into balls, using about 1 tbsp (15 mL) dough per cookie, and place 2 inches (5 cm) apart on prepared baking sheets.

4. Bake in preheated oven for 10 to 12 minutes or until lightly browned and crisp. Let cool on baking sheet on a wire rack for 5 minutes, then remove to rack to cool completely.

NUTRIENTS PER SERVING	
Calories	91
Carbohydrate	13 g
Fiber	0 g
Protein	1 g
Fat, total	4 g
Fat, saturated	0 g
Cholesterol	6 mg
Sodium	77 mg

AMERICA'S EXCHANGES	
1	Other Carbohydrates
1	Fat

CANADA'S CHOICES	
1	Carbohydrate
1	Fat

Vanilla Almond Snaps

**MAKES 30 COOKIES
(3 COOKIES PER
SERVING)**

*Use a pastry bag with
a star tip and pipe the
mixture onto baking sheet
for an elegant cookie.*

BARB'S NUTRITION NOTE

When separating the eggs,
be careful not to allow any
egg yolk to escape into the
whites. If it does, they will
not beat properly.

- ▦ Preheat oven to 275°F (140°C)
- ▦ Baking sheet, lined with parchment paper and sprayed with baking spray

¾ cup	whole blanched almonds	175 mL
¼ cup	granulated sugar	50 mL
¼ tsp	salt	1 mL
2	egg whites	2
2 tbsp	granulated sugar	25 mL
½ tsp	vanilla	2 mL
	Sliced almonds (optional)	

1. In a food processor, grind almonds with ¼ cup (50 mL) sugar and salt until as fine as possible. Transfer to a bowl and set aside.

2. In another bowl, beat egg whites until soft peaks form. Gradually add 2 tbsp (25 mL) sugar, beating until stiff peaks form. Fold in vanilla. Fold into ground nut mixture until blended. Drop by teaspoonfuls (5 mL) onto prepared baking sheet. If desired, sprinkle with a few sliced almonds.

3. Bake for 25 minutes or until golden.

NUTRIENTS PER SERVING	
Calories	97
Carbohydrate	10 g
Fiber	1 g
Protein	3 g
Fat, total	6 g
Fat, saturated	1 g
Cholesterol	0 mg
Sodium	70 mg

AMERICA'S EXCHANGES	
½	Other Carbohydrates
1	Fat

CANADA'S CHOICES	
½	Carbohydrate
1	Fat

Charlie and Emma's Favorite Carrot Cookies

MAKES 24 COOKIES (1 COOKIE PER SERVING)

These cookies are great for a healthy snack, as they are made with whole grains that provide fiber and they are lower in sugar than typical cookies.

TIP

When using margarine, choose a non-hydrogenated version to limit consumption of trans fats.

■ Preheat oven to 350°F (180°C)
■ Baking sheets, lightly greased

1 cup	whole wheat flour	250 mL
¾ cup	quick-cooking rolled oats	175 mL
½ cup	ground flaxseed	125 mL
1 tsp	ground cinnamon	5 mL
½ tsp	baking soda	2 mL
1	egg	1
¾ cup	lightly packed brown sugar	175 mL
½ cup	margarine	125 mL
1 tsp	vanilla	5 mL
1 cup	grated carrots	250 mL

1. In a medium bowl, combine flour, oats, flaxseed, cinnamon and baking soda.

2. In a large bowl, using an electric mixer, beat egg, brown sugar, margarine and vanilla until smooth. Fold in flour mixture. Stir in carrots.

3. Drop dough by heaping tablespoonfuls (15 mL), about 2 inches (5 cm) apart, onto prepared baking sheets.

4. Bake in preheated oven for 10 to 15 minutes or until lightly browned. Let cool on baking sheet on a wire rack for 5 minutes.

NUTRIENTS PER SERVING	
Calories	103
Carbohydrate	13 g
Fiber	2 g
Protein	2 g
Fat, total	5 g
Fat, saturated	1 g
Cholesterol	8 mg
Sodium	86 mg

AMERICA'S EXCHANGES	
1	Other Carbohydrates
1	Fat

CANADA'S CHOICES	
1	Carbohydrate
1	Fat

Bars, Squares and Brownies

Apple Cinnamon Bars

**MAKES 36 BARS
(1 BAR PER SERVING)**

TIP
Dust lightly with
confectioner's (icing)
sugar if desired.

■ Preheat oven to 350°F (180°C)
■ 9-inch (2.5 L) square cake pan, greased

Crust

1 cup	unbleached all-purpose flour	250 mL
1 cup	whole wheat flour	250 mL
½ cup	granulated sugar	125 mL
½ tsp	baking powder	2 mL
¼ tsp	salt	1 mL
⅔ cup	cold butter, cubed	150 mL
1	egg, beaten	1

Filling

⅓ cup	granulated sugar	75 mL
2 tbsp	all-purpose flour	25 mL
1 tsp	cinnamon	5 mL
2 lb	tart cooking apples, peeled, cored and thinly sliced (5½ cups/1.375 L)	1 kg
1 tbsp	freshly squeezed lemon juice	15 mL

1. *Crust:* In a bowl, combine all-purpose and whole wheat flours, sugar, baking powder and salt. Using a pastry blender, 2 knives or your fingers, cut in butter until mixture resembles coarse crumbs. Add egg and, using a fork, mix until thoroughly blended. Press half of the mixture (about 2 cups/500 mL) evenly into prepared pan. Set aside remainder.

NUTRIENTS PER SERVING	
Calories	87
Carbohydrate	13 g
Fiber	1 g
Protein	1 g
Fat, total	4 g
Fat, saturated	2 g
Cholesterol	14 mg
Sodium	57 mg

AMERICA'S EXCHANGES	
1	Other Carbohydrates
1	Fat

CANADA'S CHOICES	
1	Carbohydrate
1	Fat

2. *Filling:* In a large bowl, combine sugar, flour, cinnamon, apples and lemon juice, mixing well. Layer evenly over crust. Sprinkle remaining crumble mixture over top.

3. Bake in preheated oven until apples are tender and crust is golden, 45 to 50 minutes. Let cool completely in pan on rack. Cut into bars.

BARB'S NUTRITION NOTE

Fashion affects not only clothing and footwear, but also food — and in both instances, the fashion may not always be good for us. No one knows when we first began to mill wheat into flour, but the product certainly did not resemble the white all-purpose flour most people now have in their kitchens. Like today's whole wheat flour, the original contained the bran and germ portions of the grain.

About 150 years ago, millers started to produce a "higher-quality" flour by sifting out the bran and germ. These nutritious leftovers, rich in fiber and important nutrients, became animal feed. White flour became a culinary status symbol, and whole-grain flour was scorned as "peasant food." Later, a bleaching process (which destroys any remaining vitamin E) was added to make the flour even whiter.

As more and more people used white flour, they began to experience nutritional deficiencies. Today, white flour, whether bleached or not, must by law be enriched — some of the vitamins and iron are added back, but the fiber is not.

Berry Cheesecake Bars

**MAKES 20 BARS
(1 BAR PER SERVING)**

These bars offer the decadent taste of cheesecake without all the calories.

TIPS

When lining the baking pan, make sure the foil extends 1 inch (2.5 cm) beyond the edge for easy removal.

We tested these bars with raspberries, blueberries and mixed berries. All versions tasted great.

■ Preheat oven to 350°F (180°C)
■ 13- by 9-inch (3 L) baking pan, lined with greased foil

Crumb Mixture

1 cup	all-purpose flour	250 mL
1 cup	packed brown sugar	250 mL
½ cup	ground almonds	125 mL
¼ cup	melted butter	50 mL
2 tbsp	cold water	25 mL

Filling

2	eggs	2
1	egg white	1
1	package (8 oz/250 g) light cream cheese, softened	1
¾ cup	granulated sugar	175 mL
½ cup	low-fat plain yogurt	125 mL
1½ tsp	almond extract	7 mL
1 tsp	grated orange zest	5 mL
1½ cups	fresh or frozen berries (see tip, at left)	375 mL

1. *Crumb mixture:* In a medium bowl, combine flour, brown sugar, almonds, butter and water.

2. *Filling:* In a large bowl, using an electric mixer on high speed, beat eggs, egg white, cream cheese, sugar, yogurt, almond extract and orange zest until fluffy.

NUTRIENTS PER SERVING	
Calories	171
Carbohydrate	26 g
Fiber	1 g
Protein	3 g
Fat, total	6 g
Fat, saturated	3 g
Cholesterol	32 g
Sodium	121 mg

AMERICA'S EXCHANGES	
½	Starch
1	Other Carbohydrates
1	Fat

CANADA'S CHOICES	
2	Carbohydrate
1	Fat

VARIATION

If you prefer, replace the almond extract with vanilla and the orange zest with lemon.

3. Press half of the crumb mixture into prepared pan. Pour in filling and spread evenly. Sprinkle with berries. Drop remaining crumb mixture by tablespoonfuls (15 mL) over berries. Using a knife, swirl filling, berries and crumb mixture.

4. Bake in preheated oven for 35 minutes or until a tester inserted in the center comes out clean. Let cool completely in pan on a wire rack. Remove from pan by lifting foil and transfer to a cutting board. Remove foil and cut into bars.

BARB'S NUTRITION NOTE

As you prepare the recipes in this book, you will become familiar with the appropriate portion sizes for different types of desserts and the approximate Exchanges or Choices assigned to them. Use this knowledge to help you choose wisely when you're eating away from home.

Mixed Fruit Bran Bars

**MAKES 36 BARS
(1 BAR PER SERVING)**

TIP

For added fiber, substitute whole wheat flour for all or half of the all-purpose.

VARIATIONS

Replace lemon zest with orange or tangerine zest.

Replace dried cranberries with chopped dried cherries or raisins.

- Preheat oven to 375°F (190°C)
- 13- by 9-inch (3 L) cake pan, greased

2 cups	bran flakes cereal	500 mL
1 cup	unbleached all-purpose flour	250 mL
⅔ cup	packed brown sugar	150 mL
2 tsp	baking soda	10 mL
¼ tsp	salt	1 mL
1 cup	buttermilk	250 mL
2 tbsp	vegetable oil	25 mL
2	eggs	2
1 tbsp	grated lemon zest	15 mL
¾ cup	chopped dried apricots	175 mL
½ cup	chopped dried apples	125 mL
½ cup	chopped dates	125 mL
½ cup	dried cranberries	125 mL
⅓ cup	chopped pecans	75 mL

1. In a food processor fitted with a metal blade, combine cereal, flour, brown sugar, baking soda and salt. Pulse until coarsely chopped, about 1 minute. Add buttermilk, vegetable oil, eggs and lemon zest and process until cereal is crushed and mixture is blended. Stir in apricots, apples, dates, cranberries and pecans. Spread evenly in prepared pan.

2. Bake in preheated oven until set and golden, 20 to 25 minutes. Let cool completely in pan on rack. Cut into bars.

NUTRIENTS PER SERVING	
Calories	79
Carbohydrate	15 g
Fiber	1 g
Protein	1 g
Fat, total	2 g
Fat, saturated	0 g
Cholesterol	11 mg
Sodium	114 mg

AMERICA'S EXCHANGES	
½	Fruit
½	Other Carbohydrates
½	Fat

CANADA'S CHOICES	
1	Carbohydrate
½	Fat

Pick-Me-Up Bars

**MAKES 24 BARS
(1 BAR PER SERVING)**

TIP

When baking, you can usually use 1 whole egg in place of 2 egg whites or vice versa. However, in desserts like custards, where the yolk is needed for thickening, this rule doesn't apply.

VARIATIONS

Replace whole wheat flour with all-purpose, but be aware that you'll lose some of the health benefits, such as added fiber.

Replace sunflower seeds with a mixture of sesame and flaxseeds.

■ Preheat oven to 350°F (180°C)
■ 8-inch (2 L) square cake pan, greased

1 cup	graham wafer crumbs	250 mL
2/3 cup	packed brown sugar	150 mL
1/2 cup	whole wheat flour	125 mL
1/2 cup	butterscotch chips	125 mL
1/3 cup	quick-cooking rolled oats	75 mL
1/3 cup	sunflower seeds	75 mL
1 tsp	baking powder	5 mL
2	egg whites (see Tip)	2
1 tbsp	vegetable oil	15 mL
1 1/2 tsp	vanilla	7 mL

1. In a bowl, combine graham wafer crumbs, brown sugar, flour, butterscotch chips, oats, sunflower seeds and baking powder.

2. In a separate bowl, whisk egg whites, oil and vanilla until blended. Stir into dry ingredients, mixing well. Press evenly into prepared pan.

3. Bake in preheated oven until top is golden, about 20 minutes. Let cool completely in pan on rack. Cut into bars.

NUTRIENTS PER SERVING	
Calories	97
Carbohydrate	15 g
Fiber	1 g
Protein	2 g
Fat, total	3 g
Fat, saturated	1 g
Cholesterol	0 mg
Sodium	44 mg

AMERICA'S EXCHANGES	
1	Other Carbohydrates
1/2	Fat

CANADA'S CHOICES	
1	Carbohydrate
1/2	Fat

Apricot Coconut Bars

**MAKES 36 BARS
(1 BAR PER SERVING)**

TIP

When using margarine, choose a non-hydrogenated version to limit consumption of trans fats.

■ Preheat oven to 350°F (180°C)
■ 13- by 9-inch (3 L) baking pan, greased

2 cups	whole wheat flour	500 mL
1½ cups	quick-cooking rolled oats	375 mL
1⅓ cups	lightly packed brown sugar	325 mL
½ cup	oat bran	125 mL
½ cup	natural wheat bran	125 mL
½ tsp	baking soda	2 mL
½ cup	margarine or butter, softened	125 mL
½ cup	vegetable oil	125 mL
2 cups	chopped dried apricots	500 mL
1½ cups	water	375 mL
½ cup	granulated sugar	125 mL
2 tbsp	all-purpose flour	25 mL
1 cup	unsweetened shredded coconut	250 mL

1. In a large bowl, combine flour, oats, brown sugar, oat bran, wheat bran and baking soda.

2. In a small bowl, combine margarine and oil. Stir into flour mixture until mixture resembles coarse crumbs. Reserve 1 cup (250 mL) crumb mixture. Press remaining crumb mixture into bottom of prepared pan. Set aside.

3. In a large saucepan, over medium high heat, combine apricots and water; bring to a boil. Reduce heat, cover and simmer for 5 minutes, until softened.

4. Meanwhile, combine sugar and flour. Stir into apricot mixture. Cook, stirring, for 1 minute or until thick. Stir in coconut.

NUTRIENTS PER SERVING	
Calories	173
Carbohydrate	27 g
Fiber	3 g
Protein	2 g
Fat, total	7 g
Fat, saturated	2 g
Cholesterol	0 mg
Sodium	57 mg

AMERICA'S EXCHANGES	
½	Starch
½	Fruit
½	Other Carbohydrates
1½	Fat

CANADA'S CHOICES	
1½	Carbohydrate
1½	Fat

VARIATION
Replace the apricots with your favorite dried fruit.

5. Spread apricot mixture over crumbs in the pan and sprinkle evenly with reserved crumb mixture.

6. Bake for 35 minutes or until golden brown on top. Let cool completely in pan on a wire rack, then cut into bars.

BARB'S NUTRITION NOTE
When planning what to eat, we need to take into account both the type of food and the portion size. Getting the correct portion size (in other words, the right number of bars or squares) from a cake baked in a rectangular or square pan is easy: just look at how many bars are specified in the yield and cut the cake into that many portions. For example, this recipe makes 36 bars. To get that number, you would cut the cake lengthwise 3 times and crosswise 8 times. Make sure all your bars are the same size, or the nutrients per serving and Exchanges or Choices will not be accurate.

Apricot Seed Bars

**MAKES 36 BARS
(1 BAR PER SERVING)**

*Packed full of dried fruits
and seeds, these bars
make a great addition
to a backpack, if you're
hiking or biking.*

TIPS

To prevent sticking, use
cooking spray to get a
light, even coating of
grease on baking pans.

To ease cleanup, rather
than combining the dry
ingredients in a bowl (in
Step 1), place a large piece
of waxed paper on the
counter. Spread the flour
on the paper and sprinkle
the baking soda, salt and
cinnamon over it. Using the
paper as a funnel, transfer
the dry ingredients to the
egg mixture.

VARIATION

Replace cranberries
with chopped dried
figs or raisins.

- Preheat oven to 350°F (180°C)
- 13- by 9-inch (3 L) cake pan, greased

¾ cup	butter, softened	175 mL
¾ cup	packed brown sugar	175 mL
1	egg	1
1 cup	unbleached all-purpose flour	250 mL
½ tsp	baking soda	2 mL
¼ tsp	salt	1 mL
¾ tsp	cinnamon	4 mL
1 cup	quick-cooking rolled oats	250 mL
¾ cup	finely chopped dried apricots	175 mL
¾ cup	dried cranberries	175 mL
¼ cup	sesame seeds	50 mL
¼ cup	flaxseeds	50 mL
¼ cup	sunflower seeds	50 mL

1. In a bowl, using an electric mixer on medium speed,
   beat butter, brown sugar and egg until smooth and
   creamy. Combine flour, baking soda, salt and cinnamon.
   Stir into creamed mixture, mixing well. Stir in rolled
   oats, apricots, cranberries, sesame seeds, flaxseeds and
   sunflower seeds. Spread evenly in prepared pan.

2. Bake in preheated oven until top is set and golden,
   25 to 30 minutes. Let cool completely in pan on rack.
   Cut into bars.

NUTRIENTS PER SERVING	
Calories	111
Carbohydrate	14 g
Fiber	1 g
Protein	2 g
Fat, total	6 g
Fat, saturated	3 g
Cholesterol	16 mg
Sodium	77 mg

AMERICA'S EXCHANGES	
1	Other Carbohydrates
1	Fat

CANADA'S CHOICES	
1	Carbohydrate
1	Fat

Clockwise from top left:
Apricot Coconut Bars (page 126),
Toffee Bars (page 136) and
Berry Cheesecake Bars (page 122)

Chocolate-Wrapped Ginger Biscotti (page 76)

Lemon Poppy Seed Loaf (page 52)

Apricot Seed Bars (page 128)

Chocolate Marble Vanilla Cheesecake (page 192)

White Chocolate Cranberry Hazelnut Brownies (page 146)

Chunky Chocolate Shortbread (page 84)

Cream Cheese–Filled Brownies (page 150)

Date Nut Bars

**MAKES 16 BARS
(1 BAR PER SERVING)**

**BARB'S
NUTRITION NOTE**
Cut dried fruit into small pieces to spread its flavor through a batter or dough.

■ 8-inch square (2 L) baking dish

1 1/3 cups	chopped dates	325 mL
1/4 cup	walnut pieces	50 mL
1/4 cup	whole almonds	50 mL
1/2 cup	granola	125 mL

1. In a food processor, combine dates, walnuts and almonds; process until mixture begins to come together.

2. Sprinkle half of granola over bottom of baking dish. Press date mixture firmly and evenly over granola. Top with remaining granola, pressing down slightly to embed in date mixture. Chill.

3. Cut into squares.

NUTRIENTS PER SERVING	
Calories	80
Carbohydrate	14 g
Fiber	2 g
Protein	1 g
Fat, total	3 g
Fat, saturated	0 g
Cholesterol	0 mg
Sodium	4 mg

AMERICA'S EXCHANGES	
1	Fruit
1/2	Fat

CANADA'S CHOICES	
1	Carbohydrate
1/2	Fat

Granola Bars

**MAKES 18 BARS
(1 BAR PER SERVING)**

*I got tired of the cost
of the dried-out granola
bars you find in stores.
I created my own for a
healthy treat.*

TIP

After cutting into bars,
wrap each bar in its own
plastic wrap and store in a
cool, dry place or a cookie
jar for easy serving.

VARIATION

You can replace dates with
any dried fruit.

■ Preheat oven to 350°F (180°C)
■ 13- by 9-inch (3 L) metal baking pan, lined with foil, sprayed
with nonstick spray, then lined with parchment paper

1/3 cup	unsalted butter, softened	75 mL
3/4 cup	honey	175 mL
1/2 cup	packed brown sugar	125 mL
2 cups	old-fashioned rolled oats	500 mL
1 cup	natural bran	250 mL
1 cup	sunflower seeds	250 mL
1 cup	dates, pitted and chopped	250 mL
1/2 cup	pecans, toasted and chopped	125 mL
1/4 cup	sesame seeds	50 mL
2 tsp	ground cinnamon	10 mL

1. In a small saucepan over medium heat, melt butter. Stir
in honey and brown sugar. Bring to a boil, about 3 minutes.
Simmer over low heat for 5 minutes. Let cool slightly.

2. In a large bowl, combine rolled oats, bran, sunflower
seeds, dates, pecans, sesame seeds and cinnamon.
Gradually stir in sugar mixture. Firmly press into
prepared baking pan. Bake in preheated oven until
golden brown, 15 to 18 minutes. Let cool completely
in baking pan before cutting into bars.

NUTRIENTS PER SERVING	
Calories	250
Carbohydrate	37 g
Fiber	5 g
Protein	5 g
Fat, total	12 g
Fat, saturated	3 g
Cholesterol	9 mg
Sodium	5 mg

AMERICA'S EXCHANGES	
1	Starch
1/2	Fruit
1	Other Carbohydrates
2 1/2	Fat

CANADA'S CHOICES	
2	Carbohydrate
2 1/2	Fat

Peanut Butter-Coconut-Raisin Granola Bars

**MAKES 24 BARS
(1 BAR PER SERVING)**

TIPS

Corn flakes can replace bran flakes. Chopped dates can replace raisins.

When using margarine, choose a soft (non-hydrogenated) version to limit consumption of trans fats.

MAKE AHEAD

Prepare these up to 2 days ahead and keep tightly closed in a cookie tin. These freeze for up to 2 weeks.

■ Preheat oven to 350°F(180°C)
■ 9-inch square (2.5 L) pan sprayed with vegetable spray

1 1/3 cups	rolled oats	325 mL
2/3 cup	raisins	150 mL
1/2 cup	bran flakes cereal	125 mL
1/3 cup	unsweetened shredded coconut	75 mL
3 tbsp	chocolate chips	45 mL
2 tbsp	chopped pecans	25 mL
1 tsp	baking soda	5 mL
1/4 cup	peanut butter	50 mL
1/4 cup	brown sugar	50 mL
3 tbsp	margarine or butter	45 mL
3 tbsp	honey	45 mL
1 tsp	vanilla	5 mL

1. Put oats, raisins, bran flakes, coconut, chocolate chips, pecans and baking soda in bowl. Combine until well mixed.

2. In a small saucepan, whisk together peanut butter, brown sugar, margarine, honey and vanilla over medium heat for approximately 30 seconds or just until sugar dissolves and mixture is smooth. Pour over dry ingredients and stir to combine. Press into prepared pan and bake for 15 to 20 minutes or until browned. Let cool completely before cutting into bars.

NUTRIENTS PER SERVING	
Calories	99
Carbohydrate	14 g
Fiber	1 g
Protein	2 g
Fat, total	5 g
Fat, saturated	1 g
Cholesterol	0 mg
Sodium	92 mg

AMERICA'S EXCHANGES	
1	Other Carbohydrates
1	Fat

CANADA'S CHOICES	
1	Carbohydrate
1	Fat

Nutty Shortbread Bars

**MAKES 48 BARS
(1 BAR PER SERVING)**

*These bars, which are not
too sweet, have a nice
nutty flavor and a very
"short" texture.*

■ Preheat oven to 300°F (150°C)
■ 9-inch (2.5 L) square cake pan, ungreased

1 cup	butter, softened	250 mL
1/3 cup	granulated sugar	75 mL
2 tbsp	cornstarch	25 mL
1 tsp	vanilla	5 mL
2 cups	all-purpose flour	500 mL
1/3 cup	finely chopped walnuts	75 mL
1/3 cup	finely chopped pecans	75 mL

1. In a bowl, using an electric mixer on medium speed, beat butter, sugar, cornstarch and vanilla until light and creamy. Stir in flour, walnuts and pecans, mixing well. Using your hands, knead to form a smooth dough. Press evenly into pan.

2. Bake in preheated oven until light golden around edges, 40 to 45 minutes. Cut into bars just as the pan comes out of the oven, then let cool completely in pan on rack. Recut.

NUTRIENTS PER SERVING	
Calories	71
Carbohydrate	6 g
Fiber	0 g
Protein	1 g
Fat, total	5 g
Fat, saturated	2 g
Cholesterol	10 mg
Sodium	39 mg

AMERICA'S EXCHANGES	
1/2	Starch
1	Fat

CANADA'S CHOICES	
1/2	Carbohydrate
1	Fat

Chocolate Shortbread Bars

MAKES 36 BARS
(1 BAR PER SERVING)

Because there are so many chocolate lovers in the world, I've always believed you should have a chocolate version of every cookie to satisfy them all. These bars are thin, crisp and chocolaty.

- Preheat oven to 300°F (150°C)
- 13- by 9-inch (3.5 L) cake pan, ungreased

1 cup	butter, softened	250 mL
½ cup	granulated sugar	125 mL
2 cups	all-purpose flour	500 mL
2	squares (1 oz/28 g each) semisweet chocolate, melted and cooled	2

1. In a bowl, using an electric mixer on medium speed, beat butter and sugar until light and creamy, about 3 minutes. Stir in flour, mixing well. Stir in melted chocolate, mixing well. Using your hands, knead to form a smooth dough. Press evenly into pan.

2. Bake in preheated oven until firm and dry, 35 to 40 minutes. Cut into bars just as the pan comes out of the oven, then let cool completely in pan on rack. Recut.

NUTRIENTS PER SERVING	
Calories	112
Carbohydrate	11 g
Fiber	1 g
Protein	1 g
Fat, total	7 g
Fat, saturated	4 g
Cholesterol	14 mg
Sodium	52 mg

AMERICA'S EXCHANGES	
1	Other Carbohydrates
1½	Fat

CANADA'S CHOICES	
1	Carbohydrate
1½	Fat

Hazelnut Shortbread Bars

MAKES 25 BARS (1 BAR PER SERVING)

Hazelnuts have a unique flavor that really shines in a shortbread dough.

BARB'S NUTRITION NOTE

Shortbread recipes all have three basic ingredients: flour, sugar and butter. Other fats will not produce the typical shortbread texture. Do remember, however, that butter is high in saturated fat.

■ Preheat oven to 300°F (150°C)
■ 9-inch (2.5 L) square cake pan, ungreased

1 cup	butter, softened	250 mL
½ cup	superfine granulated sugar	125 mL
1½ cups	all-purpose flour	375 mL
¾ cup	cornstarch	175 mL
½ cup	finely chopped hazelnuts	125 mL

1. In a bowl, using an electric mixer on medium speed, beat butter and sugar until light and creamy, about 3 minutes. Stir in flour, cornstarch and hazelnuts, mixing well. Using your hands, knead to form a smooth dough. Press evenly into pan. Prick surface all over with a fork.

2. Bake in preheated oven until lightly browned, 30 to 35 minutes. Cut into bars just as the pan comes out of the oven, then let cool completely in pan on rack. Recut.

NUTRIENTS PER SERVING	
Calories	137
Carbohydrate	14 g
Fiber	0 g
Protein	1 g
Fat, total	9 g
Fat, saturated	5 g
Cholesterol	20 mg
Sodium	76 mg

AMERICA'S EXCHANGES	
½	Starch
½	Other Carbohydrates
2	Fat

CANADA'S CHOICES	
1	Carbohydrate
2	Fat

Chocolate Hazelnut Bars

**MAKES 60 BARS
(1 BAR PER SERVING)**

These yummy bars taste like a big chocolate chip oatmeal cookie. They're easy to make and a good choice if you're in a hurry.

TIPS

For a softer cookie, prepare these bars the day before you intend to serve them.

Hazelnuts are also called filberts. If you prefer, remove the outer brown skin before using them in baking. Toast the nuts on a rimmed baking sheet at 350°F (180°C) for about 5 minutes. Transfer the warm nuts to a towel and rub together. The skins should come off in the towel.

VARIATION

Macadamia nuts make a wonderful substitution for the hazelnuts in this bar.

■ Preheat oven to 375°F (190°C)
■ 17- by 11- by 1-inch (3 L) jelly-roll pan, greased

1 cup	butter, softened	250 mL
1 cup	packed brown sugar	250 mL
½ cup	granulated sugar	125 mL
2	eggs	2
1 tsp	vanilla	5 mL
1¾ cups	all-purpose flour	425 mL
1 cup	quick-cooking rolled oats	250 mL
1 tsp	baking soda	5 mL
¼ tsp	salt	1 mL
2 cups	semisweet chocolate chips	500 mL
1½ cups	coarsely chopped hazelnuts	375 mL

1. In a bowl, using an electric mixer on medium speed, beat butter and brown and granulated sugars until light and creamy, about 3 minutes. Add eggs, one at a time, beating well after each addition. Beat in vanilla. Stir in flour, oats, baking soda and salt, mixing well. Stir in chocolate chips and hazelnuts. Spread dough evenly in prepared pan.

2. Bake in preheated oven until golden, about 15 minutes. Let cool completely in pan on rack. Cut into bars.

NUTRIENTS PER SERVING	
Calories	114
Carbohydrate	13 g
Fiber	1 g
Protein	2 g
Fat, total	7 g
Fat, saturated	3 g
Cholesterol	14 mg
Sodium	66 mg

AMERICA'S EXCHANGES	
1	Other Carbohydrates
1½	Fat

CANADA'S CHOICES	
1	Carbohydrate
1½	Fat

Toffee Bars

**MAKES 24 BARS
(1 BAR PER SERVING)**

TIP

When using margarine, choose a non-hydrogenated version to limit consumption of trans fats.

VARIATION

You can substitute any kind of chip for the chocolate chips — white chocolate, butterscotch, peanut butter, etc.

■ Preheat oven to 350°F (180°C)
■ 13- by 9-inch (3 L) baking pan, lined with parchment paper

2 cups	quick-cooking rolled oats	500 mL
½ cup	lightly packed brown sugar	125 mL
⅓ cup	melted butter or margarine	75 mL
¼ cup	liquid honey or corn syrup	50 mL
1½ tsp	vanilla	7 mL
½ tsp	salt	2 mL
1 cup	semisweet chocolate chips	250 mL
½ cup	finely chopped nuts (pecans, walnuts, peanuts, etc.) or unsweetened shredded coconut	125 mL

1. In a large bowl, combine oats, brown sugar, butter, honey, vanilla and salt; mix thoroughly. Stir in chocolate chips and nuts until evenly mixed.

2. Pour mixture into prepared pan. Press down with clean, damp hands to compact evenly.

3. Bake in preheated oven for 25 minutes or until brown and crisp. Let cool in pan on a wire rack for 5 minutes. Remove from pan by lifting parchment and transfer to a cutting board. Remove parchment and cut into bars.

NUTRIENTS PER SERVING	
Calories	131
Carbohydrate	18 g
Fiber	1 g
Protein	2 g
Fat, total	7 g
Fat, saturated	3 g
Cholesterol	7 mg
Sodium	78 mg

AMERICA'S EXCHANGES	
1	Other Carbohydrates
1½	Fat

CANADA'S CHOICES	
1	Carbohydrate
1½	Fat

Date Oatmeal Squares

MAKES 16 SQUARES (1 SQUARE PER SERVING)

TIPS

For easier preparation, use scissors to cut the dates. Try half dates and half pitted, chopped prunes for a change.

When using margarine, choose a soft (non-hydrogenated) version.

- Preheat oven to 350°F (180°C)
- 8-inch (2 L) square cake pan, sprayed with nonstick vegetable spray

½ lb	pitted dates, chopped	250 g
1 cup	water or orange juice	250 mL
1 cup	all-purpose flour	250 mL
1 cup	rolled oats	250 mL
⅔ cup	brown sugar	150 mL
½ cup	bran cereal*	125 mL
½ tsp	baking powder	2 mL
½ tsp	baking soda	2 mL
½ cup	soft margarine	125 mL

* Use a wheat bran breakfast cereal.

1. In a saucepan, cover and cook dates and water over low heat, stirring often, for approximately 15 minutes or until dates are soft and liquid absorbed. Set aside.

2. In a bowl, combine flour, rolled oats, brown sugar, cereal, baking powder and baking soda; cut in margarine until crumbly.

3. Pat half onto bottom of cake pan; spoon date mixture over top. Pat remaining crumb mixture over date mixture. Bake for 20 to 25 minutes or until golden.

NUTRIENTS PER SERVING	
Calories	181
Carbohydrate	31 g
Fiber	3 g
Protein	2 g
Fat, total	6 g
Fat, saturated	1 g
Cholesterol	0 mg
Sodium	147 mg

AMERICA'S EXCHANGES	
1	Starch
½	Fruit
½	Other Carbohydrates
1	Fat

CANADA'S CHOICES	
2	Carbohydrate
1	Fat

Raisin and Applesauce Squares

MAKES 25 SQUARES (1 SQUARE PER SERVING)

This moist square has a soft, cake-like texture. It gets its wonderful flavor from applesauce and dates.

TIP

To ease cleanup, rather than combining the dry ingredients in a bowl (Step 2), place a large piece of waxed paper on the counter. Spread the flours on the paper. Sprinkle with the baking powder, baking soda, cinnamon and cloves. Using the paper as a funnel, transfer the dry ingredients to the butter mixture.

VARIATIONS

Replace orange zest with lemon zest.

Replace raisins with dried cranberries or cherries.

- Preheat oven to 350°F (180°C)
- 8-inch (2 L) square cake pan, greased

¼ cup	butter, softened	50 mL
½ cup	packed brown sugar	125 mL
1	egg	1
1 tbsp	grated orange zest	15 mL
1 tsp	vanilla	5 mL
1 cup	unbleached all-purpose flour	250 mL
½ cup	whole wheat flour	125 mL
½ tsp	baking powder	2 mL
½ tsp	baking soda	2 mL
1 tsp	cinnamon	5 mL
¼ tsp	ground cloves	1 mL
1 cup	unsweetened applesauce	250 mL
¾ cup	raisins	175 mL

1. In a large bowl, using an electric mixer on low speed, beat butter, brown sugar, egg, orange zest and vanilla until blended, about 3 minutes.

2. Combine all-purpose and whole wheat flours, baking powder, baking soda, cinnamon and cloves. Stir into creamed mixture alternately with applesauce, making 3 additions and mixing lightly after each addition. Stir in raisins. Spread evenly in prepared pan.

3. Bake in preheated oven until a toothpick inserted in center comes out clean, 25 to 30 minutes. Let cool completely in pan on rack. Cut into squares.

NUTRIENTS PER SERVING	
Calories	82
Carbohydrate	15 g
Fiber	1 g
Protein	1 g
Fat, total	2 g
Fat, saturated	1 g
Cholesterol	12 mg
Sodium	54 mg

AMERICA'S EXCHANGES	
½	Fruit
½	Other Carbohydrates
½	Fat

CANADA'S CHOICES	
1	Carbohydrate
½	Fat

Lemon Poppy Seed Squares

MAKES 20 SQUARES (1 SQUARE PER SERVING)

TIPS

Try substituting lime juice and zest for the lemon.

When using margarine, choose a soft (non-hydrogenated) version.

■ Preheat oven to 350°F (180°C)
■ 8-inch square (2 L) baking pan, sprayed with vegetable spray

Cake

½ cup	granulated sugar	125 mL
1 tbsp	margarine or butter	15 mL
2 tsp	poppy seeds	10 mL
1½ tsp	grated lemon zest	7 mL
1	egg	1
¾ cup	cake and pastry flour	175 mL

Topping

⅔ cup	granulated sugar	150 mL
2 tsp	grated lemon zest	10 mL
⅓ cup	freshly squeezed lemon juice	75 mL
1 tbsp	cornstarch	15 mL
1	egg	1
1	egg white	1

1. *Cake:* In a bowl, whisk together sugar, margarine, poppy seeds, lemon zest and egg until smooth. Add wet ingredients to flour and stir just until mixed. Pat into prepared pan; set aside.

2. *Topping:* In a bowl, stir together sugar, lemon zest, lemon juice, cornstarch, whole egg and egg white. Pour over cake batter in pan.

3. Bake 20 to 25 minutes or until set with center still slightly soft. Cool to room temperature on a wire rack.

NUTRIENTS PER SERVING	
Calories	77
Carbohydrate	16 g
Fiber	0 g
Protein	1 g
Fat, total	1 g
Fat, saturated	0 g
Cholesterol	19 mg
Sodium	17 mg

AMERICA'S EXCHANGES		CANADA'S CHOICES
1	Other Carbohydrates	1 Carbohydrate

Almond Shortbread Squares

**MAKES 24 SQUARES
(1 SQUARE PER
SERVING)**

*Tender but crisp, the
crunchy almonds give
these squares an unusual
texture for shortbread.*

■ Preheat oven to 325°F (160°C)
■ 13- by 9-inch (3 L) cake pan, ungreased

¾ cup	sliced almonds, toasted	175 mL
2 cups	all-purpose flour	500 mL
1 cup	cold butter, cubed	250 mL
½ cup	granulated sugar	125 mL
½ cup	cornstarch	125 mL
2 tbsp	grated orange zest	25 mL
¾ tsp	almond extract	3 mL

1. In a food processor, pulse almonds until coarsely chopped. Add flour, butter, sugar, cornstarch, orange zest and almond extract and pulse until crumbly. Press evenly into pan.

2. Bake in preheated oven until lightly browned around edges, 30 to 35 minutes. Cut into squares just as the pan comes out of the oven, then let cool completely in pan on rack. Recut.

NUTRIENTS PER SERVING	
Calories	151
Carbohydrate	15 g
Fiber	1 g
Protein	2 g
Fat, total	9 g
Fat, saturated	5 g
Cholesterol	21 mg
Sodium	79 mg

AMERICA'S EXCHANGES	
1	Other Carbohydrates
2	Fat

CANADA'S CHOICES	
1	Carbohydrate
2	Fat

Coconut Seeds Cereal Squares

*A combination of
coconut and seeds
adds fiber and flavor.*

TIP

Teach kids how to measure
brown sugar properly.
Unlike granulated sugar,
which is simply scooped
into a dry measuring cup,
then leveled off, brown
sugar is packed into the
cup. To test if they did it
right, turn the cup upside
down on a piece of waxed
paper. When you remove
the cup, the sugar should
hold its shape.

VARIATION

Use other kinds of seeds.
Pumpkin seeds add an
interesting appearance,
texture and flavor.

■ Preheat oven to 375°F (190°C)
■ 15- by 10- by 1-inch (2 L) jelly-roll pan, greased

¾ cup	butter	175 mL
1¼ cups	packed brown sugar	300 mL
1 tsp	vanilla	5 mL
2¼ cups	quick-cooking rolled oats	550 mL
¼ cup	sesame seeds	50 mL
¼ cup	flaxseeds	50 mL
¼ cup	sunflower seeds	50 mL
¼ cup	unsweetened flaked coconut	50 mL
¾ tsp	baking powder	3 mL
¼ tsp	salt	1 mL

1. In a large saucepan, melt butter over medium heat.
   Stir in brown sugar and vanilla. Cook, stirring often,
   until mixture is bubbly, about 2 minutes. Remove
   from heat. Stir in rolled oats, sesame seeds, flaxseeds,
   sunflower seeds, coconut, baking powder and salt,
   mixing well until all ingredients are moistened. Press
   evenly into prepared pan.

2. Bake in preheated oven until light golden, about
   10 minutes. Let cool completely in pan on rack.
   Cut into squares.

NUTRIENTS PER SERVING	
Calories	160
Carbohydrate	19 g
Fiber	2 g
Protein	2 g
Fat, total	9 g
Fat, saturated	4 g
Cholesterol	16 mg
Sodium	97 mg

AMERICA'S EXCHANGES	
1	Other Carbohydrates
2	Fat

CANADA'S CHOICES	
1	Carbohydrate
2	Fat

Almond Butter Cereal Squares

■ 9-inch (2.5 L) square baking pan, lightly greased

½ cup	crunchy almond butter	125 mL
½ cup	brown rice syrup	125 mL
½ cup	liquid honey	125 mL
1 tsp	vanilla	5 mL
1 cup	chopped dried apricots	250 mL
½ cup	sliced almonds	125 mL
¼ cup	sesame seeds	50 mL
¼ cup	ground flaxseed	50 mL
¼ cup	sunflower seeds	50 mL
2½ cups	high-fiber cereal, such as bran flakes	625 mL
1¼ cups	old-fashioned rolled oats	300 mL

1. In a large saucepan, over low heat, cook almond butter, rice syrup, honey and vanilla until blended. Add apricots, almonds, sesame seeds, flaxseed and sunflower seeds; mix well. Add cereal and oats; mix well.

2. Pour mixture into prepared pan. Press down with clean, damp hands to compact evenly. Let stand for 30 minutes, until firm, then cut into squares.

NUTRIENTS PER SERVING	
Calories	241
Carbohydrate	37 g
Fiber	4 g
Protein	5 g
Fat, total	10 g
Fat, saturated	1 g
Cholesterol	0 mg
Sodium	90 mg

AMERICA'S EXCHANGES	
½	Starch
½	Fruit
1½	Other Carbohydrates
2	Fat

CANADA'S CHOICES	
2	Carbohydrate
2	Fat

Moist 'n' Chewy Chocolate Brownies

MAKES 24 BROWNIES (1 BROWNIE PER SERVING)

These brownies contain a little less chocolate than some of the more luscious ones, but they still have rich chocolate flavor. Their texture is pleasantly moist and chewy.

TIPS

These brownies are quite dense and chewy. If you prefer them more cake-like, add an egg.

Instead of greasing pans, line them with parchment paper that extends up the sides and over the edges so you can lift out the brownies in a block. Spraying the pan lightly with cooking spray or greasing it lightly before adding the parchment helps the paper to stick, preventing it from shifting.

■ Preheat oven to 375°F (190°C)
■ 9-inch (2.5 L) square cake pan, greased

½ cup	butter	125 mL
3	squares (1 oz/28 g each) unsweetened chocolate, chopped	3
1¼ cups	granulated sugar	300 mL
1½ tsp	vanilla	7 mL
3	eggs	3
⅔ cup	all-purpose flour	150 mL
½ tsp	baking powder	2 mL
¼ tsp	salt	1 mL

1. In a saucepan over low heat, melt butter and chocolate, stirring constantly, until smooth. Remove from heat. Stir in sugar and vanilla, mixing well. Whisk in eggs, one at a time, beating lightly after each addition.

2. Combine flour, baking powder and salt. Stir into chocolate mixture until well blended. Spread evenly in prepared pan.

3. Bake in preheated oven just until set, 25 to 30 minutes. Let cool completely in pan on rack. Cut into bars.

NUTRIENTS PER SERVING	
Calories	113
Carbohydrate	16 g
Fiber	0 g
Protein	1 g
Fat, total	5 g
Fat, saturated	3 g
Cholesterol	34 mg
Sodium	77 mg

AMERICA'S EXCHANGES	
1	Other Carbohydrates
1	Fat

CANADA'S CHOICES	
1	Carbohydrate
1	Fat

Chocolate Chunk Banana Brownies

MAKES 36 BROWNIES (1 BROWNIE PER SERVING)

This very chocolaty brownie is flavored with mashed bananas and filled with chunks of chocolate and walnuts.

TIPS

These brownies are nice plain or dusted with confectioner's (icing) sugar.

For recipes calling for chopped chocolate, I like to buy large bittersweet chocolate bars and chop them to the size of chips.

VARIATIONS

Replace chocolate chunks with chocolate chips.

Substitute peanut butter chips for the chopped chocolate and coarsely chopped peanuts for the walnuts.

- Preheat oven to 350°F (180°C)
- 13- by 9-inch (3 L) cake pan, greased

1 cup	granulated sugar	250 mL
1/3 cup	vegetable oil	75 mL
2	eggs	2
1 cup	mashed ripe banana (2 large bananas)	250 mL
3/4 cup	unsweetened cocoa powder, sifted	175 mL
1 cup	all-purpose flour	250 mL
1 tsp	baking powder	5 mL
1/2 tsp	baking soda	2 mL
1/4 tsp	salt	1 mL
1 1/2 cups	chopped semisweet chocolate	375 mL
1 1/3 cups	coarsely chopped walnuts	325 mL

1. In a large bowl, using an electric mixer on medium speed, beat sugar, oil and eggs until thick and light, about 2 minutes. Add banana and cocoa and beat on low speed.

2. Combine flour, baking powder, baking soda and salt. Add to cocoa mixture, beating on low speed just to blend. Stir in chopped chocolate and walnuts. Spread evenly in prepared pan.

3. Bake in preheated oven just until set, 25 to 30 minutes. Let cool completely in pan on rack. Cut into bars or squares.

NUTRIENTS PER SERVING	
Calories	128
Carbohydrate	16 g
Fiber	1 g
Protein	2 g
Fat, total	7 g
Fat, saturated	2 g
Cholesterol	10 mg
Sodium	46 mg

AMERICA'S EXCHANGES	
1	Other Carbohydrates
1 1/2	Fat

CANADA'S CHOICES	
1	Carbohydrate
1 1/2	Fat

Triple Chocolate Brownies

**MAKES 16 BROWNIES
(1 BROWNIE PER
SERVING)**

TIPS

When using margarine,
choose a soft (non-
hydrogenated) version
to limit consumption
of trans fats.

**BARB'S
NUTRITION NOTE**

Enjoy these brownies
with or without the icing,
which supplies about
2 grams of carbohydrate
per brownie.

- Preheat oven to 350°F (180°C)
- 8-inch square (2 L) cake pan sprayed with vegetable spray

½ cup	granulated sugar	125 mL
⅓ cup	margarine or butter	75 mL
1	egg	1
1 tsp	vanilla	5 mL
½ cup	all-purpose flour	125 mL
⅓ cup	unsweetened cocoa powder	75 mL
1 tsp	baking powder	5 mL
¼ cup	2% milk	50 mL
¼ cup	chocolate chips	50 mL
Icing		
¼ cup	confectioner's (icing) sugar	50 mL
1½ tbsp	unsweetened cocoa powder	20 mL
1 tbsp	milk	15 mL

1. In a bowl, beat together sugar and margarine. Beat
   in egg and vanilla, mixing well.

2. In another bowl, combine flour, cocoa and baking
   powder; stir into sugar and butter mixture just until
   blended. Stir in milk and chocolate chips. Pour into
   prepared pan and bake approximately 18 minutes or
   until edges start to pull away from pan and center is
   still a little wet. Let cool slightly before glazing.

3. In small bowl, whisk together confectioner's sugar,
   cocoa and milk; pour over brownies in pan.

NUTRIENTS PER SERVING	
Calories	105
Carbohydrate	14 g
Fiber	1 g
Protein	2 g
Fat, total	5 g
Fat, saturated	1 g
Cholesterol	12 mg
Sodium	74 mg

AMERICA'S EXCHANGES	
1	Other Carbohydrates
1	Fat

CANADA'S CHOICES	
1	Carbohydrate
1	Fat

White Chocolate Cranberry Hazelnut Brownies

MAKES 48 BROWNIES (1 BROWNIE PER SERVING)

I'm sure this creamy white chocolate brownie, loaded with hazelnuts and cranberries, will become one of your favorites.

TIPS

These make a nice holiday gift. Pack them in a decorative airtight cookie tin or box, tie with a festive ribbon and add the recipe with your gift tag.

If you can find orange-flavored dried cranberries, try them in this recipe. They taste particularly delicious in this brownie.

■ Preheat oven to 375°F (190°C)
■ 8-inch (2 L) square cake pan, greased

6	squares (1 oz/28 g each) white chocolate, chopped	6
¾ cup	granulated sugar	175 mL
2	eggs	2
⅓ cup	butter, melted	75 mL
1 tsp	vanilla	5 mL
1¼ cups	all-purpose flour	300 mL
¾ tsp	baking powder	3 mL
¾ cup	coarsely chopped hazelnuts	175 mL
⅓ cup	dried cranberries	75 mL

1. In a small saucepan over low heat, melt white chocolate, stirring constantly, until smooth. Remove from heat and set aside.

2. In a bowl, whisk sugar and eggs until blended. Whisk in melted butter and vanilla. Combine flour and baking powder. Stir into egg mixture alternately with melted chocolate, making 2 additions of each and mixing until smooth. Stir in hazelnuts and cranberries. Spread evenly in prepared pan.

3. Bake in preheated oven just until set and golden, 25 to 30 minutes. Let cool completely in pan on rack. Cut into bars or squares.

NUTRIENTS PER SERVING	
Calories	72
Carbohydrate	9 g
Fiber	0 g
Protein	1 g
Fat, total	4 g
Fat, saturated	2 g
Cholesterol	11 mg
Sodium	23 mg

AMERICA'S EXCHANGES	
½	Other Carbohydrates
1	Fat

CANADA'S CHOICES	
½	Carbohydrate
1	Fat

Sour Cream Brownies

**MAKES 16 BROWNIES
(1 BROWNIE PER
SERVING)**

TIPS

If desired, sprinkle 2 tbsp
(25 mL) chopped nuts over
the batter before baking.

Garnish with a sprinkling
of icing sugar after baking.

When using margarine,
choose a soft (non-
hydrogenated) version
to limit consumption
of trans fats.

MAKE AHEAD

Bake a day before or
freeze for up to 6 weeks.

■ Preheat oven to 350°F (180°C)
■ 8-inch (2 L) square cake pan, sprayed with nonstick
  vegetable spray

⅔ cup	granulated sugar	150 mL
⅓ cup	soft margarine	75 mL
1	egg	1
1 tsp	vanilla	5 mL
⅓ cup	unsweetened cocoa powder	75 mL
⅓ cup	all-purpose flour	75 mL
1 tsp	baking powder	5 mL
¼ cup	light sour cream	50 mL

1. In a bowl, beat together sugar and margarine until
    smooth. Beat in egg and vanilla, mixing well.

2. Combine cocoa, flour and baking powder; stir into
    bowl just until blended. Stir in sour cream. Pour into
    prepared pan.

3. Bake for 20 to 25 minutes or until edges start to pull
    away from pan and center is still slightly soft.

NUTRIENTS PER SERVING	
Calories	89
Carbohydrate	12 g
Fiber	1 g
Protein	1 g
Fat, total	5 g
Fat, saturated	1 g
Cholesterol	12 mg
Sodium	76 mg

AMERICA'S EXCHANGES	
1	Other Carbohydrates
1	Fat

CANADA'S CHOICES	
1	Carbohydrate
1	Fat

Orange Cream Cheese Brownies

MAKES 24 BROWNIES (1 BROWNIE PER SERVING)

This is a very moist cake-like brownie, with a nice orange flavor in every bite. It doesn't contain any butter and uses less sugar than most brownies. It looks great, too, making it a nice dessert or coffee-time treat.

TIPS

To ease cleanup, rather than combining the dry ingredients in a bowl (in Step 2), place a large piece of waxed paper on the counter. Spread the flour on the paper and sift the cocoa powder and baking powder over it. Using the paper as a funnel, transfer the dry ingredients to the egg mixture.

- ■ Preheat oven to 350°F (180°C)
- ■ 8-inch (2 L) square cake pan, greased

Filling

4 oz	light cream cheese, softened	125 g
2 tbsp	granulated sugar	25 mL
2 tbsp	2% milk	25 mL
1 tbsp	grated orange zest	15 mL

Batter

1 cup	packed brown sugar	250 mL
1/3 cup	2% plain yogurt	75 mL
1/4 cup	vegetable oil	50 mL
1	egg	1
1	egg white	1
3/4 cup	unbleached all-purpose flour	175 mL
1/2 cup	unsweetened cocoa powder, sifted	125 mL
1 tsp	baking powder	5 mL

1. *Filling:* In a small bowl, using an electric mixer on low speed, beat cream cheese and sugar until blended, about 3 minutes. Add milk and orange zest, beating until smooth. Set aside.

2. *Batter:* In a bowl, whisk brown sugar, yogurt, oil, egg and egg white until blended. Combine flour, cocoa and baking powder. Stir into egg mixture, mixing well.

NUTRIENTS PER SERVING

Calories	95
Carbohydrate	14 g
Fiber	1 g
Protein	2 g
Fat, total	4 g
Fat, saturated	1 g
Cholesterol	11 mg
Sodium	59 mg

AMERICA'S EXCHANGES

1	Other Carbohydrates
1	Fat

CANADA'S CHOICES

1	Carbohydrate
1	Fat

VARIATIONS

For thinner, less cake-like bars, bake these in a 9-inch (2.5 L) square cake pan for 20 to 25 minutes.

Replace yogurt with light sour cream.

3. Spread half of the brownie batter in prepared pan. Spread filling evenly over top. Drop remaining batter by spoonfuls over filling. Swirl batters together lightly with small spatula or knife to make a marbled effect.

4. Bake in preheated oven until set, 25 to 30 minutes. Let cool completely in pan on rack. Cut into bars or squares.

BARB'S NUTRITION NOTE

You can reduce the amount of sugar in some recipes by using a low-calorie sweetener (also known as a sugar substitute or artificial sweetener). These products contain intensely sweet ingredients that typically replace 150 to 300 times their weight in sugar. Such miniscule amounts would be impossible to measure, so the sweetening agent is combined with carriers such as dextrose and maltodextrin. These carriers are carbohydrates, but only a very small amount is required to deliver a lot of sweetness.

Typically, 1 gram (about ¼ tsp/1 mL) of a powdered low-calorie sweetener — containing only a few milligrams of the sweetening ingredient — is equivalent to 10 grams (2 tsp/10 mL) of sugar.

Low-calorie sweeteners vary considerably. For example, some are affected by cooking temperatures, while others are not. Some are sold as sachets to add to beverages and foods at the table, while others come in a granular form that "measures like sugar." Some manufacturers make both types.

Because low-calorie sweeteners vary so much, and because sugar is often an important part of a food's structure, you often can't make a simple substitution on the basis of equal sweetness. If you want to try one of these products, first try it in recipes specifically developed for that product.

You can find out more about low-calorie sweeteners, including recommendations for their use, from the American Diabetes Association (www.diabetes.org) or the Canadian Diabetes Association (www.diabetes.ca).

Cream Cheese–Filled Brownies

This tastes like a low-fat Twinkie cupcake. Children and adults devour this dessert. When pouring batter, don't worry if there's a swirling pattern — the result will be attractive.

MAKE AHEAD

Prepare up to 2 days in advance. Freeze for up to 4 weeks.

■ Preheat oven to 350°F (180°C)
■ 8-inch (2 L) square baking dish, sprayed with vegetable spray

Filling

4 oz	light cream cheese, softened	125 g
2 tbsp	granulated sugar	25 mL
2 tbsp	2% milk	25 mL
1 tsp	vanilla	5 mL

Cake

1 cup	packed brown sugar	250 mL
1/3 cup	light sour cream	75 mL
1/4 cup	vegetable oil	50 mL
1	egg	1
1	egg white	1
3/4 cup	all-purpose flour	175 mL
1/2 cup	unsweetened cocoa powder	125 mL
1 tsp	baking powder	5 mL

1. *Filling:* In a food processor or in a bowl with an electric mixer, beat together cream cheese, sugar, milk and vanilla until smooth. Set aside.

2. *Cake:* In a large bowl, whisk together brown sugar, sour cream, oil, whole egg and egg white. In a separate bowl, stir together flour, cocoa and baking powder. Add liquid ingredients to dry, blending just until mixed.

3. Pour half the cake batter into prepared pan. Spoon filling on top; spread with a wet knife. Pour remaining batter into pan. Bake for 20 to 25 minutes or until just barely loose at center.

NUTRIENTS PER SERVING	
Calories	145
Carbohydrate	22 g
Fiber	1 g
Protein	3 g
Fat, total	6 g
Fat, saturated	1 g
Cholesterol	17 mg
Sodium	91 mg

AMERICA'S EXCHANGES	
1½	Other Carbohydrates
1	Fat

CANADA'S CHOICES	
1½	Carbohydrate
1	Fat

Cakes, Coffee Cakes and Cheesecakes

Perfect Angel Food Cake

**MAKES 12 SLICES
(1 SLICE PER SERVING)**

So many feel that angel food is hard to make, but it really is a simple cake. Try it when you have extra egg whites. This really is a perfect nonfat dessert when paired with fresh berries.

■ Preheat oven to 375°F (190°C)
■ 10-inch (4 L) tube pan, ungreased

1 cup	cake flour	250 mL
1½ cups	granulated sugar, divided	375 mL
12	egg whites, very cold (about 1¼ cups/300 mL)	12
1½ tsp	cream of tartar	7 mL
1½ tsp	vanilla	7 mL
1 tsp	almond extract	5 mL
½ tsp	salt	2 mL

1. Make sure all tools, including tube pan, mixer and whip attachment, are free of any oil, very clean and dry. If any traces of oil are on any of your tools, your cake will not work.

2. Sift cake flour together with ¾ cup (175 mL) of the granulated sugar. Set aside.

3. In a mixer bowl fitted with whip attachment, whip egg whites, cream of tartar, vanilla, almond extract and salt on high speed until soft peaks form, about 4 minutes. With mixer running, gradually sprinkle in remaining sugar, beating until stiff, glossy peaks form. Using a rubber spatula, gradually fold in flour mixture just until incorporated.

4. Pour batter into pan, smoothing top and gently removing any large bubbles. Bake in preheated oven until golden brown and top springs back when lightly touched, 40 to 45 minutes. Invert pan, balancing on tube, and let cake cool completely. The cake should fall out of pan when cool. If it needs a little help, run a rubber spatula around the sides of pan to loosen.

NUTRIENTS PER SERVING	
Calories	149
Carbohydrate	33 g
Fiber	0 g
Protein	4 g
Fat, total	0 g
Fat, saturated	0 g
Cholesterol	0 mg
Sodium	152 mg

AMERICA'S EXCHANGES	
½	Starch
1½	Other Carbohydrates
½	Very Lean Meat

CANADA'S CHOICES	
2	Carbohydrate
½	Meat and Alternatives

Chocolate Angel Food Cake

**MAKES 12 SLICES
(1 SLICE PER SERVING)**

TIP

Eggs separate more easily when cold. Use 3 bowls — one to separate eggs over, one for the yolks and one to which perfectly clean whites are transferred. Make sure there's not a speck of yolk in the whites or they won't beat properly. Egg whites beat to a greater volume when at room temperature.

BARB'S NUTRITION NOTE

Strawberries and chocolate are a great combination. Two strawberries, or 2 tbsp (25 mL) strawberry purée without sugar, adds only 1 gram of carbohydrate.

- Preheat oven to 375°F (190°C
- 10-inch (4 L) tube pan, sprayed with baking spray

1 cup	cake and pastry flour	250 mL
¼ cup	unsweetened cocoa powder	50 mL
1⅓ cups	granulated sugar	325 mL
12	egg whites, at room temperature	12
½ tsp	cream of tartar	2 mL
1 tsp	vanilla	5 mL
½ tsp	almond extract	2 mL
	Strawberry purée or sliced strawberries	

1. Into a bowl, sift together flour, cocoa and ⅓ cup (75 mL) of the sugar; set aside.

2. In a large bowl, beat egg whites until foamy. Add cream of tartar; beat until soft peaks form. Gradually add remaining sugar, beating until stiff peaks form. In 2 additions, gently fold cocoa mixture into egg whites until well blended. Fold in vanilla and almond extract. Pour batter into prepared pan.

3. Bake for 35 to 40 minutes or until cake springs back when lightly touched. Turn pan upside down and place over a bottle or an inverted funnel. Cool cake completely before removing from pan. Serve with strawberry purée or sliced strawberries.

NUTRIENTS PER SERVING	
Calories	141
Carbohydrate	31 g
Fiber	1 g
Protein	5 g
Fat, total	0 g
Fat, saturated	0 g
Cholesterol	0 mg
Sodium	55 mg

AMERICA'S EXCHANGES	
½	Starch
1½	Other Carbohydrates
½	Very lean meat

CANADA'S CHOICES	
2	Carbohydrate
½	Meat and Alternatives

Chiffon Cake

TIP

Eggs separate more easily when cold. Use 3 bowls — one to separate eggs over, one for the yolks and one to hold the perfectly clean whites. Make sure there's not a speck of yolk in the whites or they won't beat properly.

BARB'S NUTRITION NOTE

Count 2 tbsp (25 mL) sliced banana or 1/4 cup (50 mL) of most other unsweetened fresh fruits as a Free Food or Extra.

■ Preheat oven to 350°F (180°C)
■ 9-inch (2.5 L) springform pan, sprayed with baking spray

1 cup	cake and pastry flour	250 mL
1/2 cup	granulated sugar	125 mL
1 1/2 tsp	baking powder	7 mL
3	medium eggs	3
2	medium egg whites	2
1/3 cup	water	75 mL
1 tsp	grated lemon zest	5 mL
1 tsp	grated orange zest	5 mL
1/2 tsp	vanilla	2 mL
1/2 cup	egg whites (about 4 medium eggs)	125 mL
1/4 tsp	cream of tartar	1 mL
	Sliced fresh fruit	

1. Sift flour, sugar and baking powder into a bowl. In another bowl, beat together whole eggs, 2 egg whites, water, lemon zest, orange zest and vanilla until well mixed. Slowly add wet ingredients to dry ingredients, mixing until combined. Set aside.

2. In a separate bowl, beat egg whites until foamy. Add cream of tartar; beat until stiff peaks form. Gently fold egg whites into batter. Pour into prepared pan. Bake for 25 to 30 minutes or until tester inserted in center comes out clean. Cool on wire rack.

3. Serve garnished with sliced fresh fruit.

NUTRIENTS PER SERVING	
Calories	108
Carbohydrate	19 g
Fiber	0 g
Protein	4 g
Fat, total	1 g
Fat, saturated	0 g
Cholesterol	49 mg
Sodium	84 mg

AMERICA'S EXCHANGES	
1/2	Starch
1/2	Other Carbohydrates
1/2	Lean Meat

CANADA'S CHOICES	
1	Carbohydrate
1/2	Meat and Alternatives

Chocolate Espresso Cake

**MAKES 12 SLICES
(1 SLICE PER SERVING)**

TIPS

To make cutting easier, dip knife in hot water before slicing.

For a chocolate liqueur flavor, try using half coffee and half chocolate liqueur.

This cake seems so dense and rich you'll never believe it is light. A small piece goes a long way.

Decorate with fresh berries.

MAKE AHEAD

Prepare up to 2 days in advance or freeze for up to 6 weeks.

■ Preheat oven to 350°F (180°C
■ 8-inch (2 L) springform pan, sprayed with vegetable spray

1/2 cup	semisweet chocolate chips	125 mL
1/4 cup	espresso or strong brewed coffee	50 mL
2	eggs, separated	2
3/4 cup	granulated sugar	175 mL
3/4 cup	2% evaporated milk	175 mL
1/2 cup	unsweetened cocoa powder	125 mL
3 tbsp	all-purpose flour	45 mL
1 tsp	vanilla	5 mL
3 tbsp	granulated sugar	45 mL

1. Melt chocolate chips with coffee; stir until smooth. Allow to cool.

2. In a large bowl, beat together egg yolks, 3/4 cup (175 mL) sugar, evaporated milk, cocoa, flour and vanilla until smooth. Beat in chocolate-coffee mixture.

3. With an electric mixer, in a separate bowl, beat egg whites until soft peaks form. Gradually add 3 tbsp (45 mL) sugar and continue beating until stiff peaks form.

4. Stir one-quarter of egg whites into chocolate batter. Gently fold in remaining egg whites. Spoon into prepared pan. Bake 30 to 35 minutes or until cake is set at the center. Chill before serving.

NUTRIENTS PER SERVING	
Calories	137
Carbohydrate	25 g
Fiber	1 g
Protein	3 g
Fat, total	4 g
Fat, saturated	2 g
Cholesterol	32 mg
Sodium	30 mg

AMERICA'S EXCHANGES	
1 1/2	Other Carbohydrates
1	Fat

CANADA'S CHOICES	
1 1/2	Carbohydrate
1	Fat

Sour Cream Orange Apple Cake

**MAKES 20 SLICES
(1 SLICE PER SERVING)**

TIPS

Try chopped pears or peaches instead of apples.

To increase fiber, use ⅔ cup (150 mL) whole wheat and 1 cup (250 mL) all-purpose flour.

Makes two 9- by 5-inch (2 L) loaves. Bake approximately 35 minutes or until tester comes out clean.

If you don't want to layer the cake, just mix apples with batter, then add topping.

When using margarine, choose a soft (non-hydrogenated) version to limit consumption of trans fats.

MAKE AHEAD

Prepare up to 2 days in advance.

Freeze for up to 6 weeks.

- Preheat oven to 350°F (180°C)
- 10-inch (3 L) springform pan, sprayed with vegetable spray

Topping

⅓ cup	packed brown sugar	75 mL
3 tbsp	chopped pecans	45 mL
1½ tbsp	all-purpose flour	22 mL
2 tsp	margarine or butter	10 mL
½ tsp	ground cinnamon	2 mL

Filling

2 cups	chopped peeled apples	500 mL
½ cup	raisins	125 mL
1 tbsp	granulated sugar	15 mL
1 tsp	ground cinnamon	5 mL

Cake

⅔ cup	packed brown sugar	150 mL
½ cup	granulated sugar	125 mL
⅓ cup	vegetable oil	75 mL
2	eggs	2
1 tbsp	grated orange zest	15 mL
2 tsp	vanilla	10 mL
1⅔ cups	all-purpose flour	400 mL
2 tsp	baking powder	10 mL
1 tsp	baking soda	5 mL
½ cup	orange juice	125 mL
½ cup	light sour cream	125 mL

1. *Topping:* In a small bowl, combine brown sugar, pecans, flour, margarine and cinnamon. Set aside.

2. *Filling:* In a bowl, mix together apples, raisins, sugar and cinnamon. Set aside.

NUTRIENTS PER SERVING	
Calories	185
Carbohydrate	32 g
Fiber	1 g
Protein	2 g
Fat, total	6 g
Fat, saturated	1 g
Cholesterol	19 mg
Sodium	113 mg

AMERICA'S EXCHANGES	
½	Starch
½	Fruit
1	Other Carbohydrates
1	Fat

CANADA'S CHOICES	
2	Carbohydrate
1	Fat

3. *Cake:* In a food processor or in a large bowl with an electric mixer, beat together brown sugar, granulated sugar and oil. Add eggs, one at a time, beating well after each. Mix in orange zest and vanilla.

4. In a separate bowl, stir together flour, baking powder and baking soda. In another bowl, stir together orange juice and sour cream. Add flour mixture and sour cream mixture alternately to beaten sugar mixture, mixing just until blended. Spoon half of batter into prepared pan. Top with half of apple mixture. Spoon remaining batter into pan. Top with remaining apple mixture; sprinkle with topping.

5. Bake 45 to 50 minutes or until a cake tester inserted in center comes out clean. Cool on a wire rack.

BARB'S NUTRITION NOTE

A little bit of confectioner's sugar (also called icing sugar or powdered sugar) can make a plain cake look elegant while adding almost no carbohydrate. One tablespoon (15 mL) — plenty for most cakes — contains only 8 grams of carbohydrate. Use a fine sieve to distribute it evenly.

You may wonder why 1 tbsp (15 mL) of confectioner's sugar contains only 8 grams of carbohydrate when other sugars contain 15 grams. Confectioner's sugar is made from finely ground granulated sugar combined with a small amount of cornstarch, which makes it fluffy. Thus, 1 tbsp (15 mL) contains only half the amount of carbohydrate found in the same amount of granulated sugar.

Blueberry Honey Cake

**MAKES 10 SLICES
(1 SLICE PER SERVING)**

**BARB'S
NUTRITION NOTE**

Honey is high in fructose, which makes up half the sucrose molecules in ordinary table sugar. Although fructose tastes sweeter than sucrose, it does not raise blood sugar as much. Like sucrose, 1 tbsp (15 mL) fructose is an Other Carbohydrate Exchange or Carbohydrate Choice.

■ Preheat oven to 350°F (180°C)
■ 9-inch (1.5 L) round cake pan, sprayed with baking spray

1 cup	fresh or frozen blueberries	250 mL
1/3 cup	liquid honey	75 mL
1/3 cup	water	75 mL
1 tbsp	cornstarch or arrowroot	15 mL
1 tbsp	water	15 mL
1 1/2 cups	whole wheat flour	375 mL
1 tsp	baking powder	5 mL
1 cup	2% milk	250 mL
1/3 cup	honey	75 mL
1 tbsp	vegetable oil	15 mL

1. In a saucepan, combine blueberries, honey and 1/3 cup (75 mL) water; bring to a boil over medium heat. Stir together cornstarch and 1 tbsp (15 mL) water; add to simmering blueberry mixture. Cook, stirring constantly, until thickened. Remove from heat; set aside.

2. In a large bowl, stir together flour and baking powder. In another bowl, whisk together milk, honey and oil until smooth; add to flour mixture, stirring to combine. Pour into prepared pan. Pour blueberry mixture on top of batter. Bake for 25 to 35 minutes or until a tester inserted in center comes out clean.

NUTRIENTS PER SERVING	
Calories	165
Carbohydrate	36 g
Fiber	3 g
Protein	3 g
Fat, total	2 g
Fat, saturated	0 g
Cholesterol	2 mg
Sodium	41 mg

AMERICA'S EXCHANGES	
1	Starch
1 1/2	Other Carbohydrates
1/2	Fat

CANADA'S CHOICES	
2	Carbohydrate
1/2	Fat

Blueberry Peach Cake

**MAKES 16 SLICES
(1 SLICE PER SERVING)**

TIP
If using frozen blueberries, thaw first, then drain off the excess liquid.

MAKE AHEAD
Bake a day before or freeze for up to 6 weeks.

**BARB'S
NUTRITION NOTE**
To dust a cake with icing sugar, use a fine sieve. One tablespoon (15 mL) will add only ½ gram of carbohydrate to a serving of this cake.

- Preheat oven to 350°F (180°C)
- 9-inch (3 L) Bundt pan, sprayed with nonstick vegetable spray

1 cup	granulated sugar	250 mL
¾ cup	applesauce	175 mL
¼ cup	vegetable oil	50 mL
2	eggs	2
1 tsp	vanilla	5 mL
1½ cups	all-purpose flour	375 mL
½ cup	whole wheat flour	125 mL
2 tsp	cinnamon	10 mL
1½ tsp	baking powder	7 mL
1 tsp	baking soda	5 mL
½ cup	2% yogurt	125 mL
1 cup	sliced peeled peaches	250 mL
1 cup	blueberries	250 mL
	Confectioner's (icing) sugar	

1. In a large bowl, beat together sugar, applesauce, oil, eggs and vanilla, mixing well.

2. Combine all-purpose and whole wheat flours, cinnamon, baking powder and baking soda; stir into bowl just until blended. Stir in yogurt; fold in peaches and blueberries. Pour into prepared pan.

3. Bake for 40 to 45 minutes or until cake tester inserted into center comes out clean. Let cool; dust with confectioner's sugar.

NUTRIENTS PER SERVING	
Calories	165
Carbohydrate	29 g
Fiber	2 g
Protein	3 g
Fat, total	4 g
Fat, saturated	1 g
Cholesterol	24 mg
Sodium	118 mg

AMERICA'S EXCHANGES	
1	Starch
1	Other Carbohydrates
1	Fat

CANADA'S CHOICES	
2	Carbohydrate
1	Fat

Banana Cake with Lemon Cream Frosting

**MAKES 25 SLICES
(1 SLICE PER SERVING)**

TIPS

For the smoothest frosting, use extra-smooth ricotta cheese.

For the most intense walnut flavor, use walnut oil in the cake and toast the walnuts for garnishing the cake.

▪ Preheat oven to 350°F (180°C)
▪ 13- by 9-inch (3.5 L) cake pan, sprayed with baking spray

Cake

1¾ cups	whole wheat flour	425 mL
2 tsp	baking powder	10 mL
¾ tsp	baking soda	4 mL
½ cup	buttermilk	125 mL
½ cup	liquid honey	125 mL
¼ cup	walnut oil or vegetable oil	50 mL
3	ripe bananas	3
4	egg whites	4

Lemon Cream Frosting

1 cup	5% ricotta cheese	250 mL
1½ tbsp	honey	22 mL
1 tbsp	grated lemon zest	15 mL
1 tbsp	lemon juice	15 mL
1½ tsp	cornstarch or arrowroot	7 mL
¼ cup	chopped walnuts	50 mL
	Lemon zest, cut into thin strips	

1. *Cake:* In a bowl, stir together flour, baking powder and baking soda; set aside. In a food processor or blender, purée buttermilk, honey, oil and bananas until smooth; stir into flour mixture just until mixed. In another bowl, beat egg whites until stiff peaks form; fold into batter. Pour into prepared pan. Bake for 20 to 30 minutes or until a tester inserted in center comes out clean. Cool in pan on wire rack.

NUTRIENTS PER SERVING	
Calories	109
Carbohydrate	17 g
Fiber	1 g
Protein	3 g
Fat, total	4 g
Fat, saturated	1 g
Cholesterol	2 mg
Sodium	86 mg

AMERICA'S EXCHANGES	
½	Starch
½	Other Carbohydrates
1	Fat

CANADA'S CHOICES	
1	Carbohydrate
1	Fat

**BARB'S
NUTRITION NOTE**
If a recipe contains both oil and a sticky ingredient such as honey or molasses, measure the oil first. The small amount of oil left in the cup or spoon will help the honey slide out smoothly.

2. *Frosting:* In a food processor, purée ricotta, honey, lemon zest, lemon juice and cornstarch until smooth. Transfer to a saucepan. Cook over medium heat, stirring constantly, until steaming hot. Remove from heat. Chill.

3. Spread cold frosting over cooled cake. Sprinkle with walnuts and strips of lemon zest.

BARB'S NUTRITION NOTE

The fat found in nuts and seeds is primarily the desirable monounsaturated type. Like other fats, however, it also contributes calories. To get the most out of nuts when using them in baking, finely chop them to distribute their flavor and texture throughout the dough or batter.

Nuts and seeds are even more flavorful when they are lightly toasted before they are combined with other ingredients. Spread them evenly in a pie plate or cake pan and toast in a 350°F (180°C) oven for 7 to 10 minutes, or until lightly toasted and fragrant. The timing varies depending on the type of nuts or seeds, so watch them carefully to make sure they don't burn.

Date Cake with Coconut Topping

**MAKES 20 SLICES
(1 SLICE PER SERVING)**

TIPS

To chop dates easily, use kitchen shears. Whole pitted dates can be used, but then use food processor to finely chop dates after they are cooked.

Chopped pitted prunes can replace dates.

When using margarine, choose a soft (non-hydrogenated) version to limit consumption of trans fats.

■ Preheat oven to 350°F (180°C)
■ 9-inch square (2.5 L) cake pan, sprayed with vegetable spray

Cake

12 oz	chopped pitted dates	375 g
1¾ cups	water	425 mL
¼ cup	margarine or butter	50 mL
1 cup	granulated sugar	250 mL
2	eggs	2
1½ cups	all-purpose flour	375 mL
1½ tsp	baking powder	7 mL
1 tsp	baking soda	5 mL

Topping

⅓ cup	unsweetened coconut	75 mL
¼ cup	brown sugar	50 mL
3 tbsp	2% milk	45 mL
2 tbsp	margarine or butter	25 mL

1. Put dates and water in saucepan; bring to a boil, cover and reduce heat to low. Cook for 10 minutes, stirring often, or until dates are soft and most of the liquid has been absorbed. Set aside to cool for 10 minutes.

2. In a large bowl or food processor, beat together margarine and sugar. Add eggs and mix well. Add cooled date mixture and mix well.

NUTRIENTS PER SERVING	
Calories	177
Carbohydrate	33 g
Fiber	2 g
Protein	2 g
Fat, total	5 g
Fat, saturated	1 g
Cholesterol	19 mg
Sodium	138 mg

AMERICA'S EXCHANGES	
1	Fruit
1	Other Carbohydrates
1	Fat

CANADA'S CHOICES	
2	Carbohydrate
1	Fat

MAKE AHEAD

Prepare up to 2 days ahead or freeze for up to 6 weeks. The dates keep this cake moist.

3. In a bowl, combine flour, baking powder and baking soda. Stir into date mixture just until blended. Pour into prepared cake pan and bake for 35 to 40 minutes or until a cake tester inserted in center comes out dry.

4. *Topping:* In a small saucepan, combine coconut, brown sugar, milk and margarine; cook over medium heat, stirring, for 2 minutes, or until sugar dissolves. Pour over cake.

BARB'S NUTRITION NOTE

When planning what to eat, we need to take into account both the type of food and the portion size. Getting the correct portion size (in other words, the right number of slices) from a cake baked in a rectangular or square pan is easy: just look at how many slices are specified in the yield and cut the cake into that many portions. For example, this recipe makes 20 slices. To get that number, you would cut the cake lengthwise 3 times and crosswise 4 times. Make sure all your slices are the same size, or the nutrients per serving and Exchanges or Choices will not be accurate.

Prune Orange Spice Cake

TIPS

To cut prunes easily, use kitchen shears, or you can use whole pitted prunes, but you'll need to finely chop prunes in food processor after they are cooked.

Chopped pitted dates can replace prunes.

When using margarine, choose a soft (non-hydrogenated) version to limit consumption of trans fats.

MAKE AHEAD

Bake up to 2 days ahead or freeze for up to 6 weeks. The dried fruit keeps this cake very moist.

- Preheat oven to 350°F (180°C)
- 9-inch square (2.5 L) baking dish, sprayed with vegetable spray

8 oz	chopped pitted prunes	250 g
1 cup	orange juice	250 mL
⅓ cup	margarine or butter	75 mL
¾ cup	granulated sugar	175 mL
2	eggs	2
2 tsp	grated orange zest	10 mL
1 tsp	vanilla	5 mL
1 cup	all-purpose flour	250 mL
½ cup	whole wheat flour	125 mL
1 tsp	baking powder	5 mL
¾ tsp	cinnamon	4 mL
½ tsp	baking soda	2 mL
⅛ tsp	nutmeg	0.5 mL
⅓ cup	2% yogurt	75 mL
Icing		
4 tsp	orange juice	20 mL
½ cup	Confectioner's (icing) sugar	125 mL

1. Put prunes and orange juice in a saucepan; bring to a boil, cover and reduce heat to low. Cook for 10 to 12 minutes, stirring often, or until prunes are soft and most of the liquid has been absorbed. Set aside.

2. In a large bowl, cream together margarine and sugar; add eggs, orange zest and vanilla and mix well. Stir in prune mixture and mix well.

NUTRIENTS PER SERVING	
Calories	181
Carbohydrate	33 g
Fiber	2 g
Protein	3 g
Fat, total	5 g
Fat, saturated	1 g
Cholesterol	24 mg
Sodium	119 mg

AMERICA'S EXCHANGES	
1	Fruit
1	Other Carbohydrates
1	Fat

CANADA'S CHOICES	
2	Carbohydrate
1	Fat

BARB'S NUTRITION NOTE

The icing (which is included in the calculations) contributes 4 grams of carbohydrate and 15 calories.

3. In a bowl, combine flour, whole wheat flour, baking powder, cinnamon, baking soda and nutmeg. Add to wet ingredients alternately with yogurt. Pour into prepared cake pan and bake for 30 to 35 minutes or until a cake tester inserted in center comes out clean.

4. *Icing:* In a small bowl, combine orange juice and icing sugar until well mixed. Pour over cake.

BARB'S NUTRITION NOTE

It's important to measure ingredients accurately. This is especially true for cakes and cookies, which may not turn out properly if ingredient quantities are changed. Also, if the amounts are incorrect, the nutrients and Exchanges or Choices per serving will not be accurate.

To measure correctly, be sure to use standard measuring cups and spoons. There are different measuring cups for dry and liquid ingredients. Dry ingredient measures, usually made of metal or plastic, come in imperial measures of 1/4 cup, 1/3 cup, 1/2 cup and 1 cup or in metric measures of 50 mL, 75 mL, 125 mL and 250 mL.

Liquid measures are usually made of glass, with the measures marked on the outside and extra space below the rim so you can measure the full amount without spilling. They often have imperial measurements on one side and metric on the other. The most common sizes are 1 cup (250 mL) and 2 cups (500 mL).

Standard measuring spoons may be used for either liquid or dry ingredients. The standard imperial set includes 1/4 tsp, 1/2 tsp, 1 tsp and 1 tbsp; a standard metric set has 1 mL, 2 mL, 5 mL, 15 mL and 25 mL spoons.

See page 65 for more information on measuring accurately.

Banana Spice Cake with Cream Cheese Frosting

**MAKES 16 SLICES
(1 SLICE PER SERVING)**

TIPS

Increase amount of spices to your taste — or omit any not on hand.

Freeze overripe bananas in their skins for up to 3 months. Defrost and use mashed in baking.

Use as a muffin batter. Bake 15 to 20 minutes or until tester comes out clean.

When using margarine, choose a soft (non-hydrogenated) version to limit consumption of trans fats.

■ Preheat oven to 350°F (180°C)
■ 10-inch (3 L) Bundt pan, sprayed with vegetable spray

Cake

1/3 cup	margarine or butter	75 mL
3/4 cup	granulated sugar	175 mL
1/2 cup	packed brown sugar	125 mL
2	eggs	2
3/4 cup	light sour cream	175 mL
2 tsp	vanilla	10 mL
1	medium ripe banana, mashed	1
1 1/2 cups	all-purpose flour	375 mL
2 tsp	baking powder	10 mL
1 1/2 tsp	ground cinnamon	7 mL
1 tsp	baking soda	5 mL
1/8 tsp	ground allspice	0.5 mL
1/8 tsp	ground ginger	0.5 mL
1/8 tsp	ground nutmeg	0.5 mL

Icing

1/3 cup	light cream cheese, softened	75 mL
2/3 cup	confectioner's (icing) sugar	150 mL
1 tbsp	2% milk	15 mL

1. *Cake:* In a food processor or in a bowl with an electric mixer, cream together margarine, sugar and brown sugar. Add eggs one at a time, beating well after each; beat in sour cream, vanilla and banana. In a separate bowl, stir together flour, baking powder, cinnamon, baking soda, allspice, ginger and nutmeg. Add liquid ingredients to dry ingredients, blending just until mixed. Pour into prepared pan.

NUTRIENTS PER SERVING	
Calories	200
Carbohydrate	33 g
Fiber	1 g
Protein	3 g
Fat, total	6 g
Fat, saturated	1 g
Cholesterol	26 mg
Sodium	221 mg

AMERICA'S EXCHANGES	
1/2	Starch
1 1/2	Other Carbohydrates
1	Fat

CANADA'S CHOICES	
2	Carbohydrate
1	Fat

MAKE AHEAD
Bake up to 2 days in
advance. Freeze for up
to 6 weeks.

2. Bake for 35 minutes or until a cake tester inserted in center comes out clean. Cool in pan on wire rack.

3. *Icing:* In a bowl or food processor, beat together cream cheese, confectioner's sugar and milk until smooth.

4. Invert cake and drizzle icing over top.

BARB'S NUTRITION NOTE
Because we are surrounded by "jumbo" and "super-size" items and ever-larger plates, it's easy to lose track of what a reasonable serving is. (Even dietitians can fall into this trap!) The information included with the recipes in this book can teach you a lot about portion sizes. It will help you learn what ingredients are in different desserts and will give you an idea of what Exchanges or Choices a reasonable serving might contain.

Banana Date Cake

**MAKES 20 SLICES
(1 SLICE PER SERVING)**

TIPS

For easier preparation, use scissors to cut dates. Be sure to buy pitted dates.

When using margarine, choose a soft (non-hydrogenated) version.

MAKE AHEAD

Prepare up to 2 days in advance or freeze for up to 6 weeks.

■ Preheat oven to 350°F (180°C)
■ 9-inch (2.5 L) square cake pan, sprayed with nonstick vegetable spray

1 tsp	baking soda	5 mL
1 cup	boiling water	250 mL
2 cups	chopped dates (about 10 oz/280 g)	500 mL
½ cup	brown sugar	125 mL
3 tbsp	margarine	45 mL
1	egg	1
1	ripe banana, mashed	1
1½ cups	all-purpose flour	375 mL
1 cup	bran cereal*	250 mL
⅓ cup	chopped pecans or walnuts	75 mL
2 tsp	cinnamon	10 mL

* Use a wheat bran breakfast cereal.

1. In a bowl, stir baking soda into water; add dates and let stand for 10 minutes.
2. In a large bowl or food processor, beat together sugar, margarine, egg and banana until well blended.
3. Combine flour, cereal, pecans and cinnamon; add to banana mixture alternately with soaked dates, mixing well. Pour into cake pan; bake for 25 to 30 minutes or until a cake tester comes out dry.

NUTRIENTS PER SERVING	
Calories	150
Carbohydrate	30 g
Fiber	3 g
Protein	2 g
Fat, total	4 g
Fat, saturated	0 g
Cholesterol	9 mg
Sodium	123 mg

AMERICA'S EXCHANGES	
1	Fruit
1	Other Carbohydrates
1	Fat

CANADA'S CHOICES	
2	Carbohydrate
1	Fat

Carrot Cake

MAKES 20 SLICES (1 SLICE PER SERVING)

Kids love to snack on this simple cake without icing, and it's a great way to add more vegetables to their menu. It would make a healthy addition to your children's lunchboxes.

TIP

Serving idea: Dust with icing sugar for a pretty presentation.

■ Preheat oven to 350°F (180°C)
■ 13- by 9-inch (3 L) baking pan, lightly greased

¾ cup	all-purpose flour	175 mL
½ cup	whole wheat flour	125 mL
1¼ tsp	baking powder	6 mL
1¼ tsp	baking soda	6 mL
1 tsp	ground cinnamon	5 mL
½ tsp	salt	2 mL
3	eggs	3
½ cup	vegetable oil	125 mL
1 cup	lightly packed brown sugar	250 mL
2 tsp	vanilla	10 mL
2 cups	grated carrots	500 mL

1. In a small bowl, combine all-purpose flour, whole wheat flour, baking powder, baking soda, cinnamon and salt.

2. In a large bowl, beat eggs, oil, brown sugar and vanilla until well combined. Fold in dry ingredients. Stir in carrots. Pour into prepared pan.

3. Bake in preheated oven for 30 to 35 minutes or until a tester inserted in the center comes out clean. Let cool completely in pan on a wire rack. Cut cake into slices and lift servings out with a flat lifter.

NUTRIENTS PER SERVING	
Calories	134
Carbohydrate	18 g
Fiber	1 g
Protein	2 g
Fat, total	6 g
Fat, saturated	1 g
Cholesterol	28 mg
Sodium	174 mg

AMERICA'S EXCHANGES	
1	Other Carbohydrates
1	Fat

CANADA'S CHOICES	
1	Carbohydrate
1	Fat

Applesauce Carrot Cake

**MAKES 16 SLICES
(1 SLICE PER SERVING)**

**BARB'S
NUTRITION NOTES**

Use whole wheat flour to boost fiber in your baking. Along with fiber, the germ of the wheat is retained in the milling and gives it a slightly nutty flavor. Buy it in small quantities and keep it tightly covered in a cool place.

If you use the Lemon Cream Frosting, use only half the recipe and count the quantity on 1 slice of cake as a Free Food or Extra.

- Preheat oven to 350°F (180°C)
- 8-inch (2 L) Bundt pan, sprayed with baking spray

2⅓ cups	whole wheat flour	575 mL
4 tsp	cinnamon	20 mL
2 tsp	baking powder	10 mL
1 tsp	baking soda	5 mL
½ tsp	nutmeg	2 mL
¼ tsp	allspice	1 mL
¼ tsp	salt	1 mL
1 cup	unsweetened applesauce	250 mL
¾ cup	liquid honey	175 mL
⅓ cup	corn oil	75 mL
3	eggs	3
2 cups	grated carrots	500 mL
	Lemon Cream Frosting (optional) (see recipe, page 160)	
	Lemon, orange and/or lime zest cut into thin strips (optional)	

1. In a large bowl, stir together flour, cinnamon, baking powder, baking soda, nutmeg, allspice and salt. In another bowl, beat together applesauce, honey, oil and eggs; gradually stir into flour mixture until well mixed. Stir in grated carrots. Pour into prepared pan.

2. Bake for 35 minutes or until a tester inserted in center comes out clean. Cool in pan for 5 minutes; invert and cool completely on wire rack. Ice with Lemon Cream Frosting and garnish with zest, if desired. Store in refrigerator.

NUTRIENTS PER SERVING	
Calories	176
Carbohydrate	29 g
Fiber	3 g
Protein	4 g
Fat, total	6 g
Fat, saturated	1 g
Cholesterol	35 mg
Sodium	169 mg

AMERICA'S EXCHANGES	
2	Other Carbohydrates
1	Fat

CANADA'S CHOICES	
2	Carbohydrate
1	Fat

Chocolate Zucchini Cake

**MAKES 12 SLICES
(1 SLICE PER SERVING)**

This tasty chocolate cake has Mexican flair. Cocoa powder adds a satisfying chocolate flavor. For a special treat, top with the Whipped Cream and Yogurt Topping on page 222.

TIPS

If you don't have self-rising flour, substitute 1 cup (250 mL) all-purpose flour and add 1½ tsp (7 mL) baking powder and ½ tsp (2 mL) salt.

If you prefer, use commercial liquid egg whites. You'll need about ¾ cup (175 mL) for this recipe.

▪ Preheat oven to 350°F (180°C)
▪ 8-inch (2 L) square baking pan, lightly greased

1 cup	self-rising flour	250 mL
⅓ cup	unsweetened cocoa powder	75 mL
1 tsp	baking soda	5 mL
1 tsp	ground cinnamon	5 mL
6	egg whites	6
1⅓ cups	firmly packed brown sugar	325 mL
1 cup	buttermilk	250 mL
2 tsp	vanilla	10 mL
¼ tsp	almond extract	1 mL
2 cups	shredded zucchini	500 mL
	Confectioner's (icing) sugar (optional)	

1. In a small bowl, sift flour, cocoa powder, baking soda and cinnamon.

2. In a large bowl, beat egg whites, brown sugar, buttermilk, vanilla and almond extract until well blended. Fold in flour mixture until evenly moistened. Stir in zucchini. Pour batter into prepared pan.

3. Bake in preheated oven for 30 to 40 minutes or until center of cake springs back when lightly pressed and a tester inserted in the center comes out clean. Let cool on a wire rack for 10 minutes before removing from pan. Turn out onto rack to cool completely. Just before serving, dust with confectioner's sugar, if desired.

NUTRIENTS PER SERVING	
Calories	155
Carbohydrate	35 g
Fiber	1 g
Protein	4 g
Fat, total	1 g
Fat, saturated	0 g
Cholesterol	1 mg
Sodium	297 mg

AMERICA'S EXCHANGES	
½	Starch
1½	Other Carbohydrates
1	Free Food

CANADA'S CHOICES	
2	Carbohydrate
1	Extra

Apple Pecan Streusel Cake

**MAKES 16 SLICES
(1 SLICE PER SERVING)**

TIPS

Try substituting pears for the apples and chopped dates for the raisins.

When measuring flour, fill a dry measure to overflowing, then level off with a knife.

When using margarine, choose a soft (non-hydrogenated) version to limit consumption of trans fats.

- Preheat oven to 350°F (180°C)
- 10-inch (3 L) Bundt pan, sprayed with nonstick vegetable spray

Topping

1/4 cup	chopped pecans	50 mL
1/4 cup	all-purpose flour	50 mL
3 tbsp	brown sugar	45 mL
1 tbsp	margarine, melted	15 mL
1 1/2 tsp	cinnamon	7 mL

Cake

1/4 cup	soft margarine	50 mL
1 cup	brown sugar	250 mL
2	eggs	2
2 tsp	vanilla	10 mL
1 1/4 cups	all-purpose flour	300 mL
3/4 cup	whole wheat flour	175 mL
2 1/2 tsp	cinnamon	12 mL
1 1/2 tsp	baking powder	7 mL
1 tsp	baking soda	5 mL
1 cup	2% yogurt or light sour cream	250 mL
2 3/4 cups	diced peeled apples	675 mL
1/4 cup	raisins	50 mL

1. *Topping:* In a small bowl, combine pecans, flour, brown sugar, margarine and cinnamon until crumbly. Set aside.

2. *Cake:* In a large bowl or food processor, cream together margarine and brown sugar. Beat in eggs and vanilla until well blended.

NUTRIENTS PER SERVING	
Calories	209
Carbohydrate	36 g
Fiber	2 g
Protein	4 g
Fat, total	6 g
Fat, saturated	1 g
Cholesterol	24 mg
Sodium	176 mg

AMERICA'S EXCHANGES	
1	Starch
1/2	Fruit
1	Other Carbohydrates
1	Fat

CANADA'S CHOICES	
2	Carbohydrate
1	Fat

MAKE AHEAD
Bake a day before or freeze for up to 6 weeks.

3. Combine all-purpose and whole wheat flours, cinnamon, baking powder and baking soda; add to bowl alternately with yogurt, mixing just until blended. Fold in apples and raisins. Pour into prepared pan.

4. Sprinkle with topping; bake for 40 to 45 minutes or until a cake tester inserted into center comes out clean.

BARB'S NUTRITION NOTE
With a few changes, many recipes can be made healthier. Here are some suggestions.

Increase fiber by substituting whole wheat flour for all-purpose flour. Start with one-quarter of the amount; you can usually replace up to half the all-purpose flour in a recipe with whole wheat.

Lower saturated fat by replacing butter with non-hydrogenated margarine. (Avoid solid margarines, which are high in saturated and/or trans fats.) You can also replace a small proportion of the vegetable shortening or lard in a recipe with non-hydrogenated margarine.

Reduce the total amount of fat by replacing one-quarter to half of the oil in a recipe with applesauce or plain yogurt.

Boost vitamins and minerals by replacing chocolate chips with an equal quantity of chopped dried fruit.

See the worksheets on pages 18–29 to calculate the Exchanges or Choices for your favorite recipes.

Apricot Date Streusel Cake

**MAKES 16 SLICES
(1 SLICE PER SERVING)**

*Dried fruits offer a
concentrated sweetness
that is completely
different from that of
their fresh counterparts.
Just compare grapes
and raisins, or plums
and prunes, and you
can imagine the sweet
intensity of dried
cranberries, cherries,
blueberries, pineapple
and mangos.*

TIPS

It's easy to chop dried fruit
when you use scissors.

Feel free to use all dates or
all apricots. Dried prunes
are delicious.

When using margarine,
choose a soft (non-
hydrogenated) version
to limit consumption
of trans fats.

- Preheat oven to 350°F (180°C)
- 10-inch (3 L) Bundt pan, sprayed with nonstick vegetable spray

Topping

¼ cup	brown sugar	50 mL
2 tbsp	all-purpose flour	25 mL
2 tbsp	wheat bran cereal, crushed	25 mL
1 tsp	cinnamon	5 mL
1 tbsp	margarine	15 mL

Cake

3 tbsp	margarine	45 mL
¾ cup	granulated sugar	175 mL
1	egg	1
2	egg whites	2
3 tbsp	lemon juice	45 mL
1 tsp	vanilla	5 mL
1¾ cups	all-purpose flour	425 mL
½ cup	wheat bran cereal	125 mL
1 tsp	cinnamon	5 mL
1 tsp	baking powder	5 mL
1 tsp	baking soda	5 mL
1⅓ cups	2% yogurt	325 mL
⅓ cup	finely chopped dates	75 mL
⅓ cup	finely chopped dried apricots	75 mL

1. *Topping:* In a small bowl, combine brown sugar, flour, cereal and cinnamon; cut in margarine until crumbly. Set aside.

2. *Cake:* In a large bowl or food processor, cream together margarine and sugar; beat in egg, egg whites, lemon juice and vanilla until well mixed.

NUTRIENTS PER SERVING

Calories	177
Carbohydrate	33 g
Fiber	2 g
Protein	4 g
Fat, total	4 g
Fat, saturated	1 g
Cholesterol	13 mg
Sodium	184 mg

AMERICA'S EXCHANGES

½	Fruit
1½	Other Carbohydrates
1	Fat

CANADA'S CHOICES

2	Carbohydrate
1	Fat

MAKE AHEAD
Bake up to a day before
or freeze for up to 6 weeks.

3. Combine flour, cereal, cinnamon, baking powder and baking soda; stir into bowl just until incorporated. Stir in yogurt; fold in dates and apricots.

4. Pour half of batter into pan. Sprinkle with half of topping. Pour remaining batter over top; sprinkle with remaining topping. Bake for 35 to 45 minutes or until a tester inserted into center comes out clean.

BARB'S NUTRITION NOTE
For help in planning your meals, ask your doctor to refer you to a diabetes education center or a dietitian. Your local public health unit and hospitals may also have referral services. On the Internet, look for the "find a dietitian" feature at www.eatright.org (in the U.S.) or www.dietitians.ca (in Canada).

Cinnamon Streusel Coffee Cake

**MAKES 16 SLICES
(1 SLICE PER SERVING)**

Serve this moist cake for a morning or afternoon coffee break.

**BARB'S
NUTRITION NOTE**

The pecans in the streusel are optional. If you use them, add ½ Fat Exchange or Choice per serving.

■ Preheat oven to 350°F (180°C)
■ 10-inch (3 L) Bundt or 10-inch (4 L) tube pan, lightly greased and floured

Streusel

½ cup	lightly packed brown sugar	125 mL
½ cup	finely chopped pecans (optional)	125 mL
1 tbsp	ground cinnamon	15 mL

Cake

1 cup	all-purpose flour	250 mL
1 cup	whole wheat flour	250 mL
1 tsp	baking powder	5 mL
¼ tsp	salt	1 mL
1 cup	low-fat or fat-free plain yogurt	250 mL
1 tsp	baking soda	5 mL
¾ cup	granulated sugar	175 mL
¾ cup	unsweetened applesauce	175 mL
¼ cup	margarine	50 mL
2	eggs	2
1 tsp	vanilla	5 mL

1. *Streusel:* In a small bowl, combine brown sugar, pecans (if using) and cinnamon. Set aside.

2. *Cake:* In a medium bowl, combine all-purpose flour, whole wheat flour, baking powder and salt. Set aside.

3. In another bowl, combine yogurt and baking soda. (Be prepared, yogurt will foam up!)

4. In a large bowl, using an electric mixer, cream sugar, applesauce and margarine until well mixed (it may look curdled). Beat in eggs, one at a time, then stir in vanilla. Stir in flour mixture alternately with yogurt, making 3 additions of flour and 2 of yogurt mixture.

NUTRIENTS PER SERVING	
Calories	167
Carbohydrate	30 g
Fiber	1 g
Protein	3 g
Fat, total	4 g
Fat, saturated	1 g
Cholesterol	24 mg
Sodium	192 mg

AMERICA'S EXCHANGES	
1	Starch
1	Other Carbohydrates
1	Fat

CANADA'S CHOICES	
2	Carbohydrate
1	Fat

When using margarine, choose a non-hydrogenated version to limit consumption of trans fats.

5. Spoon half of the batter into prepared Bundt pan. Sprinkle with three-quarters of the streusel. Cover with remaining batter and sprinkle with remaining streusel. With the back of a small spoon, pat streusel lightly into batter (to prevent streusel from falling off when cake is inverted and removed from pan).

6. Bake in preheated oven for 40 to 50 minutes or until a tester inserted in the center comes out clean. Let cool on a wire rack for 10 minutes before removing from pan. Turn out onto rack to cool completely.

BARB'S NUTRITION NOTE
As you prepare the recipes in this book, you will become familiar with the appropriate portion sizes for different types of desserts and the approximate Exchanges or Choices assigned to them. Use this knowledge to help you choose wisely when you're eating away from home.

Orange-Glazed Coffee Cake

**MAKES 16 SLICES
(1 SLICE PER SERVING)**

TIP
If you pierce the cake with a fork when warm and pour glaze over top, the icing will filter through the cake.

**BARB'S
NUTRITION NOTE**
The glaze on this coffee cake contributes about 4 grams of carbohydrate per serving.

- Preheat oven to 350°F (180°C)
- 10-inch (3 L) Bundt pan, sprayed with nonstick vegetable spray

¼ cup	soft margarine	50 mL
1 cup	granulated sugar	250 mL
2	eggs	2
1	egg white	1
1½ cups	orange juice	375 mL
1½ tsp	grated orange rind	7 mL
1 cup	whole wheat flour	250 mL
1 cup	all-purpose flour	250 mL
1 tsp	cinnamon	5 mL
1 tsp	baking powder	5 mL
1 tsp	baking soda	5 mL
Glaze		
½ cup	icing sugar	125 mL
4 tsp	frozen orange juice concentrate, thawed	20 mL

1. In large bowl or food processor, cream together margarine and sugar. Beat in eggs, egg white, orange juice and rind until well blended.

2. Combine whole wheat and all-purpose flours, cinnamon, baking powder and baking soda; add to creamed mixture and mix until well blended. Pour into pan. Bake for 35 to 40 minutes or until cake tester inserted into center comes out clean. Let cool.

3. *Glaze:* Mix icing sugar with orange juice concentrate; pour over cake, allowing to drip down sides.

NUTRIENTS PER SERVING	
Calories	166
Carbohydrate	31 g
Fiber	1 g
Protein	3 g
Fat, total	4 g
Fat, saturated	1 g
Cholesterol	23 mg
Sodium	146 mg

AMERICA'S EXCHANGES	
1	Starch
1	Other Carbohydrates
1	Fat

CANADA'S CHOICES	
2	Carbohydrate
1	Fat

Orange Coffee Cake

**MAKES 12 SLICES
(1 SLICE PER SERVING)**

BARB'S NUTRITION NOTE

Fresh unsweetened fruit is an attractive low-carbohydrate garnish. One strawberry or 4 raspberries add only 1 gram of carbohydrate.

■ Preheat oven to 350°F (180°C)
■ 8-inch (2 L) Bundt pan, sprayed with baking spray

2 cups	orange juice	500 mL
2 tsp	grated orange zest	10 mL
1 cup	granulated sugar	250 mL
¼ cup	butter	50 mL
3	medium eggs	3
1 cup	all-purpose flour	250 mL
1 cup	whole wheat flour	250 mL
2 tsp	baking soda	10 mL
	Confectioner's (icing) sugar	
	Sliced fresh strawberries	

1. In a saucepan, combine orange juice and orange zest; bring to a boil. Remove from heat, transfer to a bowl and refrigerate until cool.

2. In a bowl, cream sugar with butter; add eggs, one at a time, beating well after each. In another bowl, stir together flour, whole wheat flour and baking soda. Add to creamed mixture alternately with orange juice, making 3 additions of flour and 2 of orange juice. Pour into prepared pan. Bake for 35 to 40 minutes or until a tester inserted in center comes out clean. Cool in pan for 5 minutes; invert and cool completely on wire rack.

3. Serve dusted with sifted confectioner's sugar and garnished with sliced strawberries.

NUTRIENTS PER SERVING	
Calories	205
Carbohydrate	36 g
Fiber	2 g
Protein	4 g
Fat, total	5 g
Fat, saturated	3 g
Cholesterol	51 mg
Sodium	265 mg

AMERICA'S EXCHANGES	
1	Starch
1½	Other Carbohydrates
1	Fat

CANADA'S CHOICES	
2	Carbohydrate
1	Fat

Cinnamon Date Coffee Cake

**MAKES 16 SLICES
(1 SLICE PER SERVING)**

**BARB'S
NUTRITION NOTE**

Dried fruits are concentrated sources of carbohydrate. If you use dates to garnish this cake, remember that 2 to 3 dates (about ⅔ oz/20 g) count as a Fruit Exchange or Carbohydrate Choice.

■ Preheat oven to 350° F (180° C)
■ 8-inch (2 L) Bundt pan, sprayed with baking spray

¾ cup	granulated sugar	175 mL
3 tbsp	softened butter	45 mL
2	egg whites	2
1	egg	1
1⅓ cups	low-fat yogurt	325 mL
3 tbsp	lemon juice	45 mL
1 tsp	vanilla	5 mL
2 cups	all-purpose flour	500 mL
1 tsp	baking powder	5 mL
1 tsp	baking soda	5 mL
1 tsp	cinnamon	5 mL
⅛ tsp	nutmeg	0.5 mL
¼ cup	packed brown sugar	50 mL
⅔ cup	chopped dates	150 mL
	Confectioner's (icing) sugar	
	Extra sliced dates (optional)	

1. In a bowl, beat together sugar, butter, egg whites and egg until smooth. Beat in yogurt, lemon juice and vanilla. In another bowl, sift together flour, baking powder, baking soda, cinnamon and nutmeg; stir into yogurt mixture just until combined.

NUTRIENTS PER SERVING	
Calories	166
Carbohydrate	32 g
Fiber	1 g
Protein	4 g
Fat, total	3 g
Fat, saturated	2 g
Cholesterol	18 mg
Sodium	144 mg

AMERICA'S EXCHANGES	
1	Starch
1	Other Carbohydrates
½	Fat

CANADA'S CHOICES	
2	Carbohydrate
½	Fat

2. In a small bowl, stir together brown sugar and dates. Pour half of cake batter into prepared pan and sprinkle with half of date mixture. Repeat. Bake for 40 minutes or until a tester inserted in center comes out clean. Cool in pan for 5 minutes; invert and cool completely on wire rack. Serve dusted with sifted confectioner's sugar and garnished with sliced dates, if desired.

Chocolate Chunk Coffee Cake

**MAKES 18 SLICES
(1 SLICE PER SERVING)**

This coffee cake has been made lower in fat by using less butter, a combination of whole eggs and egg whites and yogurt or light sour cream. The resulting taste is rich and delicious. It is a little time-consuming to make but would be great for a special dinner, served with fresh berries on the side.

■ Preheat oven to 350°F (180°C)
■ 10-inch (3 L) Bundt or 10-inch (4 L) tube pan, lightly greased and floured

2 cups	all-purpose flour	500 mL
1 cup	whole wheat flour	250 mL
1½ tsp	baking powder	7 mL
¼ tsp	salt	1 mL
2 cups	plain yogurt or light sour cream	500 mL
1 tsp	baking soda	5 mL
2 oz	semisweet chocolate	60 g
2 oz	white chocolate	60 g
1¼ cups	granulated sugar	300 mL
½ cup	unsalted butter, at room temperature	125 mL
2	egg whites	2
2	whole eggs	2
2 tsp	vanilla	10 mL
⅓ cup	unsweetened cocoa powder	75 mL
¼ cup	water	50 mL

1. In a large bowl, using a fork, combine all-purpose flour, whole wheat flour, baking powder and salt until evenly blended. Set aside.

2. In a medium bowl, combine yogurt and baking soda. (Be prepared, yogurt will foam up!) Set aside.

3. Coarsely chop semisweet chocolate until pieces are about the size of chocolate chips. Repeat with white chocolate, keeping the two separate. Set aside.

NUTRIENTS PER SERVING	
Calories	236
Carbohydrate	36 g
Fiber	2 g
Protein	6 g
Fat, total	8 g
Fat, saturated	5 g
Cholesterol	36 g
Sodium	161 mg

AMERICA'S EXCHANGES	
1	Starch
1½	Other Carbohydrates
1½	Fat

CANADA'S CHOICES	
2	Carbohydrate
1½	Fat

4. In a large bowl, using an electric mixer, cream sugar and butter. Add egg whites and eggs, one at a time, beating well after each addition. Stir in vanilla. Stir in flour mixture alternately with yogurt mixture, making 3 additions of flour and 2 of yogurt.

5. To make the chocolate batter, sift cocoa powder into a medium bowl. Stir in water until a smooth paste forms. Stir in one-third of the white batter.

6. Add the white chocolate pieces to the chocolate batter and the semisweet chocolate pieces to the white batter.

7. Pour white batter into prepared Bundt pan, then pour chocolate batter on top. Using a spatula, swirl the two mixtures together to create a ribbon effect.

8. Bake in the lower third of preheated oven for 60 to 65 minutes or until a tester inserted in the center comes out clean. Let cool on a wire rack for 10 minutes before removing from pan. Turn out onto rack to cool completely.

BARB'S NUTRITION NOTE

To create a pretty pattern on the top of a cake, cover it with a paper doily and sift confectioner's sugar over it. Then carefully lift the doily straight up.

Chocolate Marble Coffee Cake

MAKES 16 SLICES
(1 SLICE PER SERVING)

TIPS

One ounce of unsweetened cocoa has 3 grams of fat, compared to 1 oz of semi-sweet chocolate, which has 9 grams of fat.

Sift confectioner's sugar over top of cooled cake to decorate.

MAKE AHEAD

Bake a day before or freeze for up to 6 weeks.

BARB'S NUTRITION NOTE

If preparing the cake in advance, don't dust with confectioner's sugar until ready to serve. A little confectioner's sugar goes a long way. One tablespoon (15 mL) is enough for this cake, adding less than $\frac{1}{2}$ gram of carbohydrate per serving.

- ■ Preheat oven to 350°F (180°C)
- ■ 8-inch (2 L) square cake pan, sprayed with nonstick vegetable spray

$\frac{1}{4}$ cup	margarine	50 mL
$\frac{3}{4}$ cup	granulated sugar	175 mL
1	egg	1
1	egg white	1
$1\frac{1}{2}$ tsp	vanilla	7 mL
$1\frac{1}{4}$ cups	all-purpose flour	300 mL
$1\frac{1}{2}$ tsp	baking powder	7 mL
1 tsp	cinnamon	5 mL
$\frac{1}{2}$ tsp	baking soda	2 mL
1 cup	2% yogurt	250 mL

Chocolate Marble

$\frac{1}{4}$ cup	granulated sugar	50 mL
3 tbsp	sifted unsweetened cocoa powder	45 mL
3 tbsp	2% milk	45 mL

1. In a large bowl or food processor, cream together margarine and sugar. Beat in egg, egg white and vanilla.

2. Combine flour, baking powder, cinnamon and baking soda; add to bowl alternately with yogurt, mixing just until blended. Do not overmix. Pour all but 1 cup (250 mL) into cake pan.

3. *Chocolate Marble:* In a small bowl, stir together sugar, cocoa and milk until blended. Add to reserved batter, mixing well. Pour over batter in pan; draw knife through mixture to create marbled effect. Bake for 35 to 40 minutes or until a cake tester inserted into center comes out clean.

NUTRIENTS PER SERVING	
Calories	131
Carbohydrate	22 g
Fiber	1 g
Protein	3 g
Fat, total	4 g
Fat, saturated	1 g
Cholesterol	13 mg
Sodium	122 mg

AMERICA'S EXCHANGES	
$1\frac{1}{2}$	Other Carbohydrates
1	Fat

CANADA'S CHOICES	
$1\frac{1}{2}$	Carbohydrate
1	Fat

La Costa Cheesecake with Strawberry Sauce

**MAKES 8 SLICES
(1 SLICE WITH
2 TBSP/25 ML SAUCE
PER SERVING)**

TIPS
Thaw unsweetened frozen strawberries for sauce or use fresh ripe berries; if using frozen, drain excess liquid before puréeing.

The milk powder gives an extra calcium boost to this cheesecake.

**BARB'S
NUTRITION NOTE**
You will have about ½ cup (125 mL) of sauce left over. It goes well with pancakes or French toast. Count 3 tbsp (45 mL) as ½ Fruit Exchange or ½ Carbohydrate Choice.

■ Preheat oven to 325° F (160° C)
■ 9-inch (23 cm) pie plate

Cheesecake

2 cups	low-fat cottage cheese	500 mL
3 tbsp	fructose	45 mL
2 tbsp	lemon juice	25 mL
2 tsp	vanilla	10 mL
2	eggs	2
2 tbsp	low-fat milk powder	25 mL

Strawberry Sauce

2 cups	strawberries	500 mL
1	ripe banana	1
	Fresh strawberries (optional)	

1. *Cheesecake:* In a blender or food processor, combine cottage cheese, fructose, lemon juice, vanilla and eggs; purée until smooth. Add milk powder; blend just until mixed. Pour into pie plate. Set pie plate in larger pan; pour in enough hot water to come halfway up sides. Bake for 30 to 35 minutes. Remove from water bath; cool on wire rack. Chill.

2. *Strawberry sauce:* In a blender or food processor, purée strawberries with banana until smooth.

3. To serve, drizzle 2 tbsp (25 mL) strawberry sauce over each slice of cheesecake. Garnish with strawberries, if desired.

NUTRIENTS PER SERVING	
Calories	118
Carbohydrate	14 g
Fiber	1 g
Protein	10 g
Fat, total	3 g
Fat, saturated	1 g
Cholesterol	51 mg
Sodium	251 mg

AMERICA'S EXCHANGES	
1	Other Carbohydrates
1	Lean Meat

CANADA'S CHOICES	
1	Carbohydrate
1	Meat and Alternatives

Raspberry Cheesecake

MAKES 12 SLICES
(1 SLICE PER SERVING)

TIP

You can substitute whole frozen raspberries for fresh. Thaw and drain before using.

BARB'S NUTRITION NOTES

Remember that the nutrients per serving and Exchanges and Choices do not include optional ingredients.

To make about ½ cup (125 mL) raspberry purée, place 2 cups (500 mL) fresh or thawed frozen unsweetened raspberries in a blender and process until smooth. If you want to remove the seeds, pass the purée through a fine-mesh sieve. Count 2 tbsp (25 mL) as a Free Food or Extra.

- Preheat oven to 350°F (180°C)
- 8-inch (2 L) springform pan, sprayed with baking spray

1 cup	5% ricotta cheese	250 mL
1 cup	low-fat cottage cheese	250 mL
⅓ cup	granulated sugar or ¼ cup (50 mL) fructose	75 mL
⅓ cup	low-fat yogurt	75 mL
2	eggs	2
1 tsp	grated lemon zest	5 mL
½ tsp	vanilla	2 mL
1 tbsp	all-purpose flour	15 mL
1½ tsp	cornstarch	7 mL
1 cup	raspberries	250 mL
	Raspberry purée (optional)	

1. In a food processor, beat together ricotta cheese, cottage cheese, sugar, yogurt, eggs, lemon zest and vanilla until smooth. Beat in flour and cornstarch. Transfer to a bowl; gently fold in raspberries. Pour into prepared pan.

2. Bake for 35 minutes or until a tester inserted in center comes out clean. Cool on a wire rack. Chill. Serve plain or, if desired, with raspberry purée.

NUTRIENTS PER SERVING	
Calories	87
Carbohydrate	9 g
Fiber	1 g
Protein	6 g
Fat, total	2 g
Fat, saturated	1 g
Cholesterol	36 mg
Sodium	118 mg

AMERICA'S EXCHANGES	
½	Other Carbohydrates
1	Lean Meat

CANADA'S CHOICES	
½	Carbohydrate
1	Meat and Alternatives

Tangy Banana Cheesecake

TIP

For an extra-nutritious dessert with a nutty flavor, coat pie plate with wheat germ after spraying with baking spray.

BARB'S NUTRITION NOTE

Count 2 tbsp (25 mL) sliced banana or ¼ cup (50 mL) of most unsweetened berries as a Free Food or Extra.

▪ Preheat oven to 375°F (190°C)
▪ 9-inch (23 cm) pie plate, sprayed with baking spray

1 cup	low-fat cottage cheese	250 mL
1 cup	low-fat yogurt	250 mL
2	egg whites	2
2 tbsp	lemon juice	25 mL
1 tsp	vanilla	5 mL
⅓ cup	whole wheat flour	75 mL
¼ cup	honey	50 mL
2	ripe bananas	2
	Berries or sliced bananas	

1. In a blender or food processor, combine cottage cheese, yogurt, egg whites, lemon juice and vanilla; purée until smooth. Add flour; blend until well mixed. With motor running, add honey through feed tube; process until smooth. Add bananas; blend until smooth. Pour into prepared pie plate.

2. Bake for 30 to 40 minutes or until firm to the touch. Cool on wire rack. Chill at least 1 hour. Serve garnished with berries or sliced bananas.

NUTRIENTS PER SERVING	
Calories	126
Carbohydrate	23 g
Fiber	1 g
Protein	7 g
Fat, total	1 g
Fat, saturated	1 g
Cholesterol	4 mg
Sodium	151 mg

AMERICA'S EXCHANGES	
½	Fruit
1	Other Carbohydrates
1	Lean Meat

CANADA'S CHOICES	
1½	Carbohydrate
½	Meat and Alternatives

Marble Mocha Cheesecake

**MAKES 12 SLICES
(1 SLICE PER SERVING)**

TIPS

Graham crackers can also be used for the crust.

Melt chocolate in microwave on Defrost or in a double boiler.

If instant coffee is unavailable, use 2 tsp (10 mL) prepared strong coffee.

When using margarine, choose a soft (non-hydrogenated) version to limit consumption of trans fats.

■ Preheat oven to 350°F (180°C)
■ 8-inch (2 L) springform pan, sprayed with vegetable spray

Crust

1½ cups	chocolate wafer crumbs	375 mL
2 tbsp	granulated sugar	25 mL
2 tbsp	water	25 mL
1 tbsp	margarine or butter	15 mL

Filling

1⅔ cups	5% ricotta cheese	400 mL
⅓ cup	light cream cheese, softened	75 mL
¾ cup	granulated sugar	175 mL
1	egg	1
⅓ cup	light sour cream or 2% yogurt	75 mL
1 tbsp	all-purpose flour	15 mL
1 tsp	vanilla	5 mL
1½ tsp	instant coffee granules	7 mL
1½ tsp	hot water	7 mL
3 tbsp	semisweet chocolate chips, melted	45 mL

1. Combine chocolate crumbs, sugar, water and margarine; mix thoroughly. Press into bottom and up sides of springform pan.

2. In a large bowl or food processor, beat together ricotta cheese, cream cheese, sugar, egg, sour cream, flour and vanilla until well blended. Dissolve coffee granules in hot water; add to batter and mix until incorporated.

NUTRIENTS PER SERVING	
Calories	209
Carbohydrate	29 g
Fiber	1 g
Protein	7 g
Fat, total	8 g
Fat, saturated	3 g
Cholesterol	25 mg
Sodium	196 mg

AMERICA'S EXCHANGES	
1	Starch
1	Other Carbohydrates
½	Lean Meat
1	Fat

CANADA'S CHOICES	
2	Carbohydrate
½	Meat and Alternatives
1	Fat

MAKE AHEAD

Bake up to 2 days ahead and keep refrigerated.

Freeze for up to 6 weeks.

3. Pour batter into springform pan and smooth top. Drizzle melted chocolate on top. Draw knife or spatula through the chocolate and batter several times to create marbling. Bake for 35 to 40 minutes; center will be slightly loose. Let cool and refrigerate several hours before serving.

BARB'S NUTRITION NOTE

When people hear the word "cheesecake," they usually think "high fat." While this is still true of many cheesecake recipes, there are now some that call for reduced-fat ingredients. This recipe calls for 5% ricotta cheese, light cream cheese and light sour cream, all of which have lower fat levels than their traditional counterparts. If this recipe were prepared with regular ricotta, cream cheese and sour cream, the total fat in each serving would increase from 8 grams to 14 grams.

Keep in mind, though, that substituting lower-fat ingredients in a recipe doesn't always produce the same results, so if you have a favorite recipe, it's often a good idea to look for a lower-fat version that has already been tested.

Fat-free versions of cream cheese, sour cream and other dairy products are also available; however, recipe developers have discovered that, in general, they are not acceptable substitutes in recipes developed for regular-fat items, likely because they are higher in moisture.

When replacing regular cream cheese with a reduced-fat variety, be sure to use the solid type that comes in a bar, not the one in the tub.

Chocolate Cheesecake with Sour Cream Topping

**MAKES 12 SLICES
(1 SLICE PER SERVING)**

TIPS

Garnish with fresh berries or sifted cocoa.

Cooking with cocoa rather than chocolate has a major advantage. One ounce (30 g) of semisweet chocolate has 140 calories and 9 grams of fat. One ounce of cocoa has 90 calories and 3 grams of fat.

When using margarine, choose a soft (non-hydrogenated) version to limit consumption of trans fats.

BARB'S NUTRITION NOTE

For the garnish, count ¼ cup (50 mL) of most unsweetened berries as a Free Food or Extra. You will need only a very light dusting of cocoa powder.

- Preheat oven to 350°F (180°C)
- 8-inch (2 L) springform pan, sprayed with nonstick vegetable spray

Crust

1½ cups	graham or chocolate wafer crumbs	375 mL
2 tbsp	water	25 mL
1 tbsp	margarine, melted	15 mL

Cake

8 oz	ricotta cheese	250 g
8 oz	2% cottage cheese	250 g
1 cup	granulated sugar	250 mL
1	large egg	1
1 tsp	vanilla	5 mL
¼ cup	sifted unsweetened cocoa powder	50 mL
1 tbsp	all-purpose flour	15 mL

Topping

1 cup	light sour cream	250 mL
2 tbsp	granulated sugar	25 mL
1 tsp	vanilla	5 mL

1. *Crust:* In a bowl, combine crumbs, water and margarine; mix well. Pat onto bottom and sides of springform pan. Refrigerate.

2. *Cake:* In a food processor, combine ricotta and cottage cheeses, sugar, egg and vanilla; process until smooth. Add cocoa and flour; process just until combined. Pour into prepared pan and bake for 30 minutes or until set around edge but still slightly loose in center.

NUTRIENTS PER SERVING	
Calories	213
Carbohydrate	32 g
Fiber	1 g
Protein	8 g
Fat, total	6 g
Fat, saturated	2 g
Cholesterol	26 mg
Sodium	212 mg

AMERICA'S EXCHANGES	
½	Starch
1½	Other Carbohydrates
1	Lean Meat
½	Fat

CANADA'S CHOICES	
2	Carbohydrate
1	Meat and Alternatives
½	Fat

MAKE AHEAD
Prepare a day before or freeze for up to 3 weeks.

3. *Topping:* Meanwhile, stir together sour cream, sugar and vanilla; pour over cheesecake. Bake for 10 more minutes. (Topping will be loose.) Let cool and refrigerate for at least 3 hours or until set.

BARB'S NUTRITION NOTE

We are all familiar with the expression "food for thought." It's equally important to give thought for food — not just to the nutrient values and Exchanges or Choices, but also to the experience of eating. Unfortunately, many meals today have become "refueling stops" on the run (both at and away from home), with little time to socialize and even less time to enjoy what we've chosen. Various strategies can help us be more thoughtful about what we eat:

Plan meals at least a day in advance, and make sure you have all the ingredients you need.

Involve other family members in planning and preparing meals.

When ordering from a menu, ask how foods are prepared, what comes with them and possible substitutions. At a buffet, survey everything before making your choices.

At home, you are able to serve yourself appropriate portions. Restaurant servings are often larger. Do not feel obliged to eat everything on your plate.

Chocolate Marble Vanilla Cheesecake

MAKES 20 SLICES
(1 SLICE PER SERVING)

TIPS

For a mocha flavor, dissolve 2 tsp (10 mL) instant coffee in same amount of water and add to batter.

When using margarine, choose a soft (non-hydrogenated) version to limit consumption of trans fats.

MAKE AHEAD

Prepare up to 2 days ahead. Freeze for up to 6 weeks.

■ Preheat oven to 350°F (180°C)
■ 9-inch (2.5 L) springform pan, sprayed with vegetable spray

Crust

2 cups	chocolate wafer crumbs	500 mL
3 tbsp	water	45 mL
1½ tbsp	margarine or butter, melted	22 mL

Filling

2 cups	ricotta cheese	500 mL
2 cups	2% cottage cheese	500 mL
1¾ cups	granulated sugar	425 mL
2	large eggs	2
⅓ cup	all-purpose flour	75 mL
⅔ cup	light sour cream	150 mL
2 tsp	vanilla	10 mL
2 oz	semisweet chocolate	50 g
2 tbsp	water	25 mL

1. *Crust:* In a bowl, combine crumbs, water and margarine; mix well. Press onto sides and bottom of springform pan; refrigerate.

2. In a food processor, combine ricotta and cottage cheeses, sugar and eggs; process until completely smooth. Add flour, sour cream and vanilla; process until well combined. Pour into pan. Melt chocolate with water and stir until smooth. Spoon onto cake in several places and swirl through lightly with a knife. Bake for 65 minutes or until set around edge but still slightly loose in center. Let cool; refrigerate until well chilled.

NUTRIENTS PER SERVING	
Calories	222
Carbohydrate	32 g
Fiber	1 g
Protein	8 g
Fat, total	7 g
Fat, saturated	3 g
Cholesterol	31 mg
Sodium	210 mg

AMERICA'S EXCHANGES	
2	Other Carbohydrates
1	Lean Meat
1	Fat

CANADA'S CHOICES	
2	Carbohydrate
1	Meat and Alternatives
1	Fat

Pies, Tarts, Crisps and Fruit Desserts

Sour Cream Apple Pie

MAKES 12 SERVINGS

TIPS

For an attractive presentation, sprinkle a little confectioner's sugar over top.

Substitute vanilla wafer crumbs for the graham crumbs for a change.

When using margarine, choose a soft (non-hydrogenated) version to limit consumption of trans fats.

BARB'S NUTRITION NOTE

A little confectioner's sugar goes a long way. One tablespoon (15 mL) sifted over this pie adds 1 gram of carbohydrate per serving.

■ Preheat oven to 350°F (180°C)
■ 8-inch (2 L) springform pan

Crust

1½ cups	graham wafer crumbs	375 mL
2 tbsp	margarine, melted	25 mL
1 tbsp	brown sugar	15 mL
1 tbsp	water	15 mL

Filling

5½ cups	sliced peeled apples (5 to 6 apples)	1.375 L
½ cup	granulated sugar	125 mL
½ cup	2% yogurt	125 mL
½ cup	light sour cream	125 mL
¼ cup	raisins	50 mL
2 tbsp	all-purpose flour	25 mL
1 tsp	cinnamon	5 mL
1	egg, lightly beaten	1
1 tsp	vanilla	5 mL

Topping

¼ cup	packed brown sugar	50 mL
3 tbsp	all-purpose flour	45 mL
2 tbsp	rolled oats	25 mL
½ tsp	cinnamon	2 mL
1 tbsp	margarine	15 mL

NUTRIENTS PER SERVING	
Calories	204
Carbohydrate	37 g
Fiber	2 g
Protein	3 g
Fat, total	5 g
Fat, saturated	1 g
Cholesterol	16 mg
Sodium	129 mg

AMERICA'S EXCHANGES	
1	Starch
½	Fruit
1	Other Carbohydrates
1	Fat

CANADA'S CHOICES	
2½	Carbohydrate
1	Fat

MAKE AHEAD
Prepare early in the day
and warm slightly before
serving. Or freeze for
up to 2 weeks.

1. *Crust:* In a bowl, combine graham crumbs, margarine, brown sugar and water; pat onto bottom and sides of pan. Refrigerate.

2. *Filling:* In a large bowl, combine apples, sugar, yogurt, sour cream, raisins, flour, cinnamon, egg and vanilla; toss together until well mixed. Pour over crust.

3. *Topping:* In a small bowl, combine brown sugar, flour, rolled oats and cinnamon; cut in margarine until crumbly. Sprinkle over pie; bake for 30 to 40 minutes or until topping is browned and apples are tender.

BARB'S NUTRITION NOTE
For help in planning your meals, ask your doctor to refer you to a diabetes education center or a dietitian. Your local public health unit and hospitals may also have referral services. On the Internet, look for the "find a dietitian" feature at www.eatright.org (in the U.S.) or www.dietitians.ca (in Canada).

Creamy Pumpkin Cheese Pie

MAKES 12 SERVINGS

TIPS

In the fall use fresh pumpkin. Bake pumpkin or squash in a 400°F (200°C) oven until tender, approximately 1 hour.

The topping is simple but highly decorative.

BARB'S NUTRITION NOTES

If you don't have a food processor, use a hand mixer.

Be sure to bring cream cheese to room temperature before combining with other ingredients.

- Preheat oven to 350° F (180° C)
- 9-inch (2.5 L) springform pan or 9-inch (23 cm) deep-dish pie plate

1½ cups	graham cracker crumbs	375 mL
2 tbsp	granulated sugar	25 mL
2 tbsp	water	25 mL
1 tbsp	vegetable oil	15 mL
4 oz	light cream cheese	125 g
½ cup	5% ricotta cheese	125 mL
⅓ cup	granulated sugar	75 mL
1	egg	1
1 tsp	vanilla	5 mL
1 cup	canned pumpkin purée (not pie filling) or mashed cooked butternut squash	250 mL
⅔ cup	2% evaporated milk	150 mL
¾ cup	packed brown sugar	175 mL
1 tsp	ground cinnamon	5 mL
¼ tsp	ground ginger	1 mL
¼ tsp	ground nutmeg	1 mL
3 tbsp	light sour cream	45 mL
2½ tsp	granulated sugar	12 mL

1. In a bowl, combine graham crumbs, sugar, water and oil; press into bottom and sides of pan; set aside.

2. In a food processor, combine cream cheese, ricotta, sugar, egg and vanilla; process until smooth. Pour into prepared crust.

3. In a food processor, combine pumpkin, evaporated milk, brown sugar, cinnamon, ginger and nutmeg until well blended. Spoon carefully over cheese filling.

NUTRIENTS PER SERVING	
Calories	207
Carbohydrate	35 g
Fiber	1 g
Protein	5 g
Fat, total	6 g
Fat, saturated	2 g
Cholesterol	25 mg
Sodium	182 mg

AMERICA'S EXCHANGES	
1	Starch
1	Other Carbohydrates
1	Fat
1	Free Food

CANADA'S CHOICES	
2	Carbohydrate
1	Fat

MAKE AHEAD
Bake up to 2 days in advance. Freeze for up to 6 weeks.

4. In a small bowl, stir together sour cream and sugar. Put in a squeeze bottle or in a small plastic sandwich bag with the very tip of corner cut off. Draw 4 concentric circles on top of pumpkin filling. Run a toothpick through the circles at regular intervals.

5. Bake for 50 minutes or until just slightly loose at the center. Cool on wire rack. Chill before serving.

BARB'S NUTRITION NOTE
As you prepare the recipes in this book, you will become familiar with the appropriate portion sizes for different types of desserts and the approximate Exchanges or Choices assigned to them. Use this knowledge to help you choose wisely when you're eating away from home.

Lemon Meringue Pie

TIPS

Separate eggs carefully for meringue — egg whites contaminated with yolk will not beat properly. Also, make sure your bowls and beaters are perfectly clean when making meringue.

When using margarine, choose a soft (non-hydrogenated) version.

BARB'S NUTRITION NOTE

Although fructose does not raise blood sugar as much as sucrose (ordinary table sugar), it is not a sugar substitute or a Free Food or Extra. As with ordinary sugar, 1 tbsp (15 mL) counts as an Other Carbohydrate Exchange or Carbohydrate Choice. You'll find fructose in specialty grocery stores and some health food stores.

■ Preheat oven to 450°F (220°C)
■ Six ¹/₂-cup (125 mL) ovenproof dishes
■ Baking sheet

Filling

1¹/₄ cups	water	300 mL
¹/₂ cup	fructose	125 mL
1 tsp	grated lemon zest	5 mL
¹/₄ cup	freshly squeezed lemon juice	50 mL
¹/₄ cup	cornstarch	50 mL
³/₄ cup	water	175 mL
1 tsp	margarine	5 mL

Meringue

2	egg whites	2
1 tbsp	fructose	15 mL

1. *Filling:* In a saucepan, combine 1¹/₄ cups (300 mL) water, fructose, lemon zest and juice. Bring to a boil. In a bowl, stir together cornstarch and ³/₄ cup (175 mL) water until dissolved. Stir into boiling lemon mixture. Cook, stirring, until thickened. Remove from heat. Stir in margarine. Divide among dishes. Cool.

2. *Meringue:* In a bowl, beat egg whites until soft peaks form. Gradually add fructose, beating until stiff peaks form. Spoon over filling; transfer dishes to baking sheet. Bake for 5 minutes or until golden. Cool to room temperature. Chill before serving.

NUTRIENTS PER SERVING	
Calories	102
Carbohydrate	24 g
Fiber	0 g
Protein	1 g
Fat, total	1 g
Fat, saturated	0 g
Cholesterol	0 mg
Sodium	30 mg

AMERICA'S EXCHANGES	
¹/₂	Starch
1	Other Carbohydrates

CANADA'S CHOICES	
1¹/₂	Carbohydrate

Fresh Fruit Tart

MAKES 8 SERVINGS

TIP
To save time, use a store-bought pre-baked pastry shell.

BARB'S NUTRITION NOTES
Remember that nutrients per serving, and Exchanges and Choices, do not include ingredients for which no quantity is specified. Topping the tart with 8 strawberries and 2 kiwifruit will add 1 Free Food or Extra per serving.

Count 3 banana slices as 1 Free Food or Extra. For most other fruits, 1/4 cup (50 mL) sliced counts as 1 Free Food or Extra.

The filling for this tart is a custard — a mixture of milk and egg and other ingredients that thickens when heated.

1	8-inch (20 cm) pastry shell, baked	1
Filling		
1 cup	skim milk	250 mL
2 tbsp	granulated sugar	25 mL
1 tsp	grated lemon zest	5 mL
1 tsp	grated orange zest	5 mL
1/2 tsp	vanilla	2 mL
1	egg, beaten	1
1 tbsp	cornstarch	15 mL
	Fresh berries and/or sliced fruit	
2 tbsp	red currant jelly	25 mL

1. *Filling:* In a saucepan, heat milk over medium heat until hot. Stir in sugar, lemon zest, orange zest and vanilla. In a bowl, beat egg with cornstarch until blended. Whisk a little of the hot milk into egg mixture, then pour back into remaining milk. Whisk constantly until mixture is thick enough to coat a spoon; do not boil. Chill.

2. Spread custard over baked crust. Decorate with fruit and berries. In a saucepan, melt jelly. Brush over fruit.

NUTRIENTS PER SERVING	
Calories	132
Carbohydrate	17 g
Fiber	0 g
Protein	3 g
Fat, total	6 g
Fat, saturated	2 g
Cholesterol	24 mg
Sodium	127 mg

AMERICA'S EXCHANGES	
1/2	Starch
1/2	Other Carbohydrates
1	Fat

CANADA'S CHOICES	
1	Carbohydrate
1	Fat

Tropical Fruit Tart

MAKES 12 SERVINGS

TIP
When using margarine, choose a soft (non-hydrogenated) version to limit consumption of trans fats.

- ■ Preheat oven to 400°F (200°C)
- ■ 9-inch (23 cm) tart or springform pan, sprayed with nonstick vegetable spray

Crust

1¼ cups	all-purpose flour	300 mL
¼ cup	confectioner's (icing) sugar	50 mL
⅓ cup	margarine	75 mL
3 tbsp	cold water (approx.)	45 mL

Filling

1¾ cups	2% yogurt	425 mL
⅔ cup	granulated sugar	150 mL
½ cup	light sour cream	125 mL
3 tbsp	frozen orange juice concentrate, thawed	45 mL
2 tbsp	all-purpose flour	25 mL
1½ tsp	orange rind	7 mL

Topping

3 cups	sliced fruit (kiwi, mangos, papayas, star fruit)	750 mL

1. *Crust:* In a bowl, combine flour with sugar; cut in margarine until crumbly. With a fork, gradually stir in water, adding 1 tbsp (15 mL) more if necessary to make dough hold together. Pat into pan and bake for 15 minutes or until browned. Reduce heat to 375°F (190°C).

2. *Filling:* Meanwhile, in a bowl, combine yogurt, sugar, sour cream, orange juice concentrate, flour and orange rind; mix well and pour over crust. Bake for 35 to 45 minutes or until filling is set. Let cool and refrigerate until chilled.

3. *Topping:* Decoratively arrange sliced fruit over filling.

NUTRIENTS PER SERVING	
Calories	218
Carbohydrate	36 g
Fiber	2 g
Protein	4 g
Fat, total	7 g
Fat, saturated	1 g
Cholesterol	3 mg
Sodium	106 mg

AMERICA'S EXCHANGES	
1	Starch
½	Fruit
1	Other Carbohydrates
1½	Fat

CANADA'S CHOICES	
2	Carbohydrate
1	Fat
1	Extra

Blueberry Apple Crisp

MAKES 8 SERVINGS

VARIATION

In season, substitute pears for the apples and use ground ginger instead of cinnamon.

BARB'S NUTRITION NOTE

Unsweetened frozen blueberries can be substituted for fresh.

■ Preheat oven to 350°F (180°C)
■ 9-inch (2.5 L) square baking dish

3	medium apples, peeled, cored and sliced	3
1 cup	fresh blueberries	250 mL
1/4 cup	apple juice	50 mL
2 tbsp	granulated sugar	25 mL
1 tbsp	lemon juice	15 mL
1 tsp	cinnamon	5 mL

Topping

1 cup	rolled oats	250 mL
1/3 cup	whole wheat flour	75 mL
1/4 cup	packed brown sugar	50 mL
2 tbsp	apple juice	25 mL
2 tbsp	butter, softened	25 mL
1/2 tsp	cinnamon	2 mL

1. In a bowl, mix together apples, blueberries, apple juice, sugar, lemon juice and cinnamon. Transfer to baking dish.

2. *Topping:* In a bowl, stir together rolled oats, flour, brown sugar, apple juice, butter and cinnamon until crumbly. Sprinkle over blueberry mixture.

3. Bake for 30 minutes or until golden. Serve warm or cold.

NUTRIENTS PER SERVING	
Calories	170
Carbohydrate	33 g
Fiber	3 g
Protein	3 g
Fat, total	4 g
Fat, saturated	2 g
Cholesterol	8 mg
Sodium	34 mg

AMERICA'S EXCHANGES	
1	Starch
1/2	Fruit
1/2	Other Carbohydrates
1	Fat

CANADA'S CHOICES	
2	Carbohydrate
1	Fat

Apple, Pear and Cranberry Crisp

MAKES 8 SERVINGS

Crisps are a great way to enjoy fruit and whole grains. Because this dessert is fairly high in fat, serve it only on special occasions.

TIP
Leftovers can be stored in an airtight container in the fridge for up to 3 days or in the freezer for up to 3 months.

VARIATION
When available, use fresh or frozen cranberries instead of dried.

BARB'S NUTRITION NOTE
This recipe includes a generous amount of crisp topping. If you use only half the amount, you will save 1 Other Carbohydrate Exchange or Carbohydrate Choice and 1 Fat Exchange or Choice.

- Preheat oven to 400°F (200°C)
- 8-inch (2 L) square baking dish, lightly greased

Topping

¾ cup	all-purpose flour	175 mL
¾ cup	packed brown sugar	175 mL
½ cup	old-fashioned rolled oats	125 mL
½ cup	cold butter	125 mL
3	apples, cored, peeled and sliced	3
2	pears, cored, peeled and sliced	2
¼ cup	dried cranberries	50 mL
1 tbsp	all-purpose flour	15 mL
1 tbsp	packed brown sugar	15 mL

1. *Topping:* In a medium bowl, combine flour, brown sugar and oats. Cut in butter until mixture resembles coarse meal.

2. Place apples, pears and cranberries in prepared baking dish. Sprinkle with flour and sugar and toss to coat. Top with oat mixture.

3. Bake in preheated oven for 30 to 45 minutes or until topping is golden and fruit is tender. Let cool for 5 minutes before serving.

NUTRIENTS PER SERVING	
Calories	315
Carbohydrate	51 g
Fiber	3 g
Protein	2 g
Fat, total	12 g
Fat, saturated	7 g
Cholesterol	31 mg
Sodium	127 mg

AMERICA'S EXCHANGES	
1	Starch
1	Fruit
1½	Other Carbohydrates
2½	Fat

CANADA'S CHOICES	
3	Carbohydrate
2½	Fat

Blueberry Strawberry Pear Crisp

MAKES 12 SERVINGS

TIP
Other fruits can be substituted, such as peaches, apples or mangos.

MAKE AHEAD
Can be baked earlier in the day, but best if baked just ahead of serving.

- Preheat oven to 350°F (180°C)
- 9-inch square (2.5 L) cake pan, sprayed with vegetable spray

1½ cups	fresh blueberries (or frozen, thawed and drained)	375 mL
1½ cups	sliced strawberries	375 mL
1½ cups	chopped peeled pears	375 mL
½ cup	granulated sugar	125 mL
2 tbsp	all-purpose flour	25 mL
2 tsp	orange juice	10 mL
1 tsp	grated orange zest	5 mL
½ tsp	cinnamon	2 mL

Topping

¾ cup	brown sugar	175 mL
¾ cup	all-purpose flour	175 mL
½ cup	rolled oats	125 mL
½ tsp	cinnamon	2 mL
¼ cup	cold butter	50 mL

1. In a large bowl, combine blueberries, strawberries, pears, sugar, flour, orange juice, orange zest and cinnamon; toss gently to mix. Spread in prepared cake pan.

2. In a small bowl, combine brown sugar, flour, oats and cinnamon; cut butter in until crumbly. Sprinkle over fruit mixture. Bake for 30 to 35 minutes or until topping is browned and fruit is tender.

NUTRIENTS PER SERVING	
Calories	195
Carbohydrate	39 g
Fiber	2 g
Protein	2 g
Fat, total	4 g
Fat, saturated	2 g
Cholesterol	10 mg
Sodium	46 mg

AMERICA'S EXCHANGES	
½	Starch
½	Fruit
1½	Other Carbohydrates
1	Fat

CANADA'S CHOICES	
2½	Carbohydrate
1	Fat

Peach and Blueberry Crisp

MAKES 8 SERVINGS

TIP

Blueberries should be removed from their carton and placed in a moisture-proof container in the refrigerator. Do not wash until just before using.

MAKE AHEAD

Although best straight from the oven, crisp can be prepared early in day and reheated slightly before serving.

■ Preheat oven to 350°F (180°C)
■ 9-inch (2.5 L) square cake pan, ungreased

½ cup	granulated sugar	125 mL
2 tbsp	all-purpose flour	25 mL
2 tsp	freshly squeezed lemon juice	10 mL
1 tsp	grated lemon zest	5 mL
1 tsp	cinnamon	5 mL
3 cups	sliced peeled ripe peaches	750 mL
2 cups	blueberries	500 mL
Topping		
½ cup	rolled oats	125 mL
⅓ cup	all-purpose flour	75 mL
3 tbsp	packed brown sugar	45 mL
½ tsp	cinnamon	2 mL
3 tbsp	soft margarine	45 mL

1. In a large bowl, combine sugar, flour, lemon juice, zest and cinnamon; stir in peaches and blueberries until well mixed. Spread in cake pan.

2. *Topping:* In a small bowl, combine rolled oats, flour, brown sugar and cinnamon; cut in margarine until crumbly. Sprinkle over fruit. Bake for 30 to 35 minutes or until topping is browned and fruit is tender. Serve warm.

NUTRIENTS PER SERVING	
Calories	204
Carbohydrate	40 g
Fiber	3 g
Protein	2 g
Fat, total	5 g
Fat, saturated	1 g
Cholesterol	0 mg
Sodium	62 mg

AMERICA'S EXCHANGES	
½	Starch
1	Fruit
1	Other Carbohydrates
1	Fat

CANADA'S CHOICES	
2½	Carbohydrate
1	Fat

Pear, Apple and Raisin Strudel

MAKES 12 SERVINGS

see Tip, page 206

TIPS
Sprinkle with confectioner's sugar for a finishing touch.

Ripen pears at room temperature in a bowl or paper bag.

BARB'S NUTRITION NOTE
If you use confectioner's sugar, remember that you need only a small quantity. One tablespoon (15 mL) sifted over this strudel adds just 1 gram of carbohydrate per serving.

- Preheat oven to 350°F (180°C)
- Baking sheet, sprayed with vegetable spray

2⅔ cups	chopped peeled apples	650 mL
2⅔ cups	chopped peeled pears	650 mL
⅓ cup	raisins	75 mL
2 tbsp	chopped pecans or walnuts	25 mL
2 tbsp	packed brown sugar	25 mL
1 tbsp	freshly squeezed lemon juice	15 mL
1 tbsp	liquid honey	15 mL
1 tsp	cinnamon	5 mL
6	sheets phyllo pastry (see Tip, page 206)	6
4 tsp	margarine, melted	20 mL

1. In a bowl, combine apples, pears, raisins, pecans, brown sugar, lemon juice, honey and cinnamon; mix well.

2. Lay out 2 sheets of phyllo; brush with some margarine. Place 2 more sheets over top; brush with margarine again. Top with remaining 2 sheets phyllo.

3. Spread filling over phyllo, leaving 1-inch (2.5 cm) border uncovered. Roll up like jelly-roll and place, seam side down, on prepared baking sheet. Brush with remaining margarine. Bake for 40 to 50 minutes or until golden and fruit is tender.

NUTRIENTS PER SERVING	
Calories	112
Carbohydrate	22 g
Fiber	2 g
Protein	1 g
Fat, total	3 g
Fat, saturated	0 g
Cholesterol	0 mg
Sodium	64 mg

AMERICA'S EXCHANGES	
½	Starch
1	Fruit
½	Fat

CANADA'S CHOICES	
1½	Carbohydrate
½	Fat

Mango Blueberry Strudel

MAKES 8 SERVINGS

TIP

Phyllo pastry is located in the freezer section of store. Handle quickly so the sheets do not dry out. Cover those not being used with a slightly damp cloth.

- ■ Preheat oven to 375°F (190°C)
- ■ Baking sheet, sprayed with vegetable spray

2 cups	fresh blueberries (or frozen, thawed and drained)	500 mL
1 tbsp	all-purpose flour	15 mL
2½ cups	peeled chopped ripe mango	625 mL
¼ cup	granulated sugar	50 mL
1 tbsp	lemon juice	15 mL
½ tsp	cinnamon	2 mL
6	sheets phyllo pastry	6
2 tsp	melted margarine or butter	10 mL
	Confectioner's (icing) sugar	

1. Toss blueberries with flour. In a large bowl, combine mango, blueberries, sugar, lemon juice and cinnamon.

2. Lay 2 phyllo sheets one on top of the other; brush with melted margarine. Layer another 2 phyllo sheets on top and brush with melted margarine. Layer last 2 sheets on top. Put fruit filling along long end of phyllo; gently roll over until all of filling is enclosed, fold sides in, and continue to roll. Put on prepared baking sheet, brush with remaining margarine and bake for 20 to 25 minutes or until golden. Sprinkle with confectioner's sugar.

NUTRIENTS PER SERVING	
Calories	167
Carbohydrate	37 g
Fiber	3 g
Protein	2 g
Fat, total	2 g
Fat, saturated	0 g
Cholesterol	0 mg
Sodium	86 mg

AMERICA'S EXCHANGES	
½	Starch
1½	Fruit
½	Other Carbohydrates
½	Fat

CANADA'S CHOICES	
2	Carbohydrate
½	Fat
1	Extra

Baked Granola Apples

MAKES 4 SERVINGS

This is a very speedy dessert that you can prepare and cook while making the rest of a meal.

TIPS

The best apples for baking are Spartan, Empire, Golden Delicious and Cortland, as they will keep their shape while cooking.

When using margarine, choose a non-hydrogenated version to limit consumption of trans fats.

Make this dessert on a night when the oven is already on for another recipe.

VARIATION

These also bake quickly in the microwave. Place on a microwave-safe plate and cover with microwave-safe plastic wrap. Cook on High for 2 to 3 minutes or until apples are tender.

- Preheat oven to 350°F (180°C)
- 9-inch (23 cm) glass pie plate, ungreased

4	apples	4
¾ cup	low-fat granola	175 mL
2 tsp	margarine	10 mL
½ cup	low-fat plain yogurt	125 mL
1 tbsp	pure maple syrup	15 mL

1. Core apples, creating a large hollow. Firmly pack with granola and dot with margarine. Place on pie plate.
2. Bake, uncovered, in preheated oven for 30 minutes or until apples are tender.
3. Meanwhile, in a small bowl, combine yogurt and maple syrup; set aside.
4. Place each apple in a dessert bowl and garnish with maple-flavored yogurt.

NUTRIENTS PER SERVING	
Calories	213
Carbohydrate	43 g
Fiber	4 g
Protein	4 g
Fat, total	4 g
Fat, saturated	1 g
Cholesterol	2 mg
Sodium	75 mg

AMERICA'S EXCHANGES	
1	Starch
1½	Fruit
1	Fat
1	Free Food

CANADA'S CHOICES	
2½	Carbohydrate
1	Fat

Pears in Tosca Sauce

MAKES 6 SERVINGS

You can't get simpler than this quick dessert made with canned pear halves. It tastes rich and decadent.

TIP

This is a pretty dessert to serve directly from the dish, so use a glass or ceramic baking dish rather than a metal pan.

VARIATION

Substitute a combination of canned peaches and fresh or frozen raspberries for the pears.

BARB'S NUTRITION NOTE

Be sure to use pears canned in juice. They contain 20% less carbohydrate than pears canned in light syrup, and 30% less than those canned in heavy syrup.

■ Preheat oven to 350°F (180°C)
■ 8-inch (2 L) square glass baking dish, ungreased

½ cup	sliced almonds	125 mL
⅓ cup	packed brown sugar	75 mL
⅓ cup	milk	75 mL
2 tbsp	unsalted butter	25 mL
1 tbsp	all-purpose flour	15 mL
1 tsp	vanilla	5 mL
1	can (28 oz/796 mL) pear halves, drained	1

1. In a small saucepan, over medium-high heat, combine almonds, brown sugar, milk, butter, flour and vanilla. Bring to a boil and cook until sauce thickens, about 5 minutes.

2. Place pears in baking dish and pour sauce over top.

3. Bake in preheated oven until browned on top, about 15 minutes.

NUTRIENTS PER SERVING	
Calories	188
Carbohydrate	26 g
Fiber	2 g
Protein	3 g
Fat, total	9 g
Fat, saturated	3 g
Cholesterol	11 g
Sodium	16 mg

AMERICA'S EXCHANGES	
½	Fruit
1	Other Carbohydrates
2	Fat
1	Free Food

CANADA'S CHOICES	
1½	Carbohydrate
2	Fat

Poached Pears in Chocolate Sauce

MAKES 6 SERVINGS

TIP
Use a firm pear such as a Bosc.

2 tbsp	lemon juice	25 mL
6	small ripe pears	6
1½ cups	pear nectar (or other fruit nectar)	375 mL
¼ cup	semisweet chocolate chips	50 mL
1 tbsp	2% evaporated milk	15 mL

1. Put lemon juice and 6 cups (1.5 L) water in a bowl. Peel pears, leaving whole with stems intact and dropping each in water mixture as it is peeled. Drain. In a saucepan, combine pears and pear nectar. Bring to a boil, reduce heat to medium-low, cover and cook, turning pears over halfway through, for 20 to 25 minutes or until tender when pierced with a knife. Transfer pears and syrup to a bowl; chill.

2. Before serving, drain pears, reserving syrup. Bring syrup to a boil; cook until reduced to ¼ cup (50 mL). Stir in chocolate chips until melted. Beat in evaporated milk until smooth.

3. Serve chilled pears on top of a pool of hot chocolate sauce.

NUTRIENTS PER SERVING	
Calories	171
Carbohydrate	38 g
Fiber	5 g
Protein	1 g
Fat, total	3 g
Fat, saturated	2 g
Cholesterol	0 mg
Sodium	6 mg

AMERICA'S EXCHANGES	
2	Fruit
½	Other Carbohydrates
½	Fat

CANADA'S CHOICES	
2	Carbohydrate
½	Fat

Key Lime Dessert

MAKES 8 SERVINGS

TIPS

To get the most juice from limes or other citrus fruit, bring fruit to room temperature before juicing.

Make sure the egg whites for the meringue are perfectly pure, without a speck of yolk, or they will not beat properly.

■ Preheat oven to 400°F (200°C)
■ 4-cup (1 L) soufflé dish or eight ½-cup (125 mL) ramekins

Filling

¾ cup	fructose	175 mL
¼ cup	cornstarch	50 mL
1½ cups	water	375 mL
2	egg whites, at room temperature	2
1	egg, at room temperature	1
2 tsp	grated lime zest	10 mL
¼ cup	freshly squeezed lime juice	50 mL

Meringue

2	egg whites	2
¼ tsp	cream of tartar	1 mL
4 tsp	fructose	20 mL

1. *Filling:* In a saucepan, stir together fructose and cornstarch. Gradually whisk in water until smooth. Bring to a boil over medium heat, stirring constantly. Continue to boil for 1 minute, stirring constantly, or until thickened. Remove from heat.

2. In a bowl, beat egg whites with egg. Gradually whisk half of hot cornstarch mixture into egg mixture. Pour back into remaining cornstarch mixture. Return saucepan to medium heat; cook, stirring, 1 minute. Remove from heat. Stir in lime zest and juice. Pour into soufflé dish.

NUTRIENTS PER SERVING	
Calories	110
Carbohydrate	25 g
Fiber	0 g
Protein	3 g
Fat, total	1 g
Fat, saturated	0 g
Cholesterol	23 mg
Sodium	37 mg

AMERICA'S EXCHANGES	
1½	Other Carbohydrates
½	Lean Meat

CANADA'S CHOICES	
2	Carbohydrate

Gram for gram, fructose is sweeter than ordinary sugar (sucrose), but it has a lower glycemic index (it does not raise blood sugar as much). It is not, however, a sugar substitute or a Free Food or Extra. Like ordinary sugar, 1 tbsp (15 mL) of fructose counts as an Other Carbohydrate Exchange or Carbohydrate Choice. Look for it in specialty grocery stores and some health food stores.

3. *Meringue:* In a bowl, beat egg whites until foamy. Add cream of tartar and beat until soft peaks form. Gradually add fructose, beating until stiff peaks form. Spoon over hot filling. Bake for 8 to 10 minutes or until golden brown.

BARB'S NUTRITION NOTE

People with type 1 diabetes do not produce insulin, the hormone required to metabolize carbohydrate (starch and sugars). Before the development of injectable insulin, they were limited to a diet consisting entirely of protein and fat. Once insulin became available, they were able to add bread and other grain products, fruit, vegetables and milk products. Experts still believed, however, that even a very small amount of sugar would seriously interfere with blood glucose control, and several generations of people with diabetes were advised to avoid it altogether. We now know that the total quantity of carbohydrate — regardless of the source — and how it's distributed throughout the day are the most important factors. With the ban on sugar lifted, people with diabetes can usually eat the same foods as everyone else. It isn't necessary to seek out special foods or recipes.

Gram for gram, sugar has the same number of calories as the carbohydrate in other foods; however, it does not provide the essential vitamins, minerals and other healthy components that they do. For this reason, high-sugar foods are often called "empty calorie foods." And that is why only a small portion of your daily carbohydrate intake should come from sugar.

Fluffy Apricot Soufflé with Raspberry Sauce

MAKES 6 SERVINGS

TIPS

For a strawberry sauce, substitute strawberries for the raspberries.

Thaw unsweetened frozen berries for sauce or use fresh ripe berries; if using frozen, drain excess liquid before puréeing.

■ Preheat oven to 300°F (150°C)
■ 8-cup (2 L) soufflé dish, sprayed with baking spray

Soufflé

8 oz	dried apricots	250 g
¼ cup	water	50 mL
¼ cup	granulated sugar	50 mL
¼ tsp	almond extract	1 mL
5	egg whites	5

Sauce

1 cup	raspberries	250 mL
½	ripe banana	½
1 tbsp	fruit jam (any flavor)	15 mL
1 tsp	lemon juice	5 mL

1. In a saucepan, combine apricots and water; cook over medium heat for 5 minutes or until all the water is absorbed. Transfer hot apricots to a food processor or blender; purée just until finely chopped. Add sugar and almond extract; purée until well mixed. Transfer to a bowl; cool mixture to room temperature.

2. In another bowl, beat egg whites until stiff peaks form. Stir one-third of egg whites into cooled apricot mixture until well mixed. Gently fold in remaining egg whites. Apricot pieces will still be evident. Pour into prepared dish.

NUTRIENTS PER SERVING	
Calories	164
Carbohydrate	39 g
Fiber	4 g
Protein	5 g
Fat, total	0 g
Fat, saturated	0 g
Cholesterol	0 mg
Sodium	50 mg

AMERICA'S EXCHANGES	
2	Fruit
½	Other Carbohydrates
½	Lean Meat

CANADA'S CHOICES	
2	Carbohydrate
1	Extra

Be sure to choose
unsweetened frozen fruit.
Sweetened varieties
generally contain about
twice as much carbohydrate
as unsweetened.

3. Set soufflé dish in larger pan; pour in enough hot water to come halfway up sides. Bake for 20 minutes. Reduce oven temperature to 250°F (120°C); bake for 12 minutes longer or until light brown and no longer loose. Meanwhile, make the raspberry sauce: In a blender or food processor, combine raspberries, banana, jam and lemon juice; purée until smooth. Strain to remove seeds.

4. Serve soufflé hot, drizzled with raspberry sauce.

BARB'S NUTRITION NOTE
Would you like to include a favorite dessert recipe in your meals? To estimate America's Exchanges or Canada's Choices for a recipe serving, use the worksheets on pages 18–29. There you will find lists of dessert ingredients and the Exchanges or Choices contained in common amounts (usually 1 cup/250 mL), as well as instructions on how to use the worksheets. To calculate America's Exchanges, use the worksheet on page 19; to calculate Canada's Choices, use the worksheet on page 25.

Melon Balls with Warm Ginger Sauce

MAKES 12 SERVINGS

TIP

If you don't have a melon baller, use a small spoon to scoop melon flesh, or cut flesh into small cubes.

MAKE AHEAD

Make sauce in advance and store, covered, in refrigerator for up to 2 days; reheat before serving.

1	small ripe honeydew melon	1
2	small ripe cantaloupes	2
Sauce		
2 cups	orange juice	500 mL
2 tbsp	minced gingerroot or ½ tsp (2 mL) ground ginger	25 mL
1 tbsp	raspberry or red wine vinegar	15 mL
1 tsp	liquid honey	5 mL
½ tsp	lemon juice	2 mL
	Fresh mint leaves	

1. Cut melons in half and discard seeds. With a melon baller, scoop out flesh. Divide melon balls among 12 individual dessert dishes.

2. In a saucepan, combine orange juice, ginger, vinegar, honey and lemon juice. Bring to a boil; cook until reduced to ½ cup (125 mL). Spoon warm sauce over melon balls and serve garnished with mint leaves.

NUTRIENTS PER SERVING	
Calories	77
Carbohydrate	19 g
Fiber	1 g
Protein	1 g
Fat, total	0 g
Fat, saturated	0 g
Cholesterol	0 mg
Sodium	16 mg

AMERICA'S EXCHANGES	CANADA'S CHOICES
1 Fruit	1 Carbohydrate

Rhubarb Bread Pudding

MAKES 6 SERVINGS

An interesting twist to an old favorite. Cold leftovers are good too!

TIP

Leftovers can be stored in an airtight container in the fridge for up to 3 days or in the freezer for up to 3 months.

VARIATION

Try making this pudding with another fruit, such as frozen berries or peaches.

BARB'S NUTRITION NOTE

If substituting frozen fruit for rhubarb in this recipe, be sure to choose those that do not contain added sugar. Add 1 Free Food or Extra per serving.

■ Preheat oven to 350°F (180°C)
■ 8-inch (2 L) square baking dish, greased

2 cups	chopped fresh or frozen rhubarb, thawed	500 mL
3 cups	torn stale white and whole wheat bread	750 mL
1	can (14 oz/385 mL) evaporated milk	1
2	eggs	2
¼ cup	granulated sugar	50 mL
1 tsp	vanilla	5 mL
1 tsp	ground cinnamon	5 mL
	Grated zest of 1 orange	

1. Place rhubarb in prepared baking dish and cover with bread pieces.

2. In a medium bowl, beat evaporated milk, eggs, sugar, vanilla, cinnamon and orange zest. Pour over bread. Let stand for 10 minutes.

3. Bake in preheated oven for 40 to 45 minutes or until a tester inserted in the center comes out clean. Serve warm.

NUTRIENTS PER SERVING	
Calories	180
Carbohydrate	27 g
Fiber	2 g
Protein	9 g
Fat, total	4 g
Fat, saturated	2 g
Cholesterol	67 mg
Sodium	197 mg

AMERICA'S EXCHANGES	
½	Starch
1	Other Carbohydrates
½	Reduced-Fat Milk

CANADA'S CHOICES	
2	Carbohydrate
½	Meat and Alternatives

Cocoa Roll with Creamy Cheese and Berries

MAKES 10 SERVINGS

TIPS

Decorate roll with fresh berries.

Substitute other fresh berries of your choice.

BARB'S NUTRITION NOTES

Berry garnishes are too good to leave on the plate. Five strawberries or 20 small raspberries (both without sugar) count as 1 Free Food or Extra.

The quantity of confectioner's sugar to be sprinkled on the cake (Step 4) is not specified in this recipe, so it's excluded from the nutrients per serving and the Exchanges and Choices. You'll need about 1½ tbsp (22 mL) confectioner's sugar in total, which will add less than 2 grams of carbohydrate per serving.

- Preheat oven to 325°F (160°C)
- Jelly-roll pan, lined with parchment paper and sprayed with vegetable spray

5	egg whites	5
⅛ tsp	cream of tartar	0.5 mL
⅔ cup	granulated sugar	150 mL
½ cup	cake and pastry flour	125 mL
4 tsp	unsweetened cocoa powder	20 mL
1½ tsp	vanilla	7 mL
	Confectioner's (icing) sugar	

Filling

1¼ cups	ricotta cheese	300 mL
¼ cup	light sour cream	50 mL
3 tbsp	confectioner's (icing) sugar	45 mL
1¼ cups	sliced strawberries and/or blueberries	300 mL

1. In a medium bowl, beat egg whites and cream of tartar until soft peaks form. Gradually beat in ⅓ cup (75 mL) of sugar until stiff peaks form.

2. Sift together remaining sugar, flour and cocoa; sift over egg whites and fold in gently along with vanilla. Do not overmix. Pour onto prepared pan and spread evenly. Bake for 15 to 20 minutes or until top springs back when lightly touched.

NUTRIENTS PER SERVING	
Calories	157
Carbohydrate	25 g
Fiber	1 g
Protein	6 g
Fat, total	4 g
Fat, saturated	2 g
Cholesterol	13 mg
Sodium	67 mg

AMERICA'S EXCHANGES	
½	Starch
1	Other Carbohydrates
1	Lean Meat

CANADA'S CHOICES	
1½	Carbohydrate
1	Meat and Alternatives

3. *Filling:* In a bowl or food processor, mix together cheese, sour cream and confectioner's sugar until smooth. Fold in berries. Set aside.

4. Sprinkle cake lightly with confectioner's sugar. Carefully invert onto surface sprinkled with confectioner's sugar. Carefully remove parchment paper. Spread filling over cake and roll up. Place on serving dish. Sprinkle with confectioner's sugar.

BARB'S NUTRITION NOTE
Wheat flour contains a protein called gluten. In bread-making, the kneading process "develops" the gluten, allowing the dough to become stretchy, easy to handle and strong enough to trap the carbon dioxide generated by the yeast when it rises. High-gluten flour is desirable for bread-making, but cake and pastry flour, which is low in gluten, is required for pastry and delicate cakes.

All-purpose flour has an intermediate gluten level and, as its name implies, can be used for most baked goods. However, yeast doughs made with all-purpose flour may not rise as much, and pastry and delicate cakes may be less tender.

Too much stirring or handling of any batter or dough will develop the gluten and result in a less tender end product. For this reason, baking recipes often caution against overmixing.

Chocolate Quesadillas

This recipe might sound a bit over the top, but trust me — it's not! If you have access to homemade or freshly made flour tortillas, by all means use them. Otherwise, store-bought flour tortillas will work just fine. Quesadillas are usually filled with cheese, but I find that chocolate makes a fine substitute.

TIP

You can double or triple this recipe.

BARB'S NUTRITION NOTE

Don't forget that the nutrients per serving, and Exchanges and Choices, are based on ½ quesadilla, not a whole one.

½ cup	chopped pecans	125 mL
1 tbsp	granulated sugar	15 mL
Pinch	salt	Pinch
2	8-inch (20 cm) flour tortillas	2
3 oz	bittersweet or semisweet chocolate, chopped	90 g
¼ cup	sour cream	50 mL
2 tsp	packed light brown sugar	10 mL

1. In a large nonstick skillet over medium-high heat, cook pecans, granulated sugar and salt, stirring with a wooden spoon, for 2 to 4 minutes or until pecans are toasted and sugar is melted and caramelized on nuts. If sugar or nuts start to burn, reduce heat. Transfer to a plate or baking sheet and let cool.

2. In a clean large nonstick skillet over medium-high heat, heat one of the tortillas until warm. Leaving tortilla in skillet, arrange half of the chocolate on one half of tortilla; fold opposite half over chocolate to cover. Cook quesadilla, turning once, for 3 to 4 minutes or until golden brown on both sides and chocolate is melted. Set aside on a plate. Repeat with remaining tortilla and chocolate.

3. In a small bowl, stir sour cream with brown sugar until smooth. Dollop over top of each quesadilla. Sprinkle candied pecans over sour cream mixture. Serve immediately.

NUTRIENTS PER SERVING	
Calories	346
Carbohydrate	35 g
Fiber	3 g
Protein	5 g
Fat, total	21 g
Fat, saturated	7 g
Cholesterol	7 mg
Sodium	133 mg

AMERICA'S EXCHANGES	
1	Starch
1	Other Carbohydrates
4	Fat
1	Free Food

CANADA'S CHOICES	
2	Carbohydrate
4	Fat

Dessert Nachos

MAKES 8 SERVINGS

For a quick and festive dessert that children love, make a platter of these cinnamon-sugar tortilla chips with fruit salsa and low-fat yogurt for dipping. It won't last very long! A great way to enjoy fruit, yogurt and whole grains.

TIP

Pick fruits of your choice to make the 4 cups (1 L) salsa, or ask your children what they would like. Fresh or canned pineapple, fresh or frozen mango, fresh strawberries, kiwi, cantaloupe and watermelon all work well. Cut your chosen fruits into small dice and combine in a bowl.

▓ Preheat oven to 450°F (230°C)
▓ Baking sheets, lightly greased

½ cup	granulated sugar	125 mL
3 tbsp	ground cinnamon	45 mL
4	10-inch (25 cm) whole wheat flour tortillas	4
4 cups	fresh fruit salsa (see tip, at left)	1 L
2 cups	low-fat fruit-flavored yogurt	500 mL

1. On a large flat plate, mix sugar and cinnamon. Dip each tortilla in water. Shake off the excess and dip one side into the sugar and cinnamon mixture. Stack tortillas on top of each other as they are dipped. When completed, cut the stack into 8 triangular wedges.

2. Spread tortilla wedges in a single layer on prepared baking sheets, without overlapping, and bake in batches in preheated oven for 4 to 5 minutes per tray or until golden and crisp.

3. Place on a large platter with a bowl of fruit salsa and another of yogurt.

NUTRIENTS PER SERVING	
Calories	270
Carbohydrate	52 g
Fiber	4 g
Protein	7 g
Fat, total	4 g
Fat, saturated	1 g
Cholesterol	3 mg
Sodium	194 mg

AMERICA'S EXCHANGES	
1½	Starch
1	Fruit
1	Other Carbohydrates
1	Fat

CANADA'S CHOICES	
3	Carbohydrate
1	Fat

Chocolate Fondue

**MAKES ABOUT
1½ CUPS (375 ML)
CHOCOLATE FONDUE
(3 TBSP/45 ML
PER SERVING)**

VARIATION

For a milder chocolate flavor, replace the semisweet with milk chocolate. Children tend to prefer milk chocolate.

**BARB'S
NUTRITION NOTE**

Remember that the nutrients per serving, and Exchanges and Choices, are for the fondue mixture only. You will need to count the fruit separately: ½ cup (125 mL) sliced fruit will add 1 Fruit Exchange or Carbohydrate Choice.

■ Fondue pot

8 oz	semisweet chocolate, chopped	250 g
½ cup	evaporated milk or whipping (35%) cream	125 mL
	A selection of chopped fruits for dipping (bananas, strawberries, apples, pears, etc.)	

1. In fondue pot, over low heat, heat chocolate and evaporated milk, stirring with a wooden spatula, until chocolate has melted, about 5 minutes. Place fondue pot over tabletop burner.

2. Arrange fruit in a serving dish and serve with fondue.

NUTRIENTS PER SERVING	
Calories	150
Carbohydrate	20 g
Fiber	2 g
Protein	2 g
Fat, total	9 g
Fat, saturated	5 g
Cholesterol	1 mg
Sodium	21 mg

AMERICA'S EXCHANGES	
1	Other Carbohydrates
2	Fat
1	Free Food

CANADA'S CHOICES	
1	Carbohydrate
2	Fat
1	Extra

Balsamic Strawberry Sauce

MAKES ABOUT 2½ CUPS (625 ML) (¼ CUP/50 ML PER SERVING)

This is the easiest dessert sauce ever! It works well with ripe berries but also offers a tasty solution for unripe berries that are lacking in color and taste. Delicious!

VARIATION

This well-known Italian sauce is traditionally served with a dash of freshly ground black pepper on top. It can also be prepared without cooking. An hour before serving, place sliced berries in a bowl and add sugar. Just before serving, add the balsamic vinegar.

4 cups	sliced hulled strawberries	1 L
3 tbsp	granulated sugar	45 mL
¼ cup	balsamic vinegar	50 mL

1. In a medium saucepan, over medium heat, cook strawberries and sugar for 2 minutes or until sugar melts and starts to form a sauce. Add balsamic vinegar; cook for 2 minutes. Remove from heat.

2. Serve warm, or cover and refrigerate to serve cold.

Grilled Fruit

One of the simplest desserts for barbecue night is grilled fruit. Once the main meal has been cooked, clean the grill to remove any residue. Cut fruit into long pieces or chunks and skewer. Grill for a few minutes on each side, just until heated through. Serve drizzled with honey or your favorite dessert sauce over frozen yogurt. Crowd pleasers are pineapple, mango, watermelon, apple and pear.

NUTRIENTS PER SERVING	
Calories	38
Carbohydrate	9 g
Fiber	1 g
Protein	0 g
Fat, total	0 g
Fat, saturated	0 g
Cholesterol	0 mg
Sodium	2 mg

AMERICA'S EXCHANGES	
½	Fruit

CANADA'S CHOICES	
½	Carbohydrate

Whipped Cream and Yogurt Topping

**MAKES ABOUT
1½ CUPS (375 ML)
(3 TBSP/45 ML
PER SERVING)**

This is Barb's multipurpose dessert topping.

**BARB'S
NUTRITION NOTE**

This whipped cream look-alike dresses up fruit and plain cakes.

½ cup	whipping (35%) cream	125 mL
1 tbsp	granulated sugar	15 mL
½ tsp	vanilla	2 mL
½ cup	low-fat plain yogurt	125 mL

1. Beat ½ cup (125 mL) whipping (35%) cream until thick. Add 1 tbsp (15 mL) granulated sugar and ½ tsp (2 mL) vanilla; beat until stiff peaks form. Gently fold in ½ cup (125 mL) low-fat plain yogurt until thoroughly combined.

NUTRIENTS PER SERVING	
Calories	65
Carbohydrate	3 g
Fiber	0 g
Protein	1 g
Fat, total	5 g
Fat, saturated	3 g
Cholesterol	20 mg
Sodium	16 mg

AMERICA'S EXCHANGES	
1	Fat
1	Free Food

CANADA'S CHOICES	
1	Fat
1	Extra

Frozen, Chilled and Other Desserts

Honey Vanilla Ice Cream with Hot Spiced Apples

MAKES 8 SERVINGS

TIP

Don't worry if you don't have an ice cream maker. Pour chilled ice cream mixture into a loaf pan lined with plastic wrap and freeze until solid. Break into small pieces; in a food processor, pulse on and off until smooth. Store in freezer until ready to serve.

BARB'S NUTRITION NOTE

A serving of the ice cream by itself counts as ½ Other Carbohydrate Exchange or Carbohydrate Choice plus 1 Fat Exchange or Choice.

The spiced apples add 1 Fruit Exchange or Carbohydrate Choice.

Ice Cream

2 cups	2% milk	500 mL
3 tbsp	liquid honey	45 mL
⅛ tsp	vanilla	0.5 mL
6	egg yolks	6

Spiced Apple Mixture

3	apples	3
2 cups	apple juice	500 mL
¼ tsp	cinnamon	1 mL
⅛ tsp	ground ginger	0.5 mL
⅛ tsp	nutmeg	0.5 mL
2 tbsp	cornstarch	25 mL
1 tbsp	water	15 mL

1. *Ice Cream:* In a saucepan bring milk, honey and vanilla to a boil; reduce heat to low. In a bowl, beat egg yolks. Whisk a little of the hot milk into yolk mixture, then pour back into remaining milk. Whisk constantly over low heat until mixture is thick enough to coat a spoon; do not boil. Remove from heat. Chill. In an ice cream maker, freeze according to manufacturer's directions.

2. *Spiced Apple Mixture:* Peel, core and thinly slice the apples. Put in a saucepan along with apple juice, cinnamon, ginger and nutmeg. Bring to a boil, reduce heat and simmer 5 minutes. Dissolve cornstarch in water; stir into simmering apple mixture and cook 1 minute longer or until thickened. Remove from heat. Cool slightly. Serve over ice cream.

NUTRIENTS PER SERVING	
Calories	162
Carbohydrate	26 g
Fiber	1 g
Protein	4 g
Fat, total	5 g
Fat, saturated	2 g
Cholesterol	147 mg
Sodium	38 mg

AMERICA'S EXCHANGES	
1	Fruit
½	Other Carbohydrates
1	Fat

CANADA'S CHOICES	
1½	Carbohydrate
1	Fat

Mocha Ice Cream

MAKES 6 SERVINGS

TIP
Omit coffee if desired.

2 cups	2% milk	500 mL
1	egg	1
½ cup	granulated sugar	125 mL
2 tbsp	sifted unsweetened cocoa powder	25 mL
1 tsp	instant coffee granules	5 mL

1. In a saucepan, heat 1 cup (250 mL) of the milk just until bubbles form around edge of pan.

2. Meanwhile, in a small bowl, beat egg with sugar until combined; stir in half of the warm milk. Pour egg mixture back into saucepan; stir in cocoa and coffee granules. Cook, stirring, on low heat for 4 minutes or until slightly thickened. (Do not let boil or egg will curdle.) Let cool completely.

3. Stir in remaining milk. Pour into ice cream machine and freeze according to manufacturer's instructions. (Or pour into cake pan and freeze until nearly solid. Chop into chunks and beat with electric mixer or process in food processor until smooth. Freeze again until solid.)

NUTRIENTS PER SERVING	
Calories	121
Carbohydrate	22 g
Fiber	1 g
Protein	4 g
Fat, total	3 g
Fat, saturated	1 g
Cholesterol	37 mg
Sodium	51 mg

AMERICA'S EXCHANGES	
1	Other Carbohydrates
½	Reduced-Fat Milk

CANADA'S CHOICES	
1½	Carbohydrate
½	Fat

Frozen Orange Cream

MAKES 4 SERVINGS

TIP

If don't have an ice cream maker, pour into a baking dish and freeze until solid. Break into small pieces; in a food processor, pulse on and off until smooth. Store in freezer until ready to serve.

1 tbsp	grated orange zest	15 mL
1⅓ cups	orange juice	325 mL
⅔ cup	skim milk	150 mL

1. In a food processor or blender, purée orange zest, orange juice and milk.
2. In an ice cream maker, freeze according to manufacturer's directions.

BARB'S NUTRITION NOTE

We are all familiar with the expression "food for thought." It's equally important to give thought for food — not just to the nutrient values and Exchanges or Choices, but also to the experience of eating. Unfortunately, many meals today have become "refueling stops" on the run (both at and away from home), with little time to socialize and even less time to enjoy what we've chosen. Various strategies can help us be more thoughtful about what we eat:

Plan meals at least a day in advance, and make sure you have all the ingredients you need.

Involve other family members in planning and preparing meals.

When ordering from a menu, ask how foods are prepared, what comes with them and possible substitutions. At a buffet, survey everything before making your choices.

At home, you are able to serve yourself appropriate portions. Restaurant servings are often larger. Do not feel obliged to eat everything on your plate.

NUTRIENTS PER SERVING	
Calories	52
Carbohydrate	11 g
Fiber	0 g
Protein	2 g
Fat, total	0 g
Fat, saturated	0 g
Cholesterol	1 mg
Sodium	22 mg

AMERICA'S EXCHANGES	CANADA'S CHOICES
½ Fruit	1 Carbohydrate

Fresh Fruit Sorbet

2½ cups	chopped peeled soft fresh fruit (bananas, peaches, strawberries, etc.)	625 mL

1. Spread fruit on baking sheet and freeze. Purée frozen fruit in food processor and serve immediately.

BARB'S NUTRITION NOTE
The first record of sorbet dates from 60 AD, when Nero served his guests a sorbet of crushed fruit, honey and snow. Is sherbet the same as sorbet? It depends who you ask. They both contain fruit and sugar. Sherbets usually contain additional ingredients, such as milk or eggs; sorbets generally do not.

NUTRIENTS PER SERVING	
Calories	52
Carbohydrate	13 g
Fiber	2 g
Protein	1 g
Fat, total	0 g
Fat, saturated	0 g
Cholesterol	0 mg
Sodium	1 mg

AMERICA'S EXCHANGES	
1	Fruit

CANADA'S CHOICES	
1	Carbohydrate

Pineapple Lime Sorbet

MAKES 4 SERVINGS

**BARB'S
NUTRITION NOTE**
To make 1¼ cups (300 mL) puréed pineapple, you will need a fresh pineapple weighing about 1½ lbs (750 g). Peel and core it and cut it into chunks, then blend at medium speed until smooth. You can also use pineapple canned in juice. About 1¾ cups (425 mL) drained canned crushed pineapple or pineapple chunks will make 1¼ cups (300 mL) purée.

1¼ cups	pineapple purée	300 mL
2 tsp	grated lime or lemon zest	10 mL
¾ cup	freshly squeezed lime or lemon juice	175 mL
¼ cup	water	50 mL
	Granulated sugar to taste (optional)	
	Thin slices lime or lemon	

1. In a bowl, stir together pineapple purée, lime zest and juice, water and, if desired, sugar.
2. In an ice cream maker, freeze according to manufacturer's directions.
3. Divide among 4 individual dessert dishes. Serve garnished with thin slices of lime.

BARB'S NUTRITION NOTE

Remember that nutrients per serving and Exchanges and Choices do not include optional ingredients. If you want to add sugar, 1 tbsp (15 mL) of sugar added to this recipe will increase the carbohydrate by 3 grams per serving. (Count as a Free Food or Extra.)

Instead of sugar, you could also use a no-calorie (artificial) sweetener, which would add neither carbohydrate nor calories. One tablespoon (15 mL) of a "measures like sugar" product, or 1½ sachets of a product used to sweeten beverages, is equivalent to 1 tbsp (15 mL) of sugar.

NUTRIENTS PER SERVING	
Calories	60
Carbohydrate	17 g
Fiber	1 g
Protein	1 g
Fat, total	0 g
Fat, saturated	0 g
Cholesterol	0 mg
Sodium	2 mg

AMERICA'S EXCHANGES	
1	Fruit

CANADA'S CHOICES	
1	Carbohydrate

Strawberry Orange Buttermilk Sorbet

MAKES 4 SERVINGS

TIP

To make soured milk, place 2 tsp (10 mL) lemon juice or vinegar in measuring cup; pour in milk to 1 cup (250 mL) level and let stand for 10 minutes, then stir.

MAKE AHEAD

Although sorbets are best prepared just before eating so they do not crystallize, they can be prepared up to 2 days in advance.

1 cup	buttermilk or soured milk	250 mL
½ cup	puréed strawberries	125 mL
¼ cup	water	50 mL
¼ cup	liquid honey	50 mL
½ tsp	grated orange zest	2 mL
1 tbsp	freshly squeezed orange juice	15 mL

1. In a bowl, mix together buttermilk, strawberries, water, honey, orange zest and juice.

2. Freeze in ice cream machine according to manufacturer's directions. (Or pour into cake pan and freeze until nearly solid. Chop into chunks and beat with electric mixer or process in food processor until smooth. Freeze again until solid.)

NUTRIENTS PER SERVING	
Calories	99
Carbohydrate	23 g
Fiber	1 g
Protein	2 g
Fat, total	1 g
Fat, saturated	0 g
Cholesterol	2 mg
Sodium	66 mg

AMERICA'S EXCHANGES	
1½	Other Carbohydrates

CANADA'S CHOICES	
1½	Carbohydrate

Tulip Cookies with Fruit Sorbet

**MAKES 20 COOKIES
(1 COOKIE PER
SERVING)**

TIPS

To save time, make the
tulip cups assembly-line
fashion. Use 2 baking
sheets; while one tray
bakes, spread the batter
on the next tray, then
put it in the oven just as
you remove the last batch.

The cookies must be
shaped while they are
warm, so work quickly.
If cookie cools and is
too firm to shape, return
to oven for 30 seconds
or until softened.

BARB'S
NUTRITION NOTE

The nutrients per serving,
Exchanges and Choices
do not include the sorbet
or fruit. Count 1/4 cup
(50 mL) of Raspberry Ice
(opposite) or commercial
sherbet as an additional
1/2 Fruit Exchange or
1/2 Carbohydrate Choice.

NUTRIENTS PER SERVING	
Calories	36
Carbohydrate	7 g
Fiber	0 g
Protein	1 g
Fat, total	0 g
Fat, saturated	0 g
Cholesterol	10 mg
Sodium	27 mg

- Preheat oven to 350°F (180°C)
- Baking sheet, sprayed with baking spray

3/4 cup	buttermilk	175 mL
1	egg	1
6 tbsp	granulated sugar	90 mL
1/3 cup	whole wheat flour	75 mL
1/3 cup	all-purpose flour	75 mL
1/8 tsp	cinnamon	0.5 mL
1/8 tsp	salt	0.5 mL
	Raspberry or mango sorbet	
	Fresh raspberries or sliced ripe mango	

1. In a bowl, stir together buttermilk, egg, sugar, whole wheat flour, flour, cinnamon and salt until smooth. Let batter rest for 20 minutes.

2. Place 1 tbsp (15 mL) batter at one end of prepared baking sheet. With the back of a spoon, spread to form a circle 5 inches (12 cm) in diameter. Repeat with another 1 tbsp (15 mL) batter on other half of baking sheet. Bake for 9 to 11 minutes or until golden. With a spatula, remove hot cookies from baking sheet and place each over bottom of a glass, pressing gently to create fluted effect. Cool completely on glass.

3. Repeat with remaining batter, respraying baking sheet between batches.

4. Serve each tulip cup with a small scoop of sorbet, garnished with fresh fruit.

AMERICA'S EXCHANGES	
1/2	Other Carbohydrates

CANADA'S CHOICES	
1/2	Carbohydrate

Raspberry Ice with Fresh Strawberries

MAKES 6 SERVINGS

4½ cups	fresh raspberries	1.125 L
	Honey to taste	
6 tbsp	low-fat yogurt (optional)	90 mL
6	large fresh strawberries	6
	Fresh mint leaves	

1. In a blender or food processor, purée raspberries. Strain to remove seeds. Stir in honey to taste. In an ice cream maker, freeze according to manufacturer's directions.

2. Divide among 6 individual dessert dishes. Spoon 1 tbsp (15 mL) yogurt on top of each serving, if desired. Garnish each serving with a strawberry and mint leaves.

BARB'S NUTRITION NOTE

If you add honey to this recipe, remember that 1 tbsp (15 mL) will contribute 17 grams of carbohydrate, equivalent to 1 Free Food or Extra per serving. A single tablespoon (15 mL) of low-fat yogurt per serving supplies negligible carbohydrate and fat.

BARB'S NUTRITION NOTE

For help in planning your meals, ask your doctor to refer you to a diabetes education center or a dietitian. Your local public health unit and hospitals may also have referral services. On the Internet, look for the "find a dietitian" feature at www.eatright.org (in the U.S.) or www.dietitians.ca (in Canada).

NUTRIENTS PER SERVING	
Calories	51
Carbohydrate	12 g
Fiber	5 g
Protein	1 g
Fat, total	1 g
Fat, saturated	0 g
Cholesterol	0 mg
Sodium	0 mg

AMERICA'S EXCHANGES		CANADA'S CHOICES	
1	Fruit	½	Carbohydrate

Frozen Jamoca Mousse

MAKES 10 SERVINGS

TIPS

Buy extra-smooth ricotta for the smoothest mousse.

If don't have an ice cream maker, pour into a baking dish and freeze until solid. Break into small pieces; in a food processor, pulse on and off until smooth. Store in freezer until ready to serve.

1 cup	5% ricotta cheese	250 mL
2 cups	low-fat yogurt	500 mL
1/2 cup	fructose	125 mL
4 tsp	unsweetened cocoa powder	20 mL
2 tsp	instant coffee granules	10 mL
1 tsp	vanilla	5 mL

1. In a food processor or blender, purée ricotta, yogurt, fructose, cocoa, coffee granules and vanilla until smooth.

2. In an ice cream maker, freeze according to manufacturer's directions.

BARB'S NUTRITION NOTE

Fructose is a sugar that occurs naturally in small amounts in many foods. It can also be refined into a pure form. Gram for gram, it is sweeter than ordinary sugar (sucrose), but it does not raise blood sugar as much. It is not, however, a sugar substitute or Free Food/Extra. As with ordinary sugar, 1 tbsp (15 mL) counts as an Other Carbohydrate Exchange or Carbohydrate Choice. Look for it in specialty grocery stores and some health food stores.

NUTRIENTS PER SERVING	
Calories	98
Carbohydrate	14 g
Fiber	0 g
Protein	6 g
Fat, total	2 g
Fat, saturated	1 g
Cholesterol	7 mg
Sodium	66 mg

AMERICA'S EXCHANGES	
1	Other Carbohydrates
1/2	Lean Meat

CANADA'S CHOICES	
1	Carbohydrate
1/2	Meat and Alternatives

Banana-Strawberry Mousse

MAKES 8 SERVINGS

TIP

For attractive orange segments, peel a whole orange with a sharp knife, removing zest, pith and membrane; cut on both sides of dividing membranes to release segments.

BARB'S NUTRITION NOTE

Many garnishes are a feast for the eyes without adding significant carbohydrate. Count 2 orange segments or 4 strawberries as a Free Food or Extra. For most fruits, ¼ cup (50 mL) sliced also counts as a Free Food or Extra.

3	small ripe bananas	3
1 cup	orange juice	250 mL
1 cup	strawberries	250 mL
6 tbsp	lemon juice	90 mL
½ cup	cold water	125 mL
1	package (1 tbsp/7 g) gelatin	1
	Orange segments or sliced strawberries	

1. In a blender, combine bananas, orange juice, strawberries and lemon juice; purée until smooth. Put water in a small saucepan; sprinkle with gelatin. Let stand for 1 minute. Heat gently, stirring until gelatin dissolves. With motor running, pour hot gelatin through blender feed tube; purée until smooth. Divide among 8 individual dessert dishes or champagne coupes.

2. Chill for 2 hours. Serve garnished with orange segments or sliced strawberries.

NUTRIENTS PER SERVING	
Calories	60
Carbohydrate	14 g
Fiber	1 g
Protein	2 g
Fat, total	0 g
Fat, saturated	0 g
Cholesterol	0 mg
Sodium	3 mg

AMERICA'S EXCHANGES		CANADA'S CHOICES	
1	Fruit	1	Carbohydrate

Sunshine Lemon Mousse

MAKES 10 SERVINGS

This recipe contains raw eggs. If the food safety of raw eggs is a concern for you, use pasteurized eggs. Many grocery stores now carry pasteurized eggs in their shells.

BARB'S NUTRITION NOTE

If you don't have a microwave, in Step 1 pour ¼ cup (50 mL) boiling (not cold) water into a measuring cup. Sprinkle gelatin on top and stir. If the gelatin is not completely dissolved after 2 minutes, set the measuring cup in a saucepan of warm water over low heat until the remaining gelatin particles dissolve.

■ Stand mixer

1	envelope (¼ oz/7 g) unflavored gelatin	1
¼ cup	cold water	50 mL
3	egg yolks	3
¾ cup	granulated sugar, divided	175 mL
2 tsp	grated lemon zest	10 mL
⅓ cup	freshly squeezed lemon juice	75 mL
1 cup	cold whipping (35%) cream	250 mL
3	egg whites, at room temperature	3

Topping

½ cup	cold whipping (35%) cream	125 mL
1 tsp	confectioner's (icing) sugar, sifted	5 mL
1	lemon, cut lengthwise into halves and thinly sliced (optional)	1

1. In a small microwave-safe bowl, sprinkle gelatin over water and let soften for 5 minutes. Microwave on High for 10 seconds. Stir, then heat for 5 seconds. The gelatin should be melted. If it isn't, heat for 5 seconds more. Stir again and set aside.

2. Place egg yolks and ½ cup (250 mL) of the sugar in the mixer bowl. Attach the whip and mixer bowl to the mixer. Set to Speed 6 and beat until thick and pale yellow. Reduce speed to Stir and mix in dissolved gelatin and lemon zest and juice until incorporated. Transfer to a large bowl. Clean the mixer bowl and whip.

NUTRIENTS PER SERVING	
Calories	203
Carbohydrate	17 g
Fiber	0 g
Protein	3 g
Fat, total	14 g
Fat, saturated	8 g
Cholesterol	103 mg
Sodium	33 mg

AMERICA'S EXCHANGES	
1	Other Carbohydrates
3	Fat

CANADA'S CHOICES	
1	Carbohydrate
3	Fat

BARB'S NUTRITION NOTE

By skipping the topping, you can reduce the Fat Exchanges or Choices from 3 to 2. This dessert may then fit more easily into your meal plan.

3. Place whipping cream in the mixer bowl. Attach the whip and mixer bowl to the mixer. Set to Speed 8 and beat until firm. Using a large rubber spatula, gently fold into the yolk mixture. Clean the mixer bowl and whip.

4. Place egg whites in the mixer bowl. Attach the whip and mixer bowl to the mixer. Set to Speed 4 and beat until foamy. Increase to Speed 8 and beat until soft peaks form. Beat in the remaining $1/4$ cup (50 mL) sugar, in 2 additions, and beat until stiff, glossy peaks form. Using a large rubber spatula, gently fold into yolk mixture until no trace of white remains.

5. Spoon mousse into 10 dessert dishes. Cover tightly and refrigerate for at least 3 hours or overnight.

6. *Topping:* Place whipping cream in a clean mixer bowl. Attach the whip and mixer bowl to the mixer. Set to Speed 8 and beat until it starts to thicken, then sprinkle with confectioner's sugar and beat until firm. Top each serving with a dollop of cream and a lemon slice, if using.

BARB'S NUTRITION NOTE

As you prepare the recipes in this book, you will become familiar with the appropriate portion sizes for different types of desserts and the approximate Exchanges or Choices assigned to them. Use this knowledge to help you choose wisely when you're eating away from home.

Mango Raspberry Fool

MAKES 10 SERVINGS

MAKE AHEAD

Store, wrapped in plastic wrap, in the refrigerator for up to 2 days.

BARB'S NUTRITION NOTES

If your mixer doesn't have a fruit/vegetable strainer attachment, process the chopped mango in a blender or food processor until smooth and then strain, reserving juice and discarding solids.

If you don't have a microwave, in Step 2 sprinkle gelatin over water in a small glass bowl. Let stand for 5 minutes, then set in a saucepan of warm water over low heat until the gelatin particles dissolve.

One-quarter cup (50 mL) rum spikes the flavor but, divided among 10 servings, adds negligible alcohol.

- Stand mixer

4	mangos, peeled and chopped	4
⅔ cup	granulated sugar	150 mL
¼ cup	freshly squeezed lime juice	50 mL
1 tsp	unflavored gelatin	5 mL
1 tbsp	cold water	15 mL
1½ cups	cold whipping (35%) cream	375 mL
¼ cup	light rum (optional)	50 mL
1½ cups	fresh raspberries	375 mL
	Additional fresh raspberries	

1. Attach the fruit/vegetable strainer to the mixer. Set to Speed 4 and run mangoes through the strainer into a large bowl, with another bowl to catch the solids. Discard solids. You should have about 2 cups (500 mL) purée. Stir in sugar and lime juice.

2. In a small microwave-safe bowl, sprinkle gelatin over water and let soften for 5 minutes. Microwave on High for 10 seconds. Stir, then heat for 5 seconds. The gelatin should be melted. If it isn't, heat for 5 seconds more. Stir again and add to mango purée.

3. Place whipping cream in the mixer bowl. Attach the whip and mixer bowl to the mixer. Set to Speed 8 and beat until firm. Reduce speed to Stir and mix in rum, if using. Using a large rubber spatula, thoroughly fold in mango purée. Fold in raspberries and spoon into 10 serving dishes. Cover and refrigerate for at least 3 hours or overnight. Serve cold, garnished with raspberries.

NUTRIENTS PER SERVING	
Calories	218
Carbohydrate	27 g
Fiber	2 g
Protein	1 g
Fat, total	13 g
Fat, saturated	8 g
Cholesterol	46 mg
Sodium	15 mg

AMERICA'S EXCHANGES	
1	Fruit
1	Other Carbohydrates
2½	Fat

CANADA'S CHOICES	
1½	Carbohydrate
2½	Fat

Orange Cappuccino Pudding Cake

MAKES 10 SERVINGS

TIPS
Use a flavored coffee mix powder, like Irish cream or vanilla, or a cappuccino mix.

Pudding cakes are fantastic because they give you the added bonus of a low-fat sauce.

MAKE AHEAD
Best served right out of the oven, but can be reheated in microwave for similar texture.

- Preheat oven to 350°F (180°C)
- 8-inch square (2 L) baking dish, sprayed with vegetable spray

1 cup	all-purpose flour	250 mL
1 cup	packed brown sugar	250 mL
2 tsp	baking powder	10 mL
2 tsp	grated orange zest	10 mL
1/2 cup	orange juice	125 mL
2 tbsp	vegetable oil	25 mL
1	egg	1
2 tsp	vanilla	10 mL
1/4 cup	semisweet chocolate chips	50 mL
1/3 cup	granulated sugar	75 mL
1/4 cup	instant coffee mix powder or hot chocolate mix	50 mL
1/4 cup	unsweetened cocoa powder	50 mL

1. In a bowl, stir together flour, brown sugar and baking powder. In a separate bowl, whisk together orange zest, orange juice, oil, egg and vanilla. Add the wet ingredients to the dry, blending just until mixed. Batter will be thick. Pour into prepared pan. Sprinkle chocolate chips over top.

2. In a bowl, whisk together $1\frac{1}{4}$ cups (300 mL) hot water, sugar, coffee mix and cocoa. Pour carefully over cake batter. Bake 35 minutes or until cake springs back when touched lightly in center. Serve warm; spoon cake and underlying sauce into individual dessert dishes.

NUTRIENTS PER SERVING	
Calories	241
Carbohydrate	47 g
Fiber	1 g
Protein	3 g
Fat, total	6 g
Fat, saturated	1 g
Cholesterol	19 mg
Sodium	101 mg

AMERICA'S EXCHANGES	
1/2	Starch
2 1/2	Other Carbohydrates
1	Fat

CANADA'S CHOICES	
3	Carbohydrate
1	Fat

Indian-Style Rice Pudding

MAKES 10 SERVINGS

Rice pudding is a comfort-food favorite that never seems to go out of style. This version uses brown rice and is enhanced with spices, dried fruits and nuts.

TIPS

For 1 cup (250 mL) cooked brown rice, cook ⅓ cup (75 mL) rice with ⅔ cup (150 mL) water.

Freshly grated nutmeg has more aroma and flavor than ground. If you only have ground, it is fine to use it, but try grinding fresh sometime — you will really taste and smell the difference.

■ Preheat oven to 350°F (180°C)
■ Glass baking dish with cover
■ Baking sheet

1 cup	cooked brown rice	250 mL
1	can (14 oz/398 mL) light coconut milk	1
3 cups	milk	750 mL
½ cup	raisins	125 mL
¼ cup	finely chopped almonds	50 mL
¼ cup	unsweetened shredded coconut	50 mL
¼ cup	granulated sugar	50 mL
½ tsp	ground cardamom	2 mL
1	cinnamon stick	1
½ tsp	grated nutmeg (see Tips)	2 mL

1. Place rice in baking dish. Add coconut milk, milk, raisins, almonds, coconut, sugar, cardamom and cinnamon stick. Cover, place dish on baking sheet and bake in preheated oven for 1 hour or until sauce has thickened.

2. Serve warm or chilled, sprinkled with nutmeg.

BARB'S NUTRITION NOTE

Coconut milk contains coconut oil, which is high in saturated fat. Always use the light version, and only as much as you really need.

NUTRIENTS PER SERVING	
Calories	148
Carbohydrate	22 g
Fiber	1 g
Protein	5 g
Fat, total	6 g
Fat, saturated	4 g
Cholesterol	3 mg
Sodium	45 mg

AMERICA'S EXCHANGES	
½	Starch
½	Other Carbohydrates
½	Reduced-Fat Milk
½	Fat

CANADA'S CHOICES	
1½	Carbohydrate
1	Fat

Lemon Blueberry Panna Cotta

MAKES 10 SERVINGS

This traditional Italian dessert means "cooked cream," and, indeed, the original is made with whipping cream. This version has the same silky texture but is a lighter end to a meal. It is a great make-ahead dessert, as it can be stored in the refrigerator for several days.

VARIATION

Vary the berries and the flavoring for a different taste: raspberries with grated orange zest; sliced strawberries with a splash of vanilla; diced mango with grated ginger. Ask your family to choose their favorites.

■ Ten ³⁄₄-cup (175 mL) custard cups or ramekins, sprayed with vegetable spray

1 cup	milk	250 mL
1½ tbsp	unflavored gelatin	22 mL
³⁄₄ cup	granulated sugar	175 mL
3 cups	evaporated milk	750 mL
1 tsp	grated lemon zest	5 mL
2 cups	fresh blueberries, divided	500 mL

1. Pour milk into a small saucepan and sprinkle with gelatin; let stand for 10 minutes. Cook over medium-low heat, stirring constantly with a whisk, until gelatin dissolves, about 2 minutes. Increase heat to medium and add sugar. Continue whisking until sugar dissolves, about 2 minutes. Remove from heat. Stir in evaporated milk and lemon zest, stirring well to combine.

2. Divide mixture evenly among prepared custard cups and add 2 tbsp (25 mL) blueberries to each cup. Cover and refrigerate for at least 4 hours or overnight.

3. To serve, slide a knife around the edge of each cup to loosen the panna cotta. Invert onto a dessert plate and spoon 2 tbsp (25 mL) blueberries onto the side of each plate.

NUTRIENTS PER SERVING

Calories	158
Carbohydrate	29 g
Fiber	1 g
Protein	8 g
Fat, total	2 g
Fat, saturated	1 g
Cholesterol	7 mg
Sodium	100 mg

AMERICA'S EXCHANGES

1	Other Carbohydrates
1	Fat-Free/1% Milk

CANADA'S CHOICES

2	Carbohydrate

Orange Sabayon with Fresh Berries

MAKES 6 SERVINGS

TIP

Use an instant-read thermometer to check the temperature of the egg yolk mixture. Food that contains eggs should be heated to at least 160°F (75°C) to ensure that any salmonella bacteria present in the eggs are destroyed.

■ Stand mixer

4	egg yolks	4
3 tbsp	granulated sugar	45 mL
	Grated zest of 1 orange	
⅓ cup	freshly squeezed orange juice	75 mL
4 cups	berries, such as blueberries, strawberries, blackberries or raspberries	1 L

1. In the mixer bowl, whisk together egg yolks, sugar, and orange zest and juice. Set over a saucepan of simmering water, making sure the bottom of the bowl doesn't touch the water. Cook, whisking constantly, until mixture reaches 160°F (75°C). Continue to cook until thick and doubled in volume, about 5 minutes. Do not overheat or the egg yolks will scramble.

2. Attach the whip and mixer bowl to the mixer. Set to Speed 6 and beat until sabayon reaches room temperature, about 5 minutes. Spoon into 6 serving bowls, garnish with berries and serve.

NUTRIENTS PER SERVING	
Calories	113
Carbohydrate	19 g
Fiber	4 g
Protein	3 g
Fat, total	4 g
Fat, saturated	1 g
Cholesterol	126 mg
Sodium	6 mg

AMERICA'S EXCHANGES	
½	Fruit
½	Other Carbohydrates
1	Fat

CANADA'S CHOICES	
1	Carbohydrate
1	Fat

Maple Flan with Walnuts

MAKES 6 SERVINGS

TIP

For extra maple flavor, omit the vanilla and use 2 tsp (10 mL) maple extract.

BARB'S NUTRITION NOTES

Remember that garnishes are not included in nutrients per serving or Exchanges and Choices, so be mindful of what they will add.

A garnish of ¼ cup (50 mL) chopped toasted walnuts will add an extra ½ Fat Exchange or Choice per serving.

If you use the Cinnamon Cream topping, count one-sixth of the recipe as a Free Food or Extra, plus ½ Fat Exchange or Choice.

- Preheat oven to 325°F (160°C)
- 4-cup (1 L) soufflé or casserole dish

2	egg whites	2
1	egg	1
2½ tbsp	maple syrup	32 mL
1 tsp	vanilla	5 mL
1 tsp	maple extract	5 mL
1½ cups	2% milk	375 mL
	Toasted chopped walnuts (optional)	
	Cinnamon Cream (optional) (see recipe, page 242)	

1. In a bowl, whisk together egg whites, whole egg, maple syrup, vanilla and maple extract until smooth. Gradually add milk, whisking constantly. Pour into soufflé dish.

2. Set dish in larger pan; pour in enough hot water to come halfway up sides. Bake for 60 minutes or until set. Remove from water bath; cool on wire rack. Chill.

3. Serve with toasted chopped walnuts and/or Cinnamon Cream, if desired.

NUTRIENTS PER SERVING	
Calories	74
Carbohydrate	9 g
Fiber	0 g
Protein	4 g
Fat, total	2 g
Fat, saturated	1 g
Cholesterol	36 mg
Sodium	60 mg

AMERICA'S EXCHANGES	
½	Other Carbohydrates
½	Fat

CANADA'S CHOICES	
½	Carbohydrate
½	Fat

Pumpkin Flan

For individual servings, use six ¾-cup (175 mL) custard cups or ramekins and bake for 20 minutes.

BARB'S NUTRITION NOTES
Be sure to use pure canned pumpkin, not pumpkin pie filling, in this recipe.

You will find fructose in specialty grocery stores and some health food stores.

■ Preheat oven to 325°F (160°C)
■ 4-cup (1 L) soufflé or casserole dish

¾ cup	canned pumpkin	175 mL
2½ tbsp	fructose	32 mL
2	egg whites	2
1	egg	1
½ tsp	almond extract	2 mL
½ tsp	vanilla	2 mL
¼ tsp	cinnamon	1 mL
⅛ tsp	ground cloves	0.5 mL
1 cup	2% milk	250 mL

Cinnamon Cream

1 cup	5% ricotta cheese	250 mL
4 tsp	maple syrup or liquid honey	20 mL
¾ tsp	cinnamon	4 mL

1. In a bowl, beat pumpkin, fructose, egg whites, whole egg, almond extract, vanilla, cinnamon and cloves until smooth. In a saucepan, heat milk until almost boiling; remove from heat. Whisk hot milk into pumpkin mixture. Pour into dish.

2. Set dish in larger pan; pour in enough hot water to come halfway up sides. Bake for 40 minutes or until set. Remove from water bath; cool on wire rack. Chill.

3. *Cinnamon Cream:* In a food processor, purée ricotta, maple syrup and cinnamon until smooth. Serve with flan.

NUTRIENTS PER SERVING	
Calories	128
Carbohydrate	14 g
Fiber	1 g
Protein	9 g
Fat, total	4 g
Fat, saturated	2 g
Cholesterol	40 mg
Sodium	103 mg

AMERICA'S EXCHANGES	
½	Vegetable
½	Other Carbohydrates
1	Lean Meat

CANADA'S CHOICES	
1	Carbohydrate
1	Meat and Alternatives

Chocolate Crêpes

MAKES 16 SERVINGS

These crêpes are easy to make and very versatile, as they can be filled with your choice of fruit and/or frozen yogurt.

TIP

You can make the crêpes the day before; wrap them in plastic wrap and refrigerate until ready to use.

BARB'S NUTRITION NOTE

The nutrients per serving, Exchanges and Choices are for the crêpe only. The taste panel chose strawberries and frozen yogurt as their favorite additions: count 2 tbsp (25 mL) low-fat frozen yogurt with $\frac{1}{4}$ cup (50 mL) unsweetened sliced strawberries as $\frac{1}{2}$ Other Carbohydrate Exchange or Carbohydrate Choice.

■ Sixteen 6-inch (15 cm) squares of parchment or waxed paper

1$\frac{1}{2}$ cups	all-purpose flour	375 mL
$\frac{1}{2}$ cup	unsweetened cocoa powder	125 mL
6 tbsp	confectioner's (icing) sugar	90 mL
Pinch	salt	Pinch
2	eggs	2
2 cups	milk	500 mL
2 tbsp	vegetable oil	25 mL
$\frac{1}{2}$ tsp	vanilla	2 mL

1. In a large bowl, sift flour, cocoa powder, sugar and salt.

2. In a medium bowl, whisk eggs, milk, oil and vanilla until blended. Add a little at a time to the flour mixture, whisking to dissolve lumps, until smooth. Cover and refrigerate for 1 hour.

3. Heat a small skillet over medium heat and spray lightly with vegetable spray. When skillet is hot, remove from heat and pour in $\frac{1}{4}$ cup (50 mL) of the batter. Swirl skillet to spread batter evenly over the bottom. Return to heat and cook for 30 to 40 seconds, until bottom is light golden. Turn crêpe over and cook for about 15 seconds, until bottom is light golden. Remove from skillet. Repeat until all batter is used, stacking crêpes between squares of parchment or waxed paper to prevent them from sticking together.

NUTRIENTS PER SERVING	
Calories	99
Carbohydrate	15 g
Fiber	1 g
Protein	3 g
Fat, total	3 g
Fat, saturated	1 g
Cholesterol	26 mg
Sodium	24 mg

AMERICA'S EXCHANGES	
$\frac{1}{2}$	Starch
$\frac{1}{2}$	Other Carbohydrates
$\frac{1}{2}$	Fat

CANADA'S CHOICES	
1	Carbohydrate
$\frac{1}{2}$	Fat

Contributing Authors

**MEREDITH DEEDS
& CARLA SNYDER**
The Mixer Bible
Recipes from this book are found on
pages 41, 49, 86, 234, 236 and 240.

DIETITIANS OF CANADA
Simply Great Food
Recipes from this book are found on
pages 35, 37–38, 40, 44–46, 50, 56,
58, 64, 78, 91, 96, 104, 106, 116, 118,
122, 126, 136, 142, 169, 171, 176,
182, 202, 207–8, 215, 219–22, 238–39
and 243.

GEORGE GEARY
The Complete Baking Cookbook
Recipes from this book are found on
pages 42, 47, 60, 62, 130 and 152.

JULIE HASSON
300 Best Chocolate Recipes
Recipes from this book are found on
pages 72, 73 and 218.

LYNN ROBLIN, NUTRITION EDITOR
500 Best Healthy Recipes
Recipes from this book are found on
pages 34, 36, 39, 43, 48, 52–55, 57,
66–67, 69, 74–75, 87, 89, 90, 92, 94,
101, 103, 105, 107, 110–12, 117, 129,
131, 137, 139, 145, 147, 150, 153–56,
158–68, 170, 172–74, 178–80, 184–88,
190–92, 194–201, 203–6, 209–10,
212–14, 216, 224–33, 237 and 241–42.

JILL SNIDER
*Bars & Squares: More Than
200 Recipes*
Recipes from this book are found on
pages 79–80, 82–84, 120, 124–25, 128,
132–35, 138, 140–41, 143–44, 146
and 148.

JILL SNIDER
Cookies: More Than 200 Recipes
Recipes from this book are found on
pages 68, 70, 76, 81, 88, 93, 97–100,
102, 108 and 113–14.

Library and Archives Canada Cataloguing in Publication

Selley, Barbara
   150 best diabetes desserts / Barbara Selley.

Includes index.
ISBN-13: 978-0-7788-0193-1. ISBN-10: 0-7788-0193-4

1. Diabetes—Diet therapy—Recipes. 2. Desserts. I. Title.
II. Title: One hundred fifty diabetes desserts.

RC662.S42 2008a   641.5'6314   C2008-902575-X

Selley, Barbara
   Canada's 150 best diabetes desserts / Barbara Selley.

Includes index.
ISBN-13: 978-0-7788-0204-4. ISBN-10: 0-7788-0204-3

1. Diabetes—Diet therapy—Recipes. 2. Desserts. I. Title.
II. Title: Canada's one hundred fifty diabetes desserts.

RC662.S42 2008   641.5'6314   C2008-902470-2

Index